family's midwestern hometown. Denker's revelations in the heart of the nation's top red states provide a needed roadmap to how Donald Trump became president, but in the end, she didn't just travel to the Right or Left of America. Denker's journey became all of ours when she returned from those many miles with a clear and vulnerable call to action, encouraging us to look beyond our ballots and past our convictions to find a deeper understanding of what it means to love thy neighbor in a wounded world."

> — Lindsey Seavert, reporter, journalist,
> storyteller, NBC KARE 11, Minneapolis

"Angela Denker, journalist and ordained pastor, is a leading millennial voice in helping Americans understand all citizens of our great country. Regardless of partisan leanings, all Americans can find something in *Red State Christians* to surprise, delight, infuriate, and educate them."

> — Deborah White, journalist and political blogger

"For a liberal nonbeliever, the journey to discover Angela Denker's *Red State Christians* is often uncomfortable. It's important we Americans try to understand each other, and Denker's cross-country exploration shines a light on a part of our country that needs to be seen. It's my hope the book also serves as a mirror to those same Christians, leading to more grace and less stridency."

> — Mark Wollemann, writer and editor

From Christian Authors and Speakers

"Angela Denker has cast a bright light on the makeup of America today, polarized between red and blue states, right-wing and left-wing voters, conservative and progressive Christians. What Denker found is that this is not a case of us against them, us insiders against those outsiders. The divide runs right through every American family, whose members share a common humanity deeper than surface differences."

> — Carl Braaten, leading theologian in American Lutheranism

Additional Praise for *Red State Christians*

From Journalists

"*Red State Christians*, a series of humane, challenging dispatches that transcend a glut of supposedly similar think pieces. Speaking hard truths to the American church, yet reserving grace for people in the pews."

— Aarik Danielsen, *Columbia Daily Tribune* arts and entertainment editor and *Fathom Mag* columnist

"By listening—really leaning in and listening, with a compassionate sense of wanting to know, rather than merely to respond with counterargument—Denker brings light to overlooked corners of the country and of the national conversation on the issues of the day. Nuanced and immensely readable, *Red State Christians* shows what a talented writer trained in both journalism and the clergy can contribute to our collective understanding."

— Charles N. Davis, journalist and dean, Henry W. Grady College of Journalism and Mass Communication at the University of Georgia

"Quite literally—Denker travels from coast to coast in search of answers to a complex question. Along the way, interviews with people of varying backgrounds and Denker's personal anecdotes help formulate a reasonable discussion. And in the days of online arguments and partisan media, a reasonable discussion is incredibly refreshing."

— Danny Davis, sports reporter, *Austin American Statesman*

"With a masterful command of the pen and the high call of the pulpit, Angela Denker is uniquely positioned to lead us into a divided America. The journalist-turned-pastor embarks on a cross-country trip fueled by curiosity and courageous moxie, offering a dissection of Donald Trump's election through the voices of Christians—in the Bible Belt, in urban megachurches, in rural chapels, and even in her

"Like an Agatha Christie whodunnit mystery, Angela Denker skillfully reveals the motives and opportunities of the unlikely Christian characters who witnessed the death of everything that embodied Christianity. A must read for every confounded voter and a wake-up call to those looking for gospel resurrection."

— Spencer Burke, founder and executive director, Hatchery LA

"Reading *Red State Christians* will remind you that we who follow Jesus must always be more focused on obedience to the gospel commission than allegiance to any American politician. You may not like what you read, but like a bitter medicinal pill, *Red State Christians* is best consumed whether you like or not."

— Wade Burleson, author and red-state pastor

"This book will help you move beyond clichés and surface judgments and into the deeper streams of careful and critical thought, as well as into compassionate listening. America is at least as interesting, insane, and nuanced as your own family reunion. A sane future depends on the humility that Angela Denker holds in this book and her invitation to see ourselves hidden in the face of the other. This book is worth your time, especially if you're longing for a little hope in our complicated and divided mess."

— Kent Dobson, former megachurch pastor and author
of *Bitten by a Camel: Leaving Church, Finding God*

"Using both her journalistic and pastoral skills, Denker crisscrossed the United States to learn the stories that have the potential to heal our nation—if we are willing to listen and understand."

— Hugh Hollowell Jr., community pastor,
Open Door Mennonite Church, Jackson Mississippi

"In *Red State Christians*, Angela Denker moves us beyond the caricatures of Evangelical voters by exploring their world and revealing their words. She gives us insight into one of the most important and powerful political subcultures in the United States. Fair and enlightening, this is a book you'll want to read."

— Carol Howard Merritt, author of *Healing Spiritual Wounds*

"Venturing far off the beaten path of partisan politics, this book guides us toward our shared humanity, which is the antidote to our disease of dehumanization."
— Jon Huckins, coauthor of *Mending the Divides: Creative Love in a Conflicted World* and cofounding director, The Global Immersion Project

"Witness Angela Denker's curiosity, courage, and listening spirit, and let her words catapult you into a lifestyle of compassionate understanding. You cannot read this book soon enough. God bless Denker, God bless this book, and may God bless you through these pages."
— Tony Kriz, author of *Neighbors and Wise Men: Sacred Encounters in a Portland Pub and Other Unexpected Places*

"Angela Denker has written a remarkable book in *Red State Christians*. Her keen observation, wry critique, deep empathy, and fierce commitment to the gospel render this book a must-read for Christians of all political and theological stripes. Well-researched and compellingly reported, *Red State Christians* will surely prove a resource for those who want to better understand America's complex manifestations of Christianity—the peculiar interplay of theology and culture—for years to come."
— Bromleigh McCleneghan, author of *Good Christian Sex: Why Chastity Isn't the Only Option—And Other Things the Bible Says about Sex*

"*Red State Christians* will surprise you, maybe even shock you. Angela Denker will take you with her to interview people in churches where you'll be shocked at what's said both in and out of the pulpit. She'll also introduce you to people who defy stereotypes and behave far better than you'd expect based on who they voted for in 2016. Whoever wins the next election, we're all neighbors, and we need to get along. Books like Angela's can help mend the tears in our social fabric—if you'll dare to let her be your guide in a tour across our nation."
— Brian D. McLaren

"*Red State Christians* has robbed me of my resentments. *Red State Christians* helps us see that there is no us and them; there's only us. The hospitality with which Denker engages those Christians who voted for Donald Trump provides the empathy necessary for those other Christians, like myself, first to listen and then maybe to understand and possibly one day learn to love the enemy who is also my neighbor. *Red State Christians* will leave Blue State Christians not only with a better understanding of the other but also with a sneaking suspicion about themselves."

— Jason Micheli, author of *Living in Sin* and *Cancer Is Funny*

"Instead of focusing on the why of Trump's election, which has obsessed analysts since 2016, she chooses to bring us the who: the many human beings, powerful and powerless alike, that fall under that particular umbrella. In her book, we meet these Christians not as a monolith but as individuals."

—— Kaya Oakes, author of *The Nones Are Alright: A New Generation of Believers, Seekers, and Those In Between*

"What Denker has accomplished in *Red State Christians* is astonishing. This is a must-read book for those of us trying to grapple with where Christianity is in our country and how to move forward."

— Joshua Pease, pastor, journalist, and author of *The God Who Wasn't There*; former pastor at Saddleback Church

"Angela Denker sets out to do what more of us should: get to know and understand (and ultimately love) those who vote or view the world differently than we do. Expertly researched and written, *Red State Christians* is a great read—no matter your position."

— Caryn Rivadeneira, author of *Gritty and Graceful: 15 Inspiring Women of the Bible*

"With the 2020 presidential campaign on the horizon, *Red State Christians* is an insightful and timely read. Angela Denker shows how being a Christian who voted for Trump looks different in Appalachia and Orange County, for men and women, for Southern Baptists and Catholics, for baby boomers and millennials. This book reminds us how God's grace squeezes through walls."

— Ellie Roscher, author of *Play Like a Girl*
and *How Coffee Saved My Life*

"You may not agree with all of her conclusions, but have no doubt, this book will help you step into the political divisions in American Christianity with empathy and hope."

— Kurt Willems, pastor, writer, and
podcaster at theologycurator.com

"What we call 'red states' are an optical illusion—places where religion has been used to pit neighbors against one another so a minority can maintain political control. But what Denker calls 'Red State Christians' are real. They've been cultivated for forty years by the Religious Right, and they've led the charge toward extremism in American public life. But they are our fellow Americans and family at God's welcome table. We need to listen closely to hear their pain and to learn how their healing is an essential part of the healing of our land."

— Jonathan Wilson-Hartgrove, author of *Reconstructing
the Gospel: Finding Freedom from Slaveholder Religion*

From Academics and Nonprofit Leaders

"Denker's work is about the pulsebeats not the polls, the mindsets not the machinery of politics. It is a picture of everyday Americans at the grassroots. Anybody who wants to save politics and/or religion in America would do well to peer through Denker's lenses and heed her descriptions and prescriptions."

— Bud Heckman, executive director, Tri-Faith Initiative

"What is most compelling about *Red State Christians* is Denker's gift for storytelling. She has the wit of Flannery O'Connor and reveals paradox like G. K. Chesterton. Her stories explore the necessity of

Christian engagement with people not like ourselves. *Red State Christians* inspires us to reconcile the tension between the flag and the cross, to understand the Bible and our current state of economics. Ultimately, Denker's story expresses hope. That through engagement and understanding one another, we can bridge divides, heal our country, and share better conversations at our Thanksgiving tables."

— Eric LeCompte, executive director, Jubilee USA Network

"Red State Christians is a sometimes jarring and always illuminating look at a country divided, but more than that, it is a call to listen, to understand, and to remember that we are better together."

— Paul C. Pribbenow, president, Augsburg University

"Red State Christians is an unflinching and perceptive account of evangelicals in the age of Trump. It paints a complicated and vivid picture, one that is not easily summarized in an exit poll or cable-news soundbite. Angela Denker shows us the humanity of Red State Christians—their contradictions, shortcomings, kindness, and quirks—and how there is a path forward *if* we endeavor to listen to each other. *Red State Christians* is an ideal place to start the conversation."

— Andrew Whitehead, associate professor
of sociology, Clemson University

From Pastors and Church Leaders

"With the neutrality of a reporter, curiosity of an investigator, grace of a pastor, and grit of an athlete, Denker seamlessly combines human experience, theological insight, and political analysis."

— Kristen Capel, pastor

"Red State Christians refuses to generalize or stereotype the Christians who voted for Trump. Denker's conversations remind readers how to show genuine interest in one another, a spiritual gift that can always use more practice in America."

— Meta Herrick Carlson, pastor and
author of *Ordinary Blessings*

"As a Jesus-follower who also identifies as a bleeding-heart liberal, I expected to be frustrated with the subject(s) of this book. *Red State Christians* has served as a great reminder that I am as much a part of the problem as the conservative Red State Christians I wanted to blame it on. I hope that everyone, liberals and conservatives, Christians, Jews, Muslims, and people of no faith can read this book and find a middle ground, coming up with candidates who can not only answer to what we want but also start to reunite this country that has become so divided."

— Bruce Ewing, Broadway actor, singer, worship leader,
and founder of Phat Pack Entertainment: Las Vegas

"In *Red State Christians* Angela Denker has delivered an impressive book about America and Christianity in the age of Trump. Anyone curious about why Red State Christians so overwhelmingly voted for and continue to support Donald Trump will want to read this book."

—Peter Geisendorfer-Lindgren, senior pastor emeritus,
Lord of Life Lutheran Church, Maple Grove, Minnesota

"If you've ever said, 'How could any Christian have voted for Trump?' this book is a must-read. At a time when we paint 'the other' with a single color, Angela Denker paints the diversity of conservative Christianity with a full color palate."

— Jeffrey J. Marian, lead pastor, Prince of Peace
Lutheran Church, Burnsville, Minnesota

"Angela Denker has written a compelling book that boldly looks at how the often diverse, dangerous, and damaging political rhetoric masked with religious and theological interpretations and misinterpretations has helped create the polarization of families, friends, and even churches. Setting aside our desire to so quickly judge and condemn those not in our tribe and of our political persuasion, Denker reminds us to create space for dialogue with those we don't agree with and encourages us to not confuse our national identity with our Christian identity."

— Bob Mooney, senior pastor, Messiah Lutheran
Church, Yorba Linda, California

"Angela Denker has taken the time to listen. Not to listen so that she can respond, but to listen for understanding about what guides how we vote and what is important to Christian voters throughout the nation. She invites her readers to step out of their echo chambers and consider different perspectives."

— Willie Rosin, pastor, First Lutheran Church, Britt, Iowa

"The book gives every thoughtful person a reason to stop and consider: does my faith in God's love, Jesus's forgiveness, and the Spirit's power inform my political stances or do my political views determine who I think should receive God's amazing grace?"

— Dr. Mark Wickstrom, senior pastor,
Community Lutheran Church, Las Vegas

RED STATE
CHRISTIANS

RED STATE CHRISTIANS

Understanding the Voters Who Elected Donald Trump

ANGELA DENKER

Fortress Press

Minneapolis

RED STATE CHRISTIANS
Understanding the Voters Who Elected Donald Trump

Cover image: Shutterstock 2018; American People by the Map Illustration by america 365
Cover design: Laura Drew

Print ISBN: 978-1-5064-4908-1
eBook ISBN: 978-1-5064-4909-8

The paper used in this publication meets the minimum requirements of American National Standard for Information Sciences — Permanence of Paper for Printed Library Materials, ANSI Z329.48-1984.

Manufactured in the U.S.A.

To my husband, Ben, my beloved Red State Christian
without whom this book would not be possible.

CONTENTS

Introduction

In August 2018, deep into research about conservative Christian support of Donald Trump, and in between travels to conservative counties across the United States to conduct interviews with Red State Christians, I got a surprising phone call from my friend Rachel.

Rachel is a PhD student studying the Old Testament at a prestigious university in the American South. We straddle many of the same lines: female ordained pastors serving a mainline denomination, married moms of little ones, sports and adventure lovers who once played together on the seminary softball team. We share a certain affinity for bucking the status quo. We sometimes push back against the growing liberalism of our own denomination but also speak out about discrimination against women in leadership in the broader American Christian world and about the harmful misogyny of conservative Christianity. An Alaska native who lived in the Midwest and on the West Coast before moving to the Bible Belt, Rachel is a fascinating combination of all the things that make America great.

Still, I was surprised she wanted to talk on the phone. Usually, we just chat via Facebook Messenger, critiquing each other's writing or sharing stories. I hadn't actually heard her voice in years, probably since we played on that long-ago softball team in Minnesota, when we both lamented the fact that you couldn't cut bad players from a seminary team.

"Angela," Rachel said, "I don't know why, but I just had to ask you about this. You have spent so much time in the conservative Christian world. What do you think?"

Rachel's daughter had been invited to participate in an after-school program that taught students about Christianity, as well as leadership and character development. Like most such programs, especially in the American South, its teachings were conservative. Its goals were noble, and it offered the classes free of charge—a welcome break for parents stretched to afford kids' activities and child care. Still, Rachel worried about some of the messages her daughter might receive through the program. Would she learn that women are capable of preaching and leading churches? Would she be told that only men are in charge of the family? What would she be taught about religious minorities or about students who might identify as gay? Rachel also worried about the minority Muslim students at the school. Would the program make them feel even more ostracized? As an academic and Bible scholar herself, Rachel felt the double weight of teaching her daughter Christianity but also letting her be a part of her school community and learn a faith that was not exclusively dependent on her mom's academic background.

As we talked, I realized that Rachel and I share many of the same worries and concerns that most parents do: Are we passing on the right lessons to our children? How can we be influential but not pushy? How should we help them fit in but also stand up against what they believe to be wrong or unjust?

In the middle of our conversation, mixed with tears and a realization of our power and impotence as parents, Rachel and I ultimately reached the same conclusion: rather than avoid people who might think differently than she did, rather than isolate her daughter, Rachel and I decided the best course of action would be to join in, listen, and start conversations. Instead of avoiding the group, Rachel resolved to volunteer. The things she was worried about, we figured, could be combated by her presence. How could the students believe that women couldn't be leaders or teachers in the church when one of their leaders was a Bible scholar and pastor herself? Even though our initial impulse when confronted with something we find disagreeable is to disengage—to block, to unfriend—through prayer and conversation, Rachel and I realized that our Christian faith was leading us in the opposite direction, toward engagement and conversation. She messaged me about a month later, attaching a photo of her wearing a green T-shirt screen-printed with a Bible verse.

"I am a full-fledged parent volunteer," Rachel wrote. "I staffed the toilet plunger/scooter game and am the small-group leader for fourth-grade boys."

This book is my answer to the same call Rachel heard—for greater engagement and conversation at a time when America feels pulled to its extremes, when our first national impulse is to block and unfriend anyone who disagrees with us. My hunch is that the truth about the Red State Christians who voted for Trump, and the truth about Americans in general, is closer to Rachel's picture of herself in that Bible verse T-shirt, heading to volunteer at the conservative Christian after-school program. We have much more opportunity for conversation and engagement than we might imagine. When we don't avoid people who think differently than we do, we gain an opportunity for growth and national renewal. My hope is that as you read stories of

Red State Christians, you will find surprising commonalities among people who seem quite different from one another, whether you are a conservative Christian or not.

Of course, when opposing viewpoints collide, the result is not always cohesion; sometimes it is combustion. I know that as a part of telling the stories of the Christians I met in red counties, I will reveal uncomfortable and hurtful truths. In addition to the many wise, kind, and genuine Red State Christians I met across America, others were committed to division, destruction, and perversion of the story of Jesus to support their own wealth and power. Most of these people were pastors, and most of the divisive and damaging rhetoric I heard from Christians across America came either from manipulative pastors or from partisan media. The victims of these power-hungry pastors and Christian leaders were often women, the poor, people of color, immigrants, refugees, and the LGBTQ community.

In spite of these voices and the damage they inflict, I hope that we can be generous and compassionate as we journey through Red State America together. Too often, in the rush to condemnation and judgment, we miss out on creating spaces for dialogue where dialogue is needed most: between people who disagree. In this book, you'll read stories of Christians who are manipulating the story of Jesus, as well as places where churches have lost the distinction between national pride and Christian identity. These stories are true, and they concern Americans and Christians of all backgrounds. The stories of manipulation you'll read about in this book paint a picture of the way Donald Trump used Christian Nationalism and distortions of the Christian gospel to earn Evangelical support.

At the same time, you'll also read stories about surprising partnerships in red counties all over America, between Christians of diverse backgrounds and political beliefs. You'll likely be surprised at the people who are working together and the ways that the story of Jesus is being told from the grassroots. Whether you are a conservative, a liberal, or one who is fed up with everything altogether, my hope is that this book gives you a reason to reengage, to be surprised, and to consider anew what the 2016 election said about American Christians, God, and country.

CHAPTER 1

Christian Nationalism and Fourth of July Church in Dallas, Texas

In 1983, John Cougar Mellencamp wrote a song that told the story of America for conservatives, liberals, and Christians alike. Mellencamp sings about a black man living in Indiana with an interstate running through his front yard. He lives in a pink shotgun house, meaning you could open the front and back doors, shoot a shotgun shell through the house, and not hit a thing. The black man is watching a woman he loves in the kitchen, and he has loved her for a long time. He thinks he has it so good, in America.

Mellencamp sings in the second verse about a young man wearing a T-shirt and listening to rock and roll. He has greasy hair and a greasy smile; maybe he's not too clean, not too rich. Still, this greasy young man believes he can be president one day—because America is a place for dreams and dreamers.

"Ain't that America?" the song demands again and again. "Ain't that America?"—where you and I might not be millionaires, but we can be born free, dream dreams, and maybe someday own a little pink house in front of an interstate in Indiana.

Thirty-three years later, newly elected US president Donald Trump gave an inauguration speech depicting a very different America:

> Washington flourished—but the people did not share in its wealth. Politicians prospered—but the jobs left, and the factories closed. The establishment protected itself, but not the citizens of our country.
>
> Their victories have not been your victories; their triumphs have not been your triumphs; and while they celebrated in our nation's capital, there was little to celebrate for struggling families all across our land. . . .
>
> For too many of our citizens, a different reality exists: mothers and children trapped in poverty in our inner cities; rusted-out factories scattered like tombstones across the landscape of our nation; an education system, flush with cash, but which leaves our young and beautiful students deprived of knowledge; and the crime and gangs and drugs that have stolen too many lives and robbed our country of so much unrealized potential.
>
> This American carnage stops right here and stops right now.[1]

Cheering his dark and dire depiction of America were millions of Red State Christians, many of them weaned on church traditions that taught Christian Nationalism, the importance of America as a Christian country, and the fear that America was being destroyed for its apostasy. Somehow, despite being raised a millionaire's kid in

New York City, Trump spoke their language. He understood their colloquialisms and appealed directly to Red State Christians across America, whether by eating a taco bowl on Cinco de Mayo, shouting "Merry Christmas," bragging about his Big Mac consumption, or saying things that sounded racist, sexist, and rude. While Trump was connecting through the power of shared language, Democrats sounded like foreigners to Red State Christians across the South and rural America. Leading liberals didn't understand the language, much less speak it.

Not so long ago, Americans spoke a shared language, before divergent strains of partisan media and sophisticated targeted advertising gave two Americas two different languages. Thirty-three years earlier—and probably still in 2016—lots of Red State Christians could recite the words to Mellencamp's song, which had been played at campaign events for Republican presidential candidate John McCain until Mellencamp's liberal beliefs became public and McCain was criticized for using the song.

"Land of the free" and dreams and little houses for everyone were sentiments that fit the sunny optimism of the Reagan/Bush Republican Party. The fact that Mellencamp's song was also played at President Barack Obama's inauguration—as well as at 2010 conservative political events opposing same-sex marriage, despite protests from Mellencamp himself—was not all that surprising in a country where most people saw America in much the same way as Mellencamp's song described, despite partisan differences.

The song's main idea, at least as most Americans heard it, was that America's a place where anyone can succeed, anyone can buy a little pink house, and anyone can be free. This is the idea of America that immigrants climbed aboard rickety steamships for, the idea of America that soldiers died for, the triumph of America that made it the beacon of the world and the great enemy of despots and dictators everywhere.

By 2016, however, this optimistic idea of America was no longer a foregone conclusion. Two years later, McCain was dead. Most rock stars were hated by most Republicans (and vice versa), and the only ones deemed eligible to sing about America for conservatives were country singers.

Among those whose idea of America had changed the most since Mellencamp's song were the 81 percent of white American Evangelical Christians who voted for Donald J. Trump.[2] In Trump's America, particularly among Red State Christians, people have lost confidence in America's Christian identity. The United States is no longer the place where resurrection seems possible because anything is possible, even pink houses for everyone. And a shared song to represent America can no longer be sung at both liberal and conservative political events.

Instead, Red State Christians consider America and American Christianity under siege, resulting in a defensive pushback. Churches today must defend not just Jesus but also America. The American flag and the Christian flag are posted side by side in sanctuaries across the country, often directly in front of the cross.

Nationalism and American Evangelical Christians

Christian conservatives across America have watched their beloved social causes lose again and again in the Supreme Court, elections, and popular-opinion polls. The majority of Americans now support same-sex marriage and government-sponsored birth control. The white male patriarchal leadership that continues to be the norm in many conservative churches and families has been challenged on the national stage, especially in the midst of the #MeToo movement and the widely publicized alleged sexual misconduct and damaging misogynistic theology of several prominent Evangelical pastors and leaders, including Willow Creek founding pastor Bill Hybels and former Southern Baptist Convention president Paige Patterson, both of whom were forced to resign from their leadership positions in the second year of Trump's presidency.

In response, Red State Christians have turned toward the flag, feeling their patriotic fervor and nostalgic desire for a more Christian America (where kids used to pray in school). This desire to turn back the clock is more about national identity than Christian identity, though the two are inextricably tied together for many Red State Christians. They want to be the ones who get to define what America is, and for them, it must be conservative, and it must be Christian. Otherwise the country—and their Christian faith—will utterly collapse.

Two years into Trump's presidency, the Pew Research Council released a new religious typology to categorize American Christians.[3] Among the 39 percent considered highly religious, 12 percent were called "God and Country Christians," for whom American conservative values and national Christianity are most important.[4] You can see this throughout the early twenty-first century at Southern Baptist churches across America, where even Christmas and Easter are subsumed by a sort of civic religion that worships God, Guns, and Country (really, the military), lifting up Veterans Day, Memorial Day, and the Fourth of July to the same place of honor as religious high holy days.

Trump, Obama, and Christian Nationalism

Donald Trump is no devout Christian; he is no fundamentalist warrior or longtime pro-life activist, as is Vice President Mike Pence.

Trump failed the Bible test when asked his favorite passage: "Two Corinthians?" he ventured, failing to realize that the biblical book is referred to as *Second* Corinthians. Trump is no Bible scholar, no pastor, no retreat leader, and no public pray-er, though he often assures his Evangelical fans that he is praying for them and for America.

Trump didn't know much about the Bible or about Evangelical Christianity. But this new civic religion, popularized in Evangelical churches across America, especially in the South—with its unique blend of nostalgia plus a little misogyny and dog-whistle race politics on the side—well, that Trump understood well. He'd been winking and nodding at it for years, suggesting that Obama is neither an American citizen nor a Christian. Trump learned the lessons that McCain hadn't. At one of his campaign events, McCain corrected a woman who said Obama was an Arab. Trump would never do such a thing. He understands instinctively the import of the connection between conservatism and Christianity, as well as the mystique of the inherent liberal threat that is not Christian and often not white. The voters who thought Obama was Muslim would be Trump voters, and Trump wasn't about to dissuade them.

For most Red State Christians, it didn't matter that Obama was a longtime attendee of Trinity United Church of Christ in Chicago. It didn't matter when he took on the cadence of a black preacher and sang "Amazing Grace" from the pulpit in a service remembering the church massacre in Charleston, South Carolina, where a twenty-one-year-old Lutheran white supremacist gunned down nine African Americans after Bible study at Emanuel African Methodist Episcopal Church.

It didn't matter because for most Red State Christians, Obama was the embodiment of the progressivism that threatened the America they'd known and loved for generations. Their fear, mixed with the sense that they are losing, results in a toxic, jingoistic stew. They were losing the culture wars, losing the young people at church, losing popular opinion, so things like actual church attendance and Bible knowledge mattered less than a politician's ability to catalog their list of perceived cultural wrongs and manufactured fears, like transgender persons using middle-school bathrooms or caravans of unruly migrants storming the southern border. Here Trump was on solid footing.

A movement had begun—quietly, first as a resistance to Obama and progressive politics, then as a reaction to lost culture wars and an attempt to reclaim American identity in the face of perceived retreat. Nationalism, the political lion we thought had died on the battlefields of World War II, had been resurrected, this time with religion mixed in. As churches fought battles with pastors to display the American flag on the altar in front of the cross, Christian Nationalism asserted its dominance on the national stage. In churches across Red State America, Christian Nationalism battled for preeminence with the universal (and not exclusively American) gospel of Jesus Christ.

Much to the consternation of national media, celebrities, and intelligentsia (most located on the coasts), Trump speaks a language that appeals to Red State Christians. I don't know if he understands them, but they definitely understand him. Ultimately, the unlikely love affair between Red State Christians and Trump comes down to a shared *language*. So I've set out to record how Red State Christians talk about their faith, their votes, their guns, and their president. Other books have tackled this issue by studying trends, polling, and social-movement theory. But in addition to being a pastor, I'm a journalist. In both of my vocations, I spend a lot of time listening to people—really listening. In the pages that follow, we will get a chance to hear from Red State Christians and, whether you like what they have to say and how they say it, the key to understanding their relationship with the most unlikely president is to listen to them, with empathy, scrutiny, and attention.

My First Fourth of July Worship

I've long been aware of this nascent power of Christian National-ism. During my pastoral internship in Las Vegas in 2011, our worship director and I dared to remove *some* of the American flag bunting that had been prominently displayed around the church for Fourth of July Sunday worship. We didn't move it all, and as a granddaughter and daughter-in-law of war veterans, as well as a former chaplain at the VA hospital in Minneapolis, I considered it important to honor those who'd sacrificed for America even as we reminded our congre-gation that we came first to worship Jesus. That is, from the perspec-tive of this Christian pastor, it is through the lens of Jesus and the gospel that we must interpret everything else, including America and its government.

I didn't think removing a few pieces of bunting would be a big deal, but we got a lot of pushback. Our worship director took the brunt of it. (I was young—and pregnant—at the time.) He forwarded me one of the angry emails he'd gotten after Fourth of July worship: "I can't believe that you are not honoring the day that meant FREE-DOM FOR THE WORLD," the parishioner wrote.

Freedom for the world? We rolled our eyes, knowing that, in fact, the fourth of July in 1776 only meant real freedom for a small, white, landowning subset of American men. The end of slavery and women's right to vote—those would come later. Also, America is not in fact the world, and it's not even mentioned in the Bible. America's gen-esis began in the hands of white, landowning men, and they had no magnificent God-drawn plan—only European conquest, murder, and the deaths of thousands of Native Americans, then slavery, lynchings, and abuse of women. I had been educated in a post-Christendom America and no longer celebrated Columbus Day. I was proud to be American, but mostly I was proud because of *who we could be.* My faith and my national identity were at odds from time to time, as I contemplated the glory of tax cuts for me as an individual taxpayer and at the same time my own rising guilt at the lack of support for people living in poverty and services for immigrants and refugees.

Trump and Red State Christians would push back against my post-Christendom education. They were tired of being ashamed, tired of learning the mercy of Jesus without participating in the Old Testament stories of conquests. They wanted to reclaim the idea of the Crusades, of a preordained battle between Christians and Muslims. Most of all, they were desperate to reclaim the idea that America was a uniquely and especially *Christian* nation, where your culture—your positions on social issues, your views on gun control and abortion—were much more important than your grasp of theology or your understanding of grace, death, and resurrection.

A Southern Baptist Pastor on Christian Nationalism

I first became aware of the power of this new Christian Nationalism during an interview at the Evangelicals for Life Conference in Washington, DC, coinciding with the March for Life, a large, predominately conservative Christian march on Washington to oppose abortion and support the reversal of *Roe v. Wade.*

My conversation partner that morning was Dean Inserra, a prominent conservative Evangelical pastor, the founder of City Church in Tallahassee, Florida, a Liberty University grad and an advisory member of the Ethics and Religious Liberty Commission of the Southern Baptist Convention.

Inserra was at first circumspect, saying that while he didn't support Obama, he also didn't vote for Trump. He insisted that Trump's presidency had not changed him as a pastor.

Inserra was a rare Evangelical critic of Trump on social media, often completing his tweets with #MoralityMatters, and he was surprised to find that many of his fellow pastors and conservative Christians, while sharing his concerns about Trump's moral fitness, were moved to support Trump anyway.

In speaking with Inserra, I was reminded of Jesus's words about Nathanael in the Gospel of John: "Here is truly an Israelite in whom there is no deceit!" (1:47). Inserra, age thirty-seven when we spoke, is cut from an older Southern Baptist cloth. He is focused on his local church, he is concerned first for the primacy of the gospel, and while he is socially conservative, he is not militaristic about his views.

Inserra is also deeply concerned about the plague of Christian Nationalism within the Southern Baptist Convention (SBC). "I think there are two kinds of Trump supporters in the SBC," Inserra told me. "One type, they didn't want Hillary Clinton because of abortion and because of the Supreme Court; the other type is a nationalistic voter. I don't think they're racist, but American patriotism has become so linked to GOP politics, and [the SBC] has so intertwined that with what it means to be a Christian, that they almost can't question anything about the GOP nominee or about Trump." He added, "If you bring a missionary from India one week to a Southern Baptist church and the next week you bring a veteran, there's no question who's going to get the bigger applause."

The near-deification of the American military in many conservative churches is a sign of growing Christian Nationalism and its influence on the local church, in some ways further isolating the military from everyday Americans. During this time when World War II and Vietnam War veterans are aging and many Americans don't have a family member on active duty, the worship of military members can lead to a misunderstanding of what it's really like to serve. As Trump selected several generals to serve in his Cabinet and on his staff ("my generals," he called them), the appearance of military support for Trump and the intertwining of nationalism and a "Christian America" increased conservative Christian support for Trump. In fact, support for America as a Christian nation may become the most prominent lesson many American Christians learn in church, rather than a focus on the gospel, on forgiveness, or even on Jesus's death and resurrection.

Inserra suggested that an internal debate was brewing within the SBC about the question of Christian Nationalism and the limits of patriotism when it subsumes the gospel of Jesus. He even suggested that SBC seminaries are divided by their embrace of Christian Nationalism. Inserra's words surprised me, coming from a leader in a denomination known for its belief in certainty and inerrancy, from a pastor who'd been shaken to see the power of Christian Nationalism within the SBC. "I find their rhetoric troubling," Inserra said. "The unapologetic Trump voter. There are people who voted for him because of the Supreme Court, and I find their decision rational and logical. But it's that unapologetic defense. Didn't Trump say he could shoot someone on Fifth Avenue in New York City and get away with it? I think he's right."

Inserra told me about a term from Southern Baptist theology that describes the current moment in American politics and religion. "In this linking of nationalism and Christianity, we are forgetting about the message of Jesus. . . . When we do that, we have a *gospel distortion*."

A gospel distortion is the idea that another ideal is impeding the truth of the gospel. Inserra said the gospel distortion in the SBC during and before Trump's presidency has its roots in Christian Nationalism. "We have to be Christian first. If you are American first, Jesus will be at odds with you," he said. "Patriotism is not a fruit of the Spirit. It's idolatry on the Fourth of July."

Inserra pointed to national holidays in the SBC that receive as much attention as Christmas and Easter. "I say there are different high holy days in the Southern Baptist Church. Some churches have Pentecost and Epiphany. We have the Fourth of July, the Sunday closest to Veterans Day, the Sunday closest to September 11. You go to a Southern Baptist Church on the Fourth of July, you'd think you were at a baseball game, eating a hot dog."

Inserra said that SBC pastors have been unable or unwilling to stem the tide of Christian Nationalism, and in their preaching, they've further encouraged the linking of American patriotism and love of Jesus. He notices this particularly in the strongly Republican South, where the idea of God, guns, and country still defines many people's faith.

It has, Inserra suggested, put the *Christian* faith of many Southern Baptists on shaky ground. Instead of backing traditional Christian social support for people in need and accepting the stranger, Christians taught in churches that embrace Christian Nationalism will instead back the American military and American strength. "You have to understand these people," Inserra said. "If you question [the idea of Christian Nationalism], it makes them question their whole faith. Their entire faith is built on being a proud American. If you take that away from them, it shakes their whole faith."

Inserra suggested that love of Jesus is so tied to love of country that it's anathema for many Red State Christians to consider that

Jesus would challenge a (conservative) government official. (In fact, Jesus was a thorn in the side of the Roman government and was even crucified by that government for suggesting loyalty to God is more important than loyalty to the empire.)

"What you win them with is what you win them *to*," Inserra concluded, suggesting that because Southern Baptist pastors and churches rely so heavily on patriotism and "God, guns, and country" to get people into their churches, they've constructed a mass of people for whom faith in Jesus is nothing more than a blind allegiance to America, nostalgia, guns, and support for the military. In the absence of preaching that challenges GOP politics, an entire generation of Southern Baptists became susceptible to a populist nationalist who claims to be supporting Christians.

I walked away from my interview with Inserra stunned. I knew I wanted to tell the story of Red State Christians, but I had no idea the underlying thread of Christian Nationalism that bound together Trump and the 81 percent of white American Evangelicals who voted for him.[5] I didn't know what that alliance might mean for American churches, which have been suffering numerical decline for generations, as many American young people have said good-bye to the church forever.

Yet I believed—with my conservative Christian brothers and sisters—that Christians have an essential role to play in modern-day America and that the Bible has something to say about politics. So I went to the only place I could go: Southern Baptist churches in Dallas, Texas, on Fourth of July weekend. I wanted to hear which would speak louder: Jesus or America.

PrestonWorld: A Dallas-Area Megachurch Celebrates Fourth of July Worship

"You know we call it PrestonWorld because they have ATMs and a coffee shop and a bookshop and who knows what else in there," said a friend who's a pastor in Dallas, prior to my trip.

"One of my friends is an angel in their Christmas show. It's unbelievable," said another friend, who went to college in Texas.

"Former SBC President's Church Defunds the SBC," screamed headlines months before I headed to Dallas on the weekend before the Fourth of July.[6]

Prestonwood Baptist Church's reputation preceded it. The church was embroiled in controversy in early 2018, when it temporarily withheld $1 million in cooperative program funds from the SBC, the largest Protestant denomination in America, of which Prestonwood pastor Jack Graham served as two-term president.[7] Graham, a member of Trump's Evangelical advisory board, told the *Baptist Message* that Prestonwood was reevaluating its commitment to the SBC in light of what Graham saw as "disrespectfulness" by the SBC's Ethics and Religious Liberty Commission president Russell Moore toward Evangelical supporters of Trump during the 2016 presidential campaign.[8]

Moore would later issue an apology, which Graham thankfully received, and the SBC initiated an investigation. But the wounds of the election and the divide in the SBC noted by Inserra were still fresh when I visited Prestonwood almost seven months later, on June 30 to July 1, 2018. In fact, when I mentioned previous quotes from Moore to Prestonwood's executive pastor, Mike Buster, after Saturday-night worship, Buster just shook his head and laughed ruefully. "Russell Moore? Are you sure he's a Red State Christian? I think he might be a Blue State Christian," Buster said dismissively. Moore remains staunchly pro-life and even patriarchal in his view of gender relations. He is no liberal. But he dared to criticize Trump, earning him the scorn of Prestonwood.

How to Celebrate the Fourth of July in Dallas

In my years as a pastor and churchgoer, I've attended my share of impressive megachurches, so at first glance, Prestonwood in Plano, about forty minutes north of downtown Dallas, didn't look too different. The massive worship center and surrounding buildings rose like a mirage miles from the interstate, down the broad roads of suburban Texas. Still, as I turned into the enormous church parking lot, I noticed a distinguishing feature. In front of the worship center, off the main road, was an impressive football stadium, as large as any high-school stadium I'd reported from as a sportswriter in football-crazy South Florida. "Five-time state champions," read the banner: 2017, 2015, 2010, 2009, and 2005. In *Friday Night Lights* territory, this was no small feat. Prestonwood Christian Academy also boasts seven state titles in boys' basketball (including three recent years in a row) and eight in competitive cheerleading. NBA power forward Julius Randle attended Prestonwood before heading to Kentucky for a one-and-done scholarship year, and former Philadelphia Phillies catcher Cameron Rupp is also a Prestonwood Academy grad. Prestonwood likes winners.

When I got there for Saturday-night worship, I found out that Prestonwood had a big Fourth of July celebration planned for that Wednesday night, the actual Independence Day. Graham promised at the beginning of Saturday worship that they'd be "celebrating our freedoms as a country . . . and singing patriotic songs," as well as offering a pastor dunk tank, games, and refreshments in the Dallas summer heat. Still, weekend worship would not be devoid of national celebration. Already when I walked in, I noticed that the entire sanctuary—an arena-style worship space that seats seven thousand—had been covered with red, white, and blue American flag bunting. Flags festooned the stage, and most of the screen designs and backgrounds were red, white, and blue.

As Graham concluded his welcome for the evening service, he said, "We're going to start with the Pledge of Allegiance, the National Anthem, and honoring our servicemembers." I had not said the Pledge of Allegiance since elementary school, and I could not help but think of the Ten Commandments—ostensibly as influential here as the Pledge of Allegiance. The First Commandment itself warns against behavior like this, against worshiping and pledging allegiance to a flag and not to God:

> I am the Lord your God, who brought you out of the land of Egypt, out of the house of slavery; you shall have no other gods before me. You shall not make for yourself an idol, whether in the form of anything that is in heaven above, or that is on the earth beneath, or that is in the water under the earth. You shall not bow down to them or worship them; for I the Lord your God am a jealous God, punishing children for the iniquity of parents, to the third and the fourth generation of those who reject me, but showing steadfast love to the thousandth generation of those who love me and keep my commandments. (Exodus 20:1–6)

These words should strike fear into the heart of any God-fearing Evangelical, especially one standing before the cross in a house of worship and pledging *allegiance* to a flag, but no one around me seemed to mind. So I put my hand on my heart and mouthed the words. I felt a strange compulsion to conform, not to draw attention to myself, as if the polite but stern-looking ushers might carry me out screaming if I dared go against the spirit of the service. We then sang the "Star-Spangled Banner." We were invited to sit as the songs for each branch of the armed forces played, and veterans and active-duty soldiers were invited to stand when their branch was called, and we applauded. In their faces, I saw the faces of so many veterans I had met while working as a chaplain at the VA hospital in Minneapolis. I knew that not all would call themselves heroes, that not all were proud or grateful for their service. I also knew that most were humble, grateful to be recognized, carrying the weight of a country's wars and conflicts in their own fragile bodies, and carrying too the wounds of those conflicts in their bodies, their minds, and their hearts.

After this display of patriotism and honor, the service went on. Another staff member came forward to share fantastical numbers that must be inconceivable to the average American church: 5,500 children attended vacation Bible school, including 312 who made decisions for Christ. More than seventy people went on global missions that summer. Seventy-eight high-school students made decisions for Christ on mission trips, and sixty were baptized in the Gulf of Mexico. Seven hundred sixty-three children attended elementary camp, and a hundred of them made decisions for Christ.

In reciting numbers, Prestonwood was merely an old-school Baptist church, emphasizing the altar call and the sinner's prayer, in which Jesus is asked into the individual heart of the believer. Once in there, though, Jesus better make room for America. And you couldn't tell which was taking up more real estate.

Pastor Graham came forward next, introducing that weekend's theme: "America, Israel, and the Road to the Future." Prestonwood had decided that in order to sanctify its American patriotism and its embrace of Trump's America First foreign policy, the preacher would make the Bible fit a narrative of American exceptionalism (not unlike American Mormons' suggestion nearly two hundred years earlier, that the twelve tribes of Israel had an American connection).

The idea of American exceptionalism having a biblical justification is not new, but Prestonwood made it fresh. They had bright and compelling red, white, and blue graphics with retro black-and-white photography, a guest preacher who specializes in travel to the Middle East, and even a special song. The video montage and song came next, followed by the guest speaker. But first, Graham had to play a little American politics. Again, he forced the Christian narrative into its Trumpian box.

"Oh, I almost forgot," Graham said casually. "Children's shelters at the border. We've been speaking almost daily with our friends at the White House . . . , who are working to reunite children with their parents. . . . Irrespective of all our problems with immigration and all the chaos, it's the call of Jesus to help hurting people." Graham spoke in 1984–style Newspeak at its best, as America had been reeling for days about the stories of thousands of immigrant children forcibly separated from their parents at the United States–Mexico border; two young children being held in detention had died. Most of them were traveling dangerous journeys from crime-ridden, poverty-stricken Central American countries such as Guatemala, Honduras, and El Salvador. Many of the families said they planned to claim asylum in America, the one country in the world founded upon the idea of "Give me your tired, your poor, your huddled masses yearning to breathe free," expressed in Emma Lazarus's words on the Statue of Liberty. Trump wished instead for your wealthy, your educated, your beautiful models yearning to invest in America, and his Homeland Security Department made a strategic decision to quell Central American migration by separating children—some infants and still breastfeeding—from their parents, according to comments from Attorney General Jeff Sessions and Trump's chief of staff, John Kelly.

Images of children in detention centers designed for criminals, stories of children being injected to keep them calm, recordings of children crying for their parents—America was abuzz with questions. Had the most generous nation on earth lost its heart? At Prestonwood, all was good. In fact, Trump's daughter Ivanka earlier that week had donated $50,000 to Prestonwood's efforts to "care for children at the border." Her donation represented an especially cunning twist, as was Graham's statement that the White House was "working to reunite children and families," when in fact American government officials had separated children from their families in the first place.

Also note Graham's euphemistic language. He referred to "children's shelters," as opposed to what these centers had been called for years, beginning with the design and construction documents: detention centers. If you want to control the narrative, control the language. Graham did that masterfully, coming across as compassionate, conservative, and patriotic. He insinuated that America was taking care of migrant kids, despite all the problems on the border. Yes, you could feel good about that. All those recordings of children crying, the devastated families: fake news.

Just as quickly, Graham turned the congregation's attention to the video screens for a return to Christian Nationalism. The images were stirring. First, cameras panned to the Iwo Jima Memorial in Washington, DC, and then we saw servicemembers saying goodbye to their children before being deployed, followed by Marines holding back tears at a military funeral. The song playing in the background, written by Prestonwood's musicians, was equally patriotic and tear-jerking. Along with the images of servicemembers, the chorus rose, repeating that we would never forget their sacrifice, never forget the way they lived and the way they died. The greatest love on earth was to serve and die in the American military, the song suggested.

It's a good song. Even hearing it months later, I could sing it and fill in the words. Watching the video, I thought of my dad's dad, who fought in the Pacific in World War II, was shot in the stomach, and nearly died. He was airlifted to Australia and lived the rest of his life with war wounds, internal and external. I thought of my father-in-law, a brave farm kid from rural Missouri drafted into the army and flown to Vietnam in 1968, just in time for the most tumultuous year in American history. My heart swelled with pride, and I nearly cried. At the end of the song, I looked around, and nearly everyone in the massive sanctuary was standing in rapt attention, staring lovingly at the flags on the stage and applauding feverishly. This time, I stayed seated, still thinking about the First Commandment. My love for my country and my love for my God warred within me.

The words of the song were dangerously close to a take on the penal substitutionary atonement theory most popular in contemporary American Evangelical theology—the idea that Jesus's death on the cross is the ultimate sacrifice, that by his blood, our sins are forgiven and we are healed. Yet tonight we had sung these words about military veterans, not Jesus. Words that fit a theological framework were being morphed into a nationalist framework instead. The sacrifice of Jesus and the sacrifice of military veterans were conflated. Whose love was greater—that of Jesus or the veterans? The song said the world knew no greater love than the love of those who had served and died for America. But surely biblical sacrifice and great love exists outside America. Surely every country has soldiers who leave their families, who sacrifice and die for what they believe to be a righteous cause. Surely we could not consider military sacrifice, as selfless as it is, akin to Jesus's sacrifice. One is particular and limited by human frailty; the other is universal and limitless.

Israel, America, and the Road to the Future

If I thought the video skewed heretical, however, I was in for a real treat as I prepared to hear the message from the guest preacher, Graham's "good friend" Gary Frazier, director of Discovery Missions and executive vice president of United in Purpose, a conservative Christian advocacy and lobbyist group "adhering to the traditional values of our founding fathers." Frazier is a frequently cited conservative source on biblical prophecy and the end of the world, often appearing in speaking engagements with *Left Behind* author Tim LaHaye. Tonight Frazier was speaking at Prestonwood to talk about the joint biblical promise of America and Israel, in a ploy to "biblicize" the growing field of Christian Nationalism.

"I believe Christ is coming soon," Frazier began. "I believe we are living in the terminal generation." He used a manipulative twist, a quick way to gain your listeners' attention, a well-executed trick of any religious charlatan or cult leader: foresee the end of the world.

"Why is it that America has been the most blessed nation on the face of this earth for the last 242 years?" Frazier started. "It begins with a promise to a man named Abram." And from there, Frazier led Prestonwood attendees on a long and winding road in which Jesus was a footnote, with America and its founders, even the discredited Christopher Columbus, playing a starring role. Among his dubious claims:

"A megachurch pastor recently said that evolution is undeniable. I'm here to tell you that he's wrong."

"Look at the nations in the dustbin of history. Look at the nation of England. It supported Palestinians against Israel and began a death spiral."

"Abraham and Sarah ran ahead of God; they had a son by the handmaiden Hagar." I mention this quote to draw attention to Frazier's use of language. The word *handmaiden* is not the usual Hebrew translation from the Bible, which more precisely means female servant or slave. The word handmaiden, however, became popular in modern American culture from the dystopian Hulu show *The Handmaid's Tale*, based on Margaret Atwood's novel, which foretells a dystopian America in which conservative Christians rule, and single women— called handmaids—are forced to bear children for married men.

"Did you know that America was divinely appointed? And it was largely due to the obedience of one man." Here I thought he was going to say George Washington. Frazier shocked me when instead he said, "Christopher Columbus." I looked around to see if anyone else was as shocked by this as I was, but the vast majority of people at worship that night were listening in rapt attention. If they thought the use of Columbus as God's instrument to America was a bit off, they certainly didn't show it.

"[Christopher Columbus] means follower of God."

"In the 1400s, the Muslims invaded Jerusalem." This refers to various conquests by Muslim tribes and Persian/Turkish tribes of Crusader-held Jerusalem during the Middle Ages. Frazier's characterization of these tribes as "Muslims" documents the undercurrent of anti-Muslim sentiment that is taken for granted in many American Evangelical churches. It also is a part of criticism of Obama and lends credence to the burgeoning idea of Christian Nationalism and the lifting up of America as an exclusively Christian nation.

"Our founding fathers saw America as another Israel. . . . They recognized the lordship of Christ." While the founding fathers were white men, they were unlike modern American Evangelicals in that a personal faith in Jesus was largely unimportant to them, despite the founders' loosely held belief in God and commitment to Christian religious freedom.

"Many people who want to stick their head in the proverbial sand . . . they're uninformed. We have substituted lawlessness for anarchy. On June 26, 2015, we legalized same-sex marriage. . . . God saw man was incomplete and made a completer for him: a woman." Even in a sermon ostensibly about Israel, Frazier managed to work in some antigay, patriarchal theology.

"Here's the good news. All of us have not lost our way. We are on the brink of a third world war. Half our country categorically has said no to God. Raise your hand if you were born after 1962. I feel sorry for you. The country I grew up in doesn't exist anymore. In 1964, we threw prayer out of public schools. In 1973, we legalized murder of the unborn." Here Frazier plays American conservative Evangelicalism's greatest hits: abortion, prayer in schools, and even a discreet generational assault against younger Americans, who tend to vote Democratic.

"If you don't know Jesus, you're never gonna know peace." Forty minutes into Frazier's sermon, Jesus makes his first—and from my notes, only—appearance, in a cliché.

And that was it. Frazier whirled himself back into the traditional closing altar call, inviting congregants to ask Jesus into their hearts and receive a free ticket to heaven. If the room was unsettled by his words, none showed it, except for a boy, who looked to be about ten, attending with a woman who appeared to be his grandma, in front of me. At Frazier's mention of Columbus, he turned to his

29

grandma, a stunned expression on his face. A few minutes later, he ran out of church, returning to an unhappy grandma when the sermon was over.

The Red State Christian and the Day Trump Won America

I was so disconcerted by the whole thing—by the pledge, the heartfelt video that conflated military sacrifice with the cross of Christ, the absence of Jesus, the manipulation of Old Testament texts to fit an Americanization of the Bible—that by the end of service at Prestonwood, I just wanted to get back in my rental car and head to the hotel. But something stopped me. As I looked around, I saw earnest Christians filing out the doors. I saw people holding doors for each other. I saw America: white people, black people, Asian people, young people, old people, Latinos, kids, seniors. I stood outside in the ninety-eight-degree heat, staring at a statue of Jesus with a handlebar mustache falling over his beard, in the fountain in the middle of the parking lot in front of the entrance to Prestonwood's worship center. Something told me to go back inside and talk to someone.

That was the whole point anyway—to get past the hurtful rhetoric and publicized inanity and actually talk to one another, as Christians and Americans. So I sidled up to a dark-haired mom and her two girls, in line at Guest Central. I was going to interview them; they seemed nice, but the mom wanted to see how to go about getting the family's baptism certificates, so she was standing in line waiting to talk to one of the young ministers. As she did so, another earnest young minister came up to me: "Hey! Welcome to Prestonwood! Can I help you?"

"I'm visiting from Minneapolis. I'm working on a book about conservative Christians. I was going to see if I could talk to one of your pastors or staff members or maybe some church members."

Thankfully, he was interested in the project and, forgoing the typical press protocol, hustled me down to meet Executive Pastor Buster, who kind of blew me off, made the remark about Moore being a "Blue State Christian," and then, sighing, turned to the couple next to him. "Well, you should talk to Keet," Buster said. "He's a Red State Christian."

The solid-looking man next to him, with salt-and-pepper hair, glasses, and a collared shirt, looked at me. "I am *the* Red State Christian," he insisted. "What do you want to ask me?"

This was Keet Lewis, a former national cochair for Senator Ted Cruz's presidential campaign and a formidable player in conservative Texas and national politics—so formidable that he'd even recently been accused of campaign finance misconduct by Texas Democrats in the *Dallas Morning News*. ("I figured you were OK to talk to because you weren't wearing a CNN badge," he told me later.)

Lewis's story, an ever-concentrating circle of politics, power, and religion, fit neatly into the story of the growth of Christian Nationalism in American politics, even though he wouldn't call himself a Christian Nationalist. He told me with a laugh that he spent one-third of his life in politics, one-third in Christian ministry, and one-third paying for the other two-thirds. Lewis is a CPA, a former president and CEO of a screen-printing company, director on the board of Salem Media Group, and co-owner of Lewis Group International. He serves on the executive committee of the Council for National Policy and on the boards of the Free Market Foundation, Heritage Alliance, Heritage Alliance PAC, Dallas Pregnancy Recourse Council, and Vanguard PAC, in addition to chairing the deacons at Prestonwood and the SBC's Committee on Nominations. His background reads, in other words, as he said: *the* Red State Christian, a profile of influence in the GOP.

While working on the reelection campaign for George H. W. Bush in 1992, Lewis first met Pastor Graham during a briefing with *National Affairs* magazine. "How many busloads did your church bring?" Graham asked Lewis.

"Man, I have, like, fourteen people," Lewis responded, laughing. At the time, he was a key elder in a smaller Fellowship Baptist congregation outside Dallas.

"You should be at Prestonwood," Graham said, the quintessential church evangelist.

Lewis weighed the offer. Six months later, as his leadership responsibilities at church wrapped up, he came to Prestonwood and has been there ever since. He enjoyed Graham's willingness to talk politics, especially conservative politics, from the pulpit.

"The thing I liked about Jack Graham is that he was unashamed of the gospel's impact on a person's whole life, including politics," Lewis said. "He had groups of people writing letters to their congressmen all the time. Our church had never had anything like that."

I was reminded of the superior organizing power of the GOP, something I had also witnessed months earlier at the March for Life. For decades now, Red State Christians have been mobilizing and organizing, often far from the traditional national power hubs of DC, New York City, Silicon Valley, and Los Angeles. They have built up a huge grassroots network that has won electoral success across the Midwest and rural America. Red State Christians had lost the cities and most urban population centers, but that didn't mean their power was diminished. They had a new strategy to win and new converts all the time. Their work came to fruition in Trump's election, even as his conduct would have been morally repugnant to many of the original conservative Christian organizers.

Both Lewis and Graham were originally Cruz supporters and organizers. "He was the straight-up Christian guy," Lewis said. "The brilliant lawyer. He was faith friendly. As a Texan, I was proud of Ted and his faith. He was the picture-perfect candidate. We just couldn't get on the Trump deal. But then all of a sudden, it was moving, and we couldn't get ahead of it."

Pastor Robert Jeffress of First Baptist Church in Dallas was one of the first significant Evangelicals to back Trump's candidacy. "I was meeting with [Jeffress] in his office, and I said, 'What are you thinking?'" Lewis remembered. "I knew one of us was going to be right, but I didn't think it would be him."

Jeffress, who later preached a sermon for Trump on Inauguration Day at a private service at Saint John's Episcopal in Washington, DC, has made headlines for his staunch support of Trump, saying it "didn't matter to Evangelicals" if Trump had an affair with porn star Stormy Daniels. Incidentally, the morning after attending Prestonwood for Saturday night service Fourth of July weekend, I attended Jeffress's service at First Baptist before heading back to Prestonwood. The service was, given the headlines about Jeffress, surprisingly innocuous. Apparently, I'd missed his sermon the previous Sunday, entitled "America Is a Christian Nation"; the Sunday I attended, Jeffress came across as mild, Bible centered, and not heretical.

Seeing the two pastors, Graham and Jeffress, preach back-to-back affirmed my impression that Prestonwood and Graham, with their glitzy, polished, popular Christian Nationalism, represent a much greater threat to the church, and to America, than Jeffress and his old-school Baptist views. It would be Graham who would convert many, Graham who could nail the *1984* Newspeak about "children's shelters" on the border.

Nevertheless, despite the nationalistic views displayed at Prestonwood that weekend, I was impressed by Lewis's down-to-earth manner and honesty. You could tell that Lewis, a Republican operative for decades, was tired of losing. He was tired of candidates who, in his words, "put themselves in the platform; McCain McCained it," which I took to mean that he made it too much about himself, "and the Bushes took things out because they thought it would offend people." In contrast, said Lewis, "Trump just let [Republicans] do their thing and didn't get involved [in writing the platform]. He did what he needed to do, and he let others take care of the rest."

Many Red State Christians embraced this idea—that Trump could win, but that given his lack of policy expertise or desire to actually govern, he could be easily controlled. This was especially important to Red State Christians when it came to impending vacancies on the Supreme Court during Trump's presidency.

But Trump, for the majority of Red State Christians, is much more than a puppet. He represents a combination of a redeemed sinner with a checkered past and a successful businessman who can get things done. When the Christian gospel has been conflated with a strong country, it's easy to see how Trump has come to be seen as a timely savior. Evangelicals love a redeemed sinner, especially when he's white, male, and rich.

Lewis said it all came together on June 21, 2016, at the United in Purpose event where five hundred Christians of influence gathered for a "conversation" with Trump and former GOP presidential candidate, later appointed Trump's Secretary of Housing and Urban Development, Ben Carson. "His scheduler said he would only stay for thirty minutes," Lewis said of Trump. "Well, he stayed for two and a half hours, and he took questions. That's the day Trump won America."

What is most appealing about Trump to Lewis and other Red State Christians, however, is not his faith but his strength, a sign they see that God is behind Trump's presidency. "His commitment to America First—we liked that. And he cannot be bullied. He is unafraid. He is unbulliable," Lewis told me in his moneyed Texas drawl, as we stood in front of Prestonwood's massive stage, surrounded by thousands of seats. As we continued to talk church and politics, another couple and Lewis's wife waited patiently to leave for Saturday-evening dinner. "There could be implications drawn from that. And that goes into the Deep State, too. He's not obligated to either party, and that's what drives them crazy. He's doing what he said he'd do. None of these guys ever do what they say they're going to do. I've been working in politics for thirty years."

Lewis credits Cruz with negotiations that helped secure Trump's Supreme Court picks, saying that in order for Cruz to endorse Trump, the Trump campaign had to agree that he'd make public the Federalist Society's list of Supreme Court picks and promise that he'd make a choice from that list. Lewis said that Trump's campaign manager, Paul Manafort, who has since been convicted of tax fraud, balked at the idea, but when Manafort was replaced by Kellyanne Conway, she accepted. Minutes later, Cruz endorsed Trump.

I found it interesting to speak with Lewis following the sermon from Frazier, which conflated Nationalism and the Christian gospel in ways that are alien to the Bible. Compared with Frazier's sermon, Lewis's views seemed to be standard conservative fare, more in the mold of former president George W. Bush than Trump. He offered a defense of Trump that seemed almost apologetic at times.

"We had to choose the best of what's offered," added Lewis's wife, Margaret, who had been standing nearby during our conversation. "If Christians don't engage, we don't have a voice. If Christians show up and vote, we win." If Christians vote, they agreed, it is a boon for

Republicans. The idea of Christians being influenced by their faith to vote Democratic was to them unimaginable, and I was reminded again of the organization gap between conservative Christians and liberal Christians, who not so long ago held political power and influence via mainline denominations.

Notably, Lewis admitted that many Christians voted for Obama in 2008; he was unique among the conservative leaders I interviewed to make such an admission. "But when it came to round two, they didn't," he said, adding that he could see the huge tide of conservatism rising in 2010, largely ignored by the Democratic leadership, whose members were clustered in large cities and on the East and West Coasts.

Lewis is devoted to the idea that Trump is on a spiritual pilgrimage, and you can see how men like him—well off, white, older—might relate to a rehabbed, born-again Christian experience, excusing Trump for the type of behavior that they abhorred in Bill Clinton. Clinton never had the "come to Jesus moment" that many Red State Christians ascribe to Trump, despite the lack of concrete evidence of a conversion experience. Lewis talks about the Christians in Trump's Cabinet—Secretary of State Mike Pompeo and National Security Advisor John Bolton—and Trump's Catholic wife, Melania, whom Lewis said led Trump in the Lord's Prayer during an audience with the pope. While many liberal Americans watch news networks and read articles decrying the lack of empathy in Trump's policies and his indecorous language, conservatives are reading stories about Trump's nascent Christianity. Lewis is convinced that Trump is researching his ancestral home in Scotland, where they held an Evangelical revival in 1948, because he wants to trace his Presbyterian faith background.

I saw in Keet Lewis what I saw in so many Trump-supporting Christians I interviewed, from the halls of power in Washington to the hollers of Appalachia: a desire to "make Trump good," a sense that they know that all is not right yet desperately want to believe that God has won in Trump, so they make all sorts of leaps. Despite these mental gymnastics regarding Trump, Lewis has a genuine love for Jesus and a desire that America might follow the Bible, at least as he understands it.

At the end of the interview, Keet and Margaret and I bragged about our kids. Margaret told me about their daughter, Caroline, who is a conservative writer, thirty-three years old, and "could sit down with a total liberal, and they'd agree with her 100 percent." I didn't sense any malice in Keet and Margaret, and they didn't speak with the anger and fear of Prestonwood Baptist Church pastor Jack Graham or guest preacher Gary Frazier.

Pastor Jack Graham and America's Brood of Vipers

Jesus did not fault the tax collectors or even the politicians he encountered in Jerusalem. He reserved his greatest vitriol for the religious leaders, the Pharisees. I see a link between the Pharisees of the first century and the conservative pastors at Prestonwood who lead Red State Christians astray of the gospel. These pastors and Christian leaders represent our American Pharisees, the disciples of Christian Nationalism.

"You brood of vipers! How can you speak good things, when you are evil? For out of the abundance of the heart the mouth speaks," says Jesus in the Gospel of Matthew. "Woe to you, scribes and Pharisees, hypocrites! For you are like whitewashed tombs, which on the outside look beautiful, but inside they are full of the bones of the dead and of all kinds of filth. So you also on the outside look righteous to others, but inside you are full of hypocrisy and lawlessness" (Matthew 12:34, 23:27–28).

The next morning, back at Prestonwood for Sunday-morning worship, I witnessed Pastor Graham turn the story of God's faithfulness to God's chosen people into the story of God's favor for nation-states, particularly Israel and America, and the kings who rule them. The service began again with an homage to the American military. As the song and video petered out again, reminding us of the unmatched and unforgettable sacrifice of the American military, this time the entire sanctuary of thousands stood and applauded. I saw zero dissenters, so this time I stood, too. I didn't think I had a choice.

Graham then began to tell his story, twisting the family of Abraham to encompass the modern nations of Israel and America. "Israel and America share a spiritual legacy: Yahweh. We are connected by our shared faith in the structure of the family"—a little red meat for the anti-gay-marriage crowd. He continued, "Our history is close because America also is a miracle. In so many ways, America is a miracle from God. In 1492, when Columbus sailed the ocean blue and discovered the new world, did you know they were financed by a Jew? And the first person to step off the boat was a Jew?

"I have met [Prime Minister Netanyahu]; he is quite a gentleman and quite a person," Graham said, establishing his Israel bona fides. He went on, "Jesus is the Jewish Messiah. Many of them rejected him, but many of them are coming to Jesus." Graham conveniently ignored the Jewish rejection of Jesus as Savior and the fact that his words would be heresy to most Israelis, including Netanyahu. He then moved quickly into full-on Christian Nationalism: "We just quoted the Pledge of Allegiance. It was beautiful. We also sang the 'Star-Spangled Banner.' We sing it at ball games, why not at church?"

From the Christian Nationalist dream, Graham began to paint a picture of another America, one likely ruled by Democrats, the "they" he references. "We have two Americas: one that is secular and godless, and another that is spiritual and of God. They say no God—no

God in the halls of our schools, no God, no Bible, no Commandments, and no sanctity of marriage, and no sanctity of life. No God."

"Our nation will be taken down by this reproach to God," he declared. "It's quite possible that the demise of America is because of our secularism," he speculated.

Graham dismisses the idea that Christian Nationalism could bring suffering to those Americans who don't fit its white, middle-class, straight Christian ideal. He dismissed sexism, racism, homophobia, discrimination, and injustice of all kinds in a single sweeping sentence: "People are in bondage today and persecuted, but the greatest bondage is the bondage of sin."

"There is another Statue of Liberty, and it's the cross of Christ," he preached. The conflation of the promise of America and the promise of the Christian gospel was indubitable after that sentence.

"If you want to know," he continued, "we are in the last days. There are wars, ruins, and moral collapse. A super sign in the Scripture will be the restoration of Israel to their land. Jesus once said this generation of people will never be dispersed again. Israel is in the land for keeps. What we are doing today"—earlier the congregation had applauded Trump moving the US Embassy to Jerusalem—"is setting in motion the final hours of history."

"We have a king, and his name is Jesus," he concluded. When Graham ended his sermon, I felt myself breathing heavily. He had mentioned Jesus, sure, but it felt like a name without a story, like a name without a gospel, as though Jesus were just a fill-in name for this ultimate king who would glorify us all, especially if we happened to be white and wealthy and American (or Israeli—and if we were Israeli, we'd better be the "right" kind of Israeli, that is, white and conservative with money), and we'd better plan on converting at the last minute. All the while, the threat of the end times hovered in the sanctuary, an omnipresent fear.

In my final analysis, Graham plays a religious leader, but he leads people away from God. He manipulates. He uses hatred of the other, fear, and submission to gain power—a distortion of the true gospel of Jesus, grounded in love, acceptance, forgiveness, and the absence of fear. Graham spoke about Jesus's supposed prophecy to this American generation, a prophecy emphasizing fear, power, strength, riches, nostalgia, and hatred of the other. But as Keet Lewis proves, not every Red State Christian at Prestonwood drips with the same anger and fear. Thank God.

CHAPTER 2

He Will Save the
Supreme Court: Abortion

Of the overriding stereotypes about Red State Christians, among the most common is that they are a backward lot—uninformed, out of touch, and uncaring about the broader world beyond their congregations and rural enclaves, clinging to their guns and religion, a basket of deplorables. The truth is quite different. The most common reason for voting for Trump cited by conservative Christians indicates both their level of information and their concern for the broader world. For many Red State Christians, voting with gritted teeth for Trump, their decision came down to a simple, heartfelt belief: he will save the Supreme Court. Conservative Christian Trump voters may not read the *Atlantic* or *Vanity Fair*, but they are well versed in the politics of the Supreme Court, particularly when it comes to abortion law. For these voters, the election of Trump meant not just an opportunity to overturn the long-detested *Roe v. Wade* but also a means to build a bulwark against a liberal Court, made possible by justice deaths or retirements during the years of a potential Trump presidency.

The Court was a contentious topic during Trump's election and presidency, and voters were right that the newly elected president would have opportunities to make multiple Supreme Court nominations. In the second year of Trump's presidency, eighty-one-year-old swing voter Justice Anthony Kennedy announced his retirement, sparking the second of two Court battles during Trump's presidency. During the same year, liberal stalwart justice Ruth Bader Ginsburg turned eighty-five, and fellow liberal justice Stephen Breyer turned seventy-nine. Trump's first Supreme Court nominee, Justice Neil Gorsuch, had already passed muster and been sworn in just three months after Trump took office in January 2017. All the while, a special counsel named Robert Mueller was on assignment for the Justice Department, in the midst of investigating potential collusion between the Trump campaign and the Russian government during the 2016 election. These newly elected justices could hold Trump's fate in their hands. But that wasn't the primary concern of Christians who voted for Trump in 2016.

Nine months before the 2016 presidential election, the conservative world was shaken by the death of famed justice Antonin Scalia, found dead at a hunting ranch in Texas. The official ruling was death by natural causes. The seventy-nine-year-old Scalia had a history of heart trouble, but that didn't stop conservative activists from musing over more nefarious reasons for his death. Republican strategist Brad Todd said he's not sure Red State Christians would have supported Trump without the death of Scalia.

"It wasn't an expected vacancy; it was Scalia. Imagine if it had been Roberts," Todd told me. "You'd wonder if a thrice-married, anatomy-grabbing candidate would have gotten Evangelicals behind him."

In the midst of court battles over gay wedding cakes and trans-friendly bathrooms, Red State Christians felt national opinion moving against them. In a show of support for Evangelical values, Trump released a list of potential Supreme Court nominees shortly after being sworn in. All were conservative; all were supported by the influential Federalist Society and Heritage Foundation. All were staunchly pro-life, and many had a record of opposing gay rights.

"More people in America became court conscious," Todd said. "People in rural America weren't dumb and drug addled, they were paying attention to the Supreme Court."

As pop culture moved against Red State Christians, they looked to someone, anyone, who would support their causes and make them winners again. George W. Bush had spoken the language of compassionate conservatism and came across as authentically born again. But his inept management of the economy and his nomination of the relatively moderate John Roberts meant Bush wasn't the Evangelicals' man anymore. Red State Christians needed a champion. Winning was more important than being pure. Most Democrats remember Trump's 1999 *Meet the Press* interview where he stated unequivocally, "I am very pro-choice." But few mainstream news outlets emphasized a story that gained prominence in pro-life circles. Back in 2011, five years before Trump would become the Republican nominee for president, he told a story to Christian Broadcasting Network's David Brody about two friends of his:

> One of the reasons I changed—one of the primary reasons—a friend of mine's wife was pregnant, in this case married. She was pregnant, and he didn't really want the baby. And he was telling me the story. He was crying as he was telling me the story. He ends up having the baby, and the baby is the apple of

his eye. It's the greatest thing that's ever happened to him. And you know, here's a baby that wasn't going to be let into life. And I heard this, and some other stories, and I am pro-life.[1]

Trump had a conversion story that Red State Christians loved to hear, and he followed it up with promises and a letter outlining his specific pro-life policies: defunding Planned Parenthood, making permanent the Hyde Amendment disallowing taxpayer funding for abortions under Medicaid, and most significantly, appointing pro-life justices to the Supreme Court. About that same time, many Americans wrote off Trump for his sexist comments on a bus with Billy Bush. But Red State Christians were hearing a story of repentance and, more importantly, a story of a powerful man who might finally advocate for them.

This conservative group, many of whom attend churches where women are not allowed to preach or serve on the board of elders, would be hard-pressed to seriously consider a female candidate for president. When that same female candidate was married to the original boor of the White House and depicted in conservative media as wanting to abort as many babies as possible, Red State Christians had fewer qualms about embracing Trump. Another Clinton presidency was unthinkable. A few Evangelicals quietly advanced a biblical theory comparing Trump to the benevolent Persian king Cyrus, called "anointed one" in Isaiah 45:1. Cyrus decreed the rebuilding of the Jerusalem temple in spite of the fact that he was not Hebrew and did not worship the God of Israel, and he allowed the return of the Jews to the promised land from their time in Babylonian captivity. Cyrus succeeded where many Hebrew kings had failed. Red State Christians began to imagine that Trump could be their own King Cyrus, who would give way eventually to the "true" Evangelical, vice presidential candidate Mike Pence, a longtime conservative Christian advocate and proven Evangelical, albeit a Catholic one. In the face of videos showing Planned Parenthood nonchalantly selling aborted baby parts for profit, what was a little "locker room talk"? Red State Christians felt lives were at stake—indeed, eternal life.

Articles by prominent Evangelicals started circulating on social media, essentially offering absolution for guilty Evangelicals who wanted to vote for Trump. While some leading Evangelicals spoke out against Trump's character, people in the pews were frustrated and impatient. Weaned by these same leaders on the easy theological selling points of American exceptionalism, support of the military, and nationalism, the less-popular tenets of Jesus's mandates to care for the poor and let the oppressed go free were a tougher sell than the seemingly obvious: Hillary wants to kill babies, and Trump has promised to save the unborn while also making us great again. The choice was clear.

Marching for Life

About a year into the great Evangelical experiment known as the presidency of Donald Trump, I wanted to see how this unequally yoked marriage between Trump and Evangelicals was working out. I booked a flight to Washington, DC, arriving a day before the March for Life, the largest gathering of pro-lifers in the country, billed as "the largest human rights demonstration in American history." As an added bonus, for the first time in history, a sitting president would address the March for Life, albeit from a few blocks away on the jumbotron. I met my first March attendees on the DC Metro at the Arlington stop, on the way downtown from Washington Reagan Airport. Many of them were young. A middle-school girl from Nebraska wearing French braids told me she was going to march with her family and friends.

"It's just such an important cause," she said. "Did you hear President Trump is going to address the march?" Hordes of Catholic school teenagers got on the Metro at Arlington Cemetery. They might have been more excited about a trip to the nation's capital than about devoting themselves to the pro-life cause. Still, at a formative time in their lives, these young people were exposed to what they called "a culture of life."

I began my March for Life morning at a conference put on by the Ethics and Religious Liberty Commission (ERLC) of the Southern Baptist Convention, a group called Evangelicals for Life. The first speaker I heard was best-selling author Ann Voskamp, listed in the program as a wife and mother. She started out by thrusting the Bible in the air with one hand, saying in a quavering but resolute voice, "This is a book about refugees," going on to quote numerous Bible passages and Evangelical heavyweight Tim Keller: "If the church doesn't identify with the marginalized, then the church will be marginalized." While surely pro-life, this group was also pro-refugee.

The March for Life happened against the backdrop of a congressional showdown between Democrats, who wanted a deal for so-called Dreamers (undocumented Americans brought to the United States as children), and Republicans, who were attempting to institute Trump's hard-line immigration policies without coming across as heartless. American Evangelicals, many of whom are nonwhite, found themselves largely allied with Democrats on immigration but allied with Trump on abortion. Many white Evangelicals, however, were hesitant to support Dreamers, whom they saw as flouting the rules their European ancestors followed. The tension was palpable during a panel discussion among Southern Baptist Ethics and Religious

Liberty Commission president Russell Moore, Focus on the Family president Jim Daly, World Relief senior vice president of advocacy Jenny Yang, and Voskamp. Moore wanted to extend a conciliatory hand to both groups, suggesting that advocacy for the unborn could lead to advocacy for refugees, and vice versa. Moore stated the obvious: "The reason we care about all of these people is because Jesus does."

When asked about tensions between social justice and pro-life groups, Moore suggested that the friction originated in the national media, and people got along in the grassroots. But Yang pushed back, pointing out that many don't think about the fact that deportations lead to separation of families, and therefore to be pro-family means to be pro-immigration. Daly, clearly sensing political tension, backtracked. "People can have myopic vision," he said. "What is our assignment, and what is the government's assignment?" The crowd murmured in approval. His statement represents a familiar trope in American Evangelicalism: the church, not the government, should provide social services and care for the poor. In this worldview, you can rationally support a government that slashes welfare and deports families while volunteering for a church that hosts refugees and supports a soup kitchen. Evangelicals justify this hypocrisy with Jesus's exhortation to "give to Caesar what belongs to Caesar" (Mark 12:17).

Nevertheless, the Evangelicals for Life conference promoted a rare, inclusive vision of what it means to be pro-life. Rather than the judgmental and disturbing signs of bloody unborn babies I'd anticipated, the ERLC created innocuous signs for its marchers to carry. On a black background with white text, the signs simply read, "All people are made in the image of God." What Christian wouldn't march with that?

Even more shocking, the next speaker, an American pastor who'd moved to Uganda when an international adoption didn't go through, sounded brazenly progressive. "This is not one more white-savior story," Smooth Via said. "If we're gonna be Evangelicals for Life, if we're gonna be pro-life, then we fight for who Jesus fought for. I want you to fight for all life. If we're gonna be pro-life, we have to fight for all lives: black, white, blue, gay, straight." I could sense a youthful momentum on the side of a movement I'd long associated with my Catholic grandmother. The pro-life movement here was truly trying to embrace life in all of its complexity. Still, if Via, Moore, Daly, Voskamp, and Yang were building a bridge, the event's final speaker reminded me of the wall that often exists between Red State Christians and everyone else. "I was pro-choice, and I wasn't a Christian," Trillia Newman said, almost perfunctorily, emphasizing the deadness of her heart before she embraced born-again Christianity and a pro-life ethic.

Those Who March for Life

My partner for the beginning of the March for Life was Pam Nicholson, a mother and grandmother from nearby Maryland. She grew up nominally Episcopalian and had been attending a nondenominational church until recently, when the worship got too contemporary for her. She and her husband began attending a Methodist church, and she came to a realization while attending the March for Life: "I must be going to a liberal church. No one said anything about the March for Life."

Nicholson was a first-time marcher who had signed up for the conference on a whim, unsure if she would actually show up. "I'm not a sign carrier," she said. "I'm not a marcher." But Nicholson told me that her personal Bible study had caused her to reexamine her pro-choice views, and she found herself growing more and more conservative, the more she studied her Bible. As a teenager, she said, "I basically thought, 'Don't tell me what to do,' and 'Abortion is no one's business.' Then I got married, and I was pregnant with a daughter. The only difference now was that I wanted a baby." It made her think about her views, she told me—"that life begins at conception, not when I want it to begin." I was struck by the humility of Nicholson's position. She had come to it not by politics or culture but rather by introspection, prayer, and Bible study. She also identified with the feeling of marginalization experienced by many Red State Christians in the Trump era.

"I've been watching how the media counts numbers, and that seems to be how they determine what matters, so I had a feeling that I needed to be counted," Nicholson said, recalling the comparison of Trump's inauguration crowd and the 2017 Women's March in Washington, DC. Her feeling was shared among Red State Christians I talked to at the March for Life. They had taken on the mantle of "deplorables," and they knew that people were looking down on them. So they wanted to stand up and be counted. Many felt as though they'd been forgotten in the modern conception of America, and they wanted to matter, more than they wanted to be "great." Nicholson hedged when asked about the breadth of her pro-life positions. She referenced one of her daughters, who was Catholic by marriage and the mother of three children, born close together. "Birth control is a tough one for me," she said. "Mother always told us, 'Don't have a lot of kids.' Being the oldest of twelve was hard for her. She was a big supporter of birth control."

As we walked on the Washington Mall, surrounded by a crowd of anti-abortion marchers, I broached the topic of Trump. "I vote, but pro-life isn't my highest priority," she admitted. "You're never really sure about a candidate. I didn't vote for Trump, but I've been thrilled with his politics." Nicholson mentioned her daughters' in-laws, both doctors who have struggled with mandates that require them to participate in medical procedures that are against their Catholic beliefs. She brought up Trump's recent expansion of the Religious Freedom Restoration Acts. "I've been thrilled with his politics," she repeated.

My interaction with Nicholson surprised me, and it encapsulated my experience at the March for Life as a whole. I'd come expecting a thinly veiled Trump rally, complete with Make America Great Again hats and chants of "Build the wall!" and "Lock her up!" What I found instead were Christians talking openly about their initial ambivalence regarding Trump. Nicholson wasn't the only march attendee I talked to who hadn't voted for him. What surprised me most was that in Trump's first year of office, widely considered a disaster by most mainstream media outlets, Red State Christians were *more* supportive of Trump than they had been before. In the same way that Nicholson was introspective and humble in explaining her pro-life journey, I noticed a similar self-consciousness on behalf of the entire pro-life movement, strikingly different from Trump himself. Where Trump was brash and cocky in courting "my Evangelicals," as he called them, the marchers themselves were cognizant, and even ashamed, of the negative opinion many in America have of them and their support of Trump. In fact, most march organizers went out of their way to be inclusive and appeal to progressives. Jeanne Mancini, president of the March for Life Education and Defense Fund, repeated this phrase over and over again about the march: "the largest annual human rights demonstration in the world."

By tying the pro-life movement to human rights, Mancini positioned the march to appeal to a new generation of voters. And as House Speaker Paul D. Ryan would later point out, the march was conspicuously made up of young people—conspicuous because conservative Christians are usually thought of as older, white baby boomers.

The opening prayer noted that "any violence," including racism, oppression, and hatred, "is the tearing of the tunic," referring to biblical mourning rituals where clothing was torn, and "to be pro-life is to understand that all violence of all time is violence of all." Mancini continued in the same vein, saying that "abortion has claimed the lives of sixty million Americans in the last forty-five years." The messaging sounded persuasive. Even as I wrote about the march later, I felt ashamed to use the word *fetus*, rather than the pro-life preferred term, *unborn baby*. The anti-abortion movement effectively claimed the moral high ground, and even for a feminist Christian, I found it difficult to argue with the movement's rhetoric.

Following the opening prayer, speakers returned to more familiar pro-life tales. A young nun told the story of a girl named Raquel, who became pregnant as a teenager and lived with the religious sisters during her pregnancy. Raquel said she would never have an abortion but would also never tell another woman what to do—a line of thinking many women can relate to. Then the nun told the story of Raquel meeting another young pregnant mom in the hospital, on her way to an abortion. "You're not having an abortion, you're having a baby," Raquel told her. Two years later, Raquel saw the same young woman again at the hospital, wheeling a stroller with twin girls, one named Raquel.

I wondered about the holes in the story, the journey the young woman had taken from pregnant teen to teen mother of twin toddlers. I wondered about the opportunities she'd given up, the support or shame she'd received, and what she really thought about her decisions. Did she feel doubly blessed or doubly cursed?

Then I saw my first red Trump hat. I didn't see more than about five all day, even as vendors attempted to hawk them. The lack of

MAGA hats pointed to the crowd's ambivalence about Trump. Evangelicals wanted to be open to and affirming of the idea that the right to life goes beyond birth. They also wanted a champion who would repeal *Roe v. Wade*, even if that champion was an unconvincing convert to the pro-life cause.

The jumbotron shifted to the Rose Garden at the White House. Vice President Mike Pence, responsible for much Evangelical support of Trump, continued his tradition of never shying away from hyperbole, introducing Trump as "the most pro-life president in American history" and "a tireless defender of life and conscience in America." While *conscience* may not be the first word many Americans think of when they think of Trump, the crowd nonetheless offered requisite cheers, though the cheers were more tepid than I'd anticipated. He began to speak in typical Trumpian fashion, extolling the "beautiful day" and "how nice" the crowd was to clap for him, his childlike need for incessant praise on full display. Trump had the fortune of looking like a sheepish little boy in need of love, and even at his most offensive, I wondered if the women and mothers in the crowd who'd managed to vote for him had done so in the same way we excused our husbands and sons, sometimes thinking of grown men as petulant, overgrown little boys.

Who Owns the Pro-Life Movement?

At his core, Trump believes in transactional relationships. You scratch my back; I'll scratch yours. Many of Trump's Evangelical supporters view their relationship with him the same way. At the march, he recited the pro-life greatest hits he was expected to, and the crowd cheered as it was expected to. But the crowd cheered much louder for other speakers, notably for Speaker Ryan. The president was tolerated, in the same way he tolerated the intrusion of Evangelical policies in his political platform of self-aggrandizement. Trump was notably more animated in the second half of his speech, when he got to talking about how great the country was doing since he took office.

Ryan spoke next, decidedly more in his element than Trump, and was more openly embraced, especially by his many fellow Catholics in the crowd. Unlike Trump, Ryan fell in line with some earlier speakers and with the Evangelicals at that morning's conference by emphasizing the inclusivity and even progressivism of the pro-life movement. He got a big cheer when he said, "Science is on our side," breaking stride with a GOP that has often been at odds with scientists, especially when it comes to climate change and vaccines. "One thing that gets lost," Ryan said, "is just how compassionate the pro-life movement is. That's why it's such a joyful crowd. You're marching with joy and love, not anger and hate. You don't see that much on the other side, do you?"

Ryan had reversed the narrative swallowed by much of American pop culture for the past year or so since Trump took office. The Democrats were supposed to be the compassionate ones, and the Republicans the ones who want to yank benefits and give away all money to the rich, the hate-filled racists and sexist pigs. Americans have rarely heard the GOP's kindness counternarrative since the failure of Bush's compassionate conservatism. But as I looked around, I had to admit that Ryan had a point. The pro-lifers were doing their darnedest to be a positive, family-friendly movement. I rarely saw or heard anything about abortion at all. When I finally saw an anti-Hillary sign, I went up to the young man carrying it, expecting to hear sexist rhetoric and Trumpian grandeur. "Well, I didn't vote for Trump," said Ben, who had driven to the march from Creighton University in Nebraska with a group of fellow college students.

The only mildly hate-filled rhetoric I heard openly was from a pair of teenagers, a brother and sister, who had traveled to the march with their family. They were wearing Trump buttons. "I have a lot of friends who are Mexican," said Madge from suburban Illinois. "But Trump just wants to separate the good from the bad; the Mexicans are coming in with gangs and drugs, and they just keep coming back. I don't want to get raped."

Trump had awakened a fear, maybe a racist fear, in this young girl, who said she was attending the march because her father had been adopted after being born to a teenage mother. But she might outgrow her words; her hatred was not yet deeply rooted. Maybe that was the saving grace of Trump: he said so many inflammatory things about so many people, but he didn't say any of them with enough depth for them to stick. Even his racism, as vile and despicable as racism is, usually reads as pragmatic rather than ideological, like his relationship with Evangelicals.

As the speakers continued on the jumbotron, each planned and precise and diverse in background, the politicians gave way to former NFL center Matt Birk, who said something else that surprised me: "Abortion advocates are our brothers and sisters." American politics have become so divisive that a universal brother/sisterhood seems elusive. It doesn't help the anti-abortion cause to suggest that abortion advocates are good people. But again, like Moore's words earlier at the Evangelicals for Life Conference, Birk's statement invited people to cross the aisle, so to speak.

I've spent much of my life in conservative communities, where you're more likely to be shamed for liberal views than conservative ones. Rhonda Green, from downtown Philly, had the opposite experience. As an African American woman, she was a distinct minority at the March for Life, yet she told me she was among like-minded people, more so than in her own neighborhood.

Green talked about her arguments with her sister, Renee. "She goes to a liberal church, and she tells me, 'Rhonda, you're all about rules.' But I never saw Trump as racist. I saw the comments he made [about the NFL kneeling protests]. I didn't agree with his comments, but people of color made comments, too. I didn't see it as a racist thing."

Green said she and her sister argued about the pro-life movement's commitment to life after birth, but it struck me that their disagreements were grounded in love and a deep Christian faith. These two women, from the same family, came to very different conclusions politically and loved each other anyway. Neither was less of a Christian than the other. Still, it wasn't easy to be a black Trump supporter in Philadelphia. "My sister asked me not to go out alone," Green said.

An America of Two Marches

The march wrapped up near the steps of the Supreme Court, and in those final blocks, I saw the horrifying graphic posters of aborted fetuses and heard recorded newborn-baby cries. These tactics worked to promote the pro-life movement by shaming women through graphic and painful imagery that felt sensationalistic and unnecessary.

The next day I'd join the Women's March, though again more as a reporter and observer than a marcher. That's another story for another book, but what surprised me there, where I'd expected to feel more at home, was that the extremes of both the conservative and liberal movements had been tainted by partisanship and greed, so that the compassion of some of their lauded goals was lost. For example, I watched a group of young black women chant slogans while a group of older white women nearby told them to be quiet.

What remains with me most from those two days was a moment just before the horrifying images and sounds at the end of the March for Life. In the chaos of salesmen and church groups and angry street preachers and curious onlookers, a man played "Amazing Grace" on an alto saxophone outside DC's Union Station. I was so grateful just to feel that grace, to taste that grace, to experience that grace— that grace that is altogether all too lacking in American politics and American life and even in American churches. I climbed atop a concrete platform near him and watched the marchers stream ahead and behind, from across the country, like me and not like me, proud and quiet, hopeful and hateful.

I watched them walk, and I forced myself to hear only that old, old, song, written by a man who once traded slaves and later worked to set them free—a song sung more than two hundred years later every weekend in churches and concert halls across America, often by the descendants of those same slaves, hoping that this land of the free will finally offer justice to them. The song reminded me of repentance, of transformation, of America's unbelievable capacity for hope, and I wondered why I'd become so hopeless, so jaded, so cynical, so limiting of the amazing grace of Jesus.

Amazing grace, how sweet the sound
That saved a wretch like me.

I walked over to the saxophonist at the end of the song. He removed his hat and said, "God bless America," in a heavy accent.

Trump was nowhere to be seen.

CHAPTER 3

God and Guns

Gun control dominated national dialogue even in Trump's America, or so it appeared on March 24, 2018, as more than a million protesters thronged the streets of Washington, DC, and eight hundred other US cities, shouting, "What do we want? Gun control! When do we want it? Now!"

The world was fascinated by the Parkland Kids, as they became known: teenagers David Hogg, Cameron Kasky, Jaclyn Corin, Alex Wind, Alfonso Calderon, and others. They were survivors of a school shooting at Marjory Stoneman Douglas High School in Parkland, Florida, outside Fort Lauderdale in Broward County. Former student Nikolas Cruz, age nineteen, killed seventeen people—fourteen students and three staff members—and wounded seventeen more. Parkland marked the eighth-deadliest mass shooting in American history, and the students decided to raise their voices, primarily on social media and news outlets, organizing nationwide school walkouts and the March for Our Lives on March 24.

Gun violence and gun rights divide Americans along party lines. Due to our militia roots, the vaunted Second Amendment, and Wild West lore, Americans love guns, even as gun violence kills thousands of Americans each year. More than eleven thousand Americans died in 2016 due to homicide by gunshot, the first major increase in fifteen years.[1] The mass shooting, a particularly American horror, has become more prevalent and deadly in recent years: of the thirty deadliest shootings in America going back to 1949, eighteen have occurred since 2007.[2] American mass shooters even have a gun of choice, the AR-15.[3]

On October 1, 2017, Stephen Paddock committed the deadliest mass shooting in America since 1949, using a cache of modified semi-automatic weapons, including AR-15s. He killed fifty-eight concert-goers and bystanders at the Route 91 Harvest country music festival in Las Vegas, and he injured 851 more. Just four months later, Cruz killed seventeen in Parkland, the deadliest shooting ever at an American high school, and another grim gun statistic for Donald Trump's young presidency.

Still, reaction to gun violence broke along party lines, despite the passion of the high-school students. Polarized opinions among politicians and their constituents only led to more inertia. Christians were among the most divided Americans, with liberal Christians championing voluntary programs to turn in guns, and conservative Christians carrying holsters to prayer meetings.

While the Bible doesn't address guns, it doesn't seem likely that Jesus would have been a gunslinger. The Old Testament prophets spoke of beating swords into plowshares, spears into pruning hooks, and praying of a world where "nation shall not lift up sword against nation, neither shall they learn war anymore" (Isaiah 2:4). And on the night before he was crucified, Jesus warned his disciple Peter against even retributive and defensive violence, as Peter sought to save Jesus from the religious hierarchy and Roman soldiers who would imprison and kill him: "Put your sword back into its place; for all who take the sword will perish by the sword," Jesus told him (Matthew 26:52).

Would Jesus advocate for gun control in America? Of course, Jesus espoused nonviolence. But he was also a sometime anarchist pacifist who rarely found solutions to problems within government bureaucracy. Maybe he would have appealed instead to people's hearts and minds, to healing communities from the inside. Mass shootings and school shootings aside, America's most stubborn and entrenched gun violence occurs primarily in impoverished urban neighborhoods, where most guns are not purchased legally anyway. The thrust of gun control legislation is more complicated than activists on either side admit, and despite fear-mongering headlines, no one wants to take away rifles from deer hunters in rural America, where owning a gun is commonplace and gun control is seen as a threat to American individualism and sovereignty.

An America Where You Need a Gun

Many Christians, following the pacifist roots of Jesus and centuries of Christian leaders, marched with the Parkland kids on March 24, 2018. But other Christians looked at the same data, the same incidence of troubling mass shootings, and took a different tack. For them, the answer was not fewer guns but more guns. President Trump gave voice to this response just a week after Parkland, defending it via tweet on February 22, the morning after meeting with people affected by school shootings, including bereaved parents, at a White House event:

> What I said was to look at the possibility of giving concealed guns to gun adept teachers with military or special training

experience—only the best. 20% of teachers, a lot, would now be able to immediately fire back if a savage sicko came to school with bad intentions. Highly trained teachers would also serve as a deterrent to the cowards that do this. Far more assets at much less cost than guards. A "gun free" school is a magnet for bad people. ATTACKS WOULD END.

Americans asked how these shootings could happen. Is it too easy to get access to a deadly weapon? Are the available guns too powerful? Is the problem caused by lax background checks or easily available ammunition at Walmart?

None of these reasons resounded with Red State Christians. For them, gun violence has nothing to do with gun laws at all. Instead, the Parkland shooting and others like it comprised evidence of society collapsing all around us. They saw broken families and lamented the exodus of prayer in schools. They saw a loss of a certain American innocence. They saw young people lacking steady ground on which to stand. They blamed social media and the internet and birth control. The shootings were rooted in people who didn't speak English and too many refugees and ISIS encroaching on American borders.

For many Red State Christians, a world in which people felt cornered led to the Parkland shooting. The "American carnage" depicted by Trump in his inauguration speech came alive in the images of students running out of their schools, hands over their heads, terrified. In this scary, unfamiliar America, Red State Christians would never surrender their guns. They had to hold them tighter. In fact, they had to arm teachers. They had already lost so much that had previously kept them safe. Guns, in this view, were one final defense against the encroachment of an amoral, irreligious outside world.

Red State Christians felt betrayed by the white, affluent Parkland students who championed gun control. They disbelieved and disliked the students' gun control advocacy so much that popular right-wing media called the Parkland kids "crisis actors" and attacked their credibility. For Red State Christians, the students, like the shooter himself, presaged a future America that looks nothing like *Happy Days*, in which no one says the pledge and no one defends the Constitution. Someone had to rise up. America is under attack.

We Are Heavily Armed—Signed, The Pastors

Two days after a gunman killed twenty-six people at a small Baptist church in Sutherland Springs, Texas, Pastor Rodney Howard-Browne, a Florida pastor and member of Trump's Evangelical Advisory Board, responded on Twitter with a photo of the signs on his church's doors:

WARNING

WELCOME TO THE RIVER AT TAMPA BAY CHURCH—RIGHT OF ADMISSION RESERVED—THIS IS PRIVATE PROPERTY. PLEASE KNOW THIS IS NOT A GUN FREE ZONE—WE ARE HEAVILY ARMED—ANY ATTEMPT WILL BE DEALT WITH DEADLY FORCE—YES WE ARE A CHURCH AND WE WILL PROTECT OUR PEOPLE.

—THE PASTORS

Pastor Allen Hawes said the signs had been up for a year before anyone noticed. Tampa police had been looking for a mass murderer, and the River was the kind of high-profile church that could be susceptible to a shooting. Pastors are not immune to death threats, and in an age of social media and easily accessible guns, maybe Howard-Browne was right to be afraid. The signs were a bit of an overstatement, too. The night I went to youth worship at the River, a few weeks after Parkland happened on the other side of Florida, Hawes told me that he wasn't actually carrying a gun while he preached. "I have a permit though," he said. "Florida has more conceal-carry permits than any other state. We aren't waiting for there to be a scary first time it happens." After Parkland and Vegas and Sutherland Springs, everyone was already scared, but we left that unspoken, hanging in the humid air that Sunday night in March 2018.

To understand the River at Tampa Bay and the unique threat it and churches like it make to American Christianity, you have to enter their world. You have to walk into church as I did, suspending judgment and disbelief and saying, as I told the bright-eyed young woman at the welcome desk, "I want to go to worship."

She first pointed me toward Pastor Allen, who looked like many Evangelical megachurch pastors: dressed in tight jeans, but not aggressively tight, and a button-up shirt cut to make clear that, yes, he does lift weights. He had slightly squinted eyes and a defensive posture, ready at any moment to swing into action and defend the gospel or Donald Trump.

If you can manage to look past the sign that tells you the pastors are heavily armed, the River feels like your run-of-the-mill American megachurch. It pops up out of nowhere on a meandering Tampa road, north of Brandon on the way to Plant City, far inland from the glitzy hotels and beaches of Tampa Bay and Clearwater. You've entered

Red State Florida, much different from the glamour of Trump's Palm Beach Mar-a-Lago Winter White House. Welcome to a place where people fish and hang gun racks in their pickups—a place that has more in common with Alabama than Miami.

But know this: the River is not a white phenomenon, nor a middle-aged one. I am visiting the youth service on Sunday night, and apparently I have chosen a big night, with fire and lots of baptisms. Nearly three thousand people "like" the River's Student Ministries Facebook page. Hundreds of them are here tonight. The young woman who greets me at the information desk has dark, wavy, natural hair and a welcoming style. She's dressed stylishly but not too carefully, as though she might wear $500 sneakers with some cutoff jeans she got at Target. Most of the young people here tonight act self-consciously cool—megachurch hipster Christian chic. They mill around, gazing at Howard-Browne's latest offering in the church library, which lacks Bibles, devotionals, or theological books. Instead, it promotes Browne's latest work, a patriotic spin-off of disgraced conservative pundit Bill O'Reilly's *Killing* series. Howard-Browne titled his work *Killing Uncle Sam: The Demise of the United States of America*, and on the cover is a bloodied American flag with a sword stuck in it, with the US Constitution in the background.

Howard-Browne has spread some wild theories recently. In an October 2017 sermon, he suggested that human sacrifice and cannibalism have been "going on for years" in Hollywood. Three months earlier, he claimed insider knowledge of a planned attack on Trump, known about at the highest levels of government. Howard-Browne is also famous for inciting Holy Spirit laughter, which is decidedly creepier than it sounds.

At this point in the evening, the River felt just like a slightly-more-guns-happy version of every Evangelical, Southern Baptist, and nondenominational church I'd ever attended: the obligatory café, kids milling around in tight jeans and T-shirts, awkward church romances, and older people trying to be cool and join in the youth group. It felt fairly innocuous, as I've experienced at most megachurches. There was a great sense of energy in worship, fantastic music and quality production, a well-planned sermon, some covert misogyny and less-covert homophobia, American flags, a feeling of us-against-the-world—but nothing that would bring down America or irreversibly taint the name of Jesus.

Trump's American Youth Group

I met Pastor Allen, and he promised to speak with me after service. He was pleasant enough, as was the woman in the Trump-Pence green T-shirt who ushered me to my seat as worship began.

As the youth group streamed in to worship, I was struck by the ways they mirrored their counterparts in Parkland. They were white and black and brown and Latino and Asian and mixed race. They were confident and connected, sending Snaps as worship began and taking selfies. They chatted confidently with one another, hugging friends. They talked about school and college and rent. They acted like any other young people you might meet at any other church across America. The worship team was diverse, too, with black and white singers in T-shirts and skinny jeans, singing familiar and unfamiliar praise music that was live-streamed and beamed all over the world. In front of me, an interracial young couple held hands as they sang about God's grace in their lives. I could see the future of progressive young Christian America, and I wondered if the Trump T-shirt was an aberration or something more. As the dancers and singers weaved back and forth through the opening songs, I noticed no cross, no altar, and no religious trappings of any kind—only the American and Floridian flags, flanked across the room by flags of all nations.

While the church is racially diverse, all the pastors and leaders I met are white. And they share a similar look. Pastor Allen and all the young men taking turns leading up front were distinguished by more than their jeans and slightly tight button-up shirts. They all sported a popular hairstyle: short on the sides and long on top. The style was made popular by rapper Macklemore, actor Brad Pitt, soccer star David Beckham—and by neo-Nazis and white nationalists. Like everything else at the church, the pastors' uniform style was normal, and also not. It elicited fear and uncertainty, placed into context with the warning on the door and the *Killing Uncle Sam* in the bookstore. Before Pastor Allen started his sermon, he invited forward his "beautiful" wife (all pastors at the River serve as married couples, though the men are the unquestioned leaders), and then he invited forward Pastor Matt, a former youth group member leading a River-related ministry in Chicago, a reminder that what happens in this Florida church is not limited to Florida.

"We had a Jewish kid saved. We had an atheist kid saved," Matt said. "You need to invite people here that are not saved. The Bible tells us that a lack of knowledge leads to sin; we are going to learn tonight how to take control of your life."

In the tradition and cadence of televangelists, Pastor Allen began in Old Testament obscurity, the relatively unknown tale of King Ahab, throwing in complex Old Testament names and glossing over their stories, leaving behind the prophets but focusing in on the narrative of Israel's kings in 1 and 2 Chronicles and 1 and 2 Kings. He mentioned people who "call themselves Christian" but aren't born again. He spoke of the kids he had in youth group who have drifted from the church, a personal grievance: "I have to question if those kids were ever saved in the first place," he says.

Then it was on to a riff about Jezebel, "Ahab's dirty old skanky wife." The world of Pastor Allen's sermon is a dichotomous one in which nothing is safe and kids must defend themselves and brace for impact. Ushers walked through the sanctuary with offering envelopes, the only piece of literature available in the worship service. As they handed out the envelopes, a girl named Crystal told the story of how she chose to work at the church, and one day out of the blue, she got a phone message offering her a free car. A young man, not older than twenty, came forward and told about how he and his wife got an unexpected influx of rent money. The message was *"Give! give! give!* and maybe you, too, can get a car or rent money." The envelope passers, including the woman in the Trump T-shirt, disappeared as quickly as they had come.

Pastor Allen talked about taking his two daughters to Disney World the day before, and then he segued into a story of Christians he knew who wore bulletproof vests. He mentioned AR-15s and kids' guns, and he was moving so fast, it was hard to keep track of the trajectory of his message. A baby was crying, and Pastor Allen was talking about demon spirits, about how even the kids at this church were filled with them, and they'd better stay away from Ouija boards because it was *all real*. Pastor Allen was intent on pressing the reality of evil, from the skanky Jezebel, to the lapsed youth, to the Pauline tale of a man sleeping with his stepmother. I heard a hint of sexual innuendo in what he preached, a dash of violence, and a tablespoon of ever-present danger.

Pastor Allen was not so intent on emphasizing the reality of God or of Jesus. In fact, he mentioned neither of them, except once, with God as an arbiter of justice and punishment. Pastor Allen said nothing about who God is, or why Jesus came, or what Jesus said. Instead, God and Jesus live in the background, and the foreground consists of sinners in an angry God's hands. I noticed, looking around at this gathering of young, hip Christians, the disproportionate number of young pregnant girls and of teenagers wearing wedding rings. A girl near me whispered about her mother, "Since I was fourteen, she's been telling me to get married." The uncomfortable marriage of glitzy technology and high-octane worship to traditional values and stifling gender roles was almost suffocating, repackaged again for the next generation of conservative American Christians.

Pastor Allen was getting ramped up. His voice took on a mocking, acerbic tone. "Grace, grace, grace," he crowed sarcastically, summoning churches he deemed insufficiently holy. "Graaaaaace. I believe in grace, but I also believe in holiness."

The congregation did not respond. "It's getting quiet in this Presbyterian youth group," he continued. "Scripture tells us we are to be light in a wicked generation!"

But this he knows: if he wants to get the congregation worked up, preach about homosexuality and gender identity: "You don't have to look in the mirror to know what gender you are. Two men cannot procreate, and it's a spiritual law to create and propagate."

I saw young people pulling out their iPhones. Someone opened the Snapchat app. Others were taking notes. Still others stared in rapt attention. What he was saying went against everything we have heard about this generation, but they stayed and listened anyway—black and white, Latino and Asian, young and on fire for fundamentalist Christianity and all the rigidity it implies. These are Trump's young people.

Pastor Allen anticipated the protests of some in the room: "'You're just intolerant,' they tell me. Well, no, I'm not. I think the same of someone who has same-sex attraction as someone who has a problem with stealing or gambling." Pastor Allen used the language of aberration, of sickness, to talk about people who identify as gay or lesbian. His language dehumanizes groups of people, sends them to so-called reparative therapy, and tells them they are diseased. Pastor Allen offers an ominous retort to "It gets better": it gets worse.

Pastor Allen moved on to talking about marriage, dating, and the #MeToo movement. He suggested that there's no need to discuss consent or compatibility. Instead, women are merely an outlet to be "plugged into," and no one ever asked the outlet for its consent. "If you're a boy, and she's a girl, you're compatible," Allen continued, spittle leaking from the corner of his mouth and sweat stains forming under his arms. "You don't have to think about it. If you don't understand, go plug a cord into the wall. That's how it works." He said that those who misunderstand relationships annoy him; presumably, this means he is annoyed by anyone who strays from the dominant male, subservient female model of sexuality.

"You're an idiot, and you're gonna go to hell," he said, with a pronounced lisp that sounded purposeful; he mocked and lisped and thundered with ease. The laid-back, hip megachurch pastor I had met before service had transformed, and he was just getting warmed up. We were about to enter hour three of the worship service, and Pastor Allen was still on a roll.

Holy Spirit Laughter and a Town Where Everyone Owns a Gun

Tonight was a "burn night," during which attendees would write whatever they wanted to remove from their lives, whatever sin was weighing on them, and bring it outside to a massive bonfire. I've done things like this before, as have many American Christians. I've never done it quite the way the River does it, however. A long queue wrapped around the back of the room. An air of "anything could happen" hung in the worship space, and the fundamentalist preaching mixed with the revolutionary fervor in the air, combining traditional values and the energy of old-fashioned tent revivals. The energy in the room was almost sexual, and even as Pastor Allen preached chastity, he practiced promiscuity, turning on every emotional receptor in everyone there. I sat still in my seat in the back, writing notes to myself on my phone and begging my battery not to die, wondering if I was missing something, feeling the palpable absence of God and the fear that settled in its place. I was startled by a hand on my shoulder. A swollen white man in his fifties, with an ill-fitting shirt and shorts straining to contain their flesh, was pressing down on me.

"Mind if I sit here?" he asked.

Jeff Duncan of Kennesaw, Georgia, stood out in this young, hipster crowd, and I wonder later if it's by design that he goes to the youth service, to stand on the edge of what he once had, to pretend he is among them even as he sticks out. Others like him, decidedly not youth but here anyway, stood with Duncan apart from the group but aflame in its fervor, dying to join in. Jeff asked me for my phone number, which struck me as a little odd, given the circumstances (people were tossing their sins in flames near us; it was not exactly speed dating). He noticed my wedding ring and was shocked. Maybe he frequents the youth service often, looking for potential young brides.

I told Jeff I'm writing a book about Christian Trump voters, and this particular chapter is about guns. He told me he's from Kennesaw, Georgia, where in 1982, gun ownership was mandated for all heads of household (except for those who couldn't afford guns, couldn't use guns, couldn't legally own guns, or didn't want to own guns). I learned more about this law by visiting the fact-checking website Snopes, which references Kennesaw as an oft-cited right-wing meme following a mass shooting in Roseburg, Oregon, at a community college in 2015. I wondered later if Jeff had as such made up his Kennesaw connection, but who knows? The law was itself mostly a political statement about Kennesaw's support of the right to bear arms.

Jeff lived in violation of Kennesaw's law. "I don't have a gun," he said. "I was mostly protected by the angels. I took martial arts when I was younger, and I've gotten by with that." I didn't know what forces Jeff had needed to fight against in rural Georgia, but I didn't get a chance to ask. As Jeff and I were talking, Pastor Allen walked through the line, pushing people on the head. They subsequently fell backward onto the ground, something up until now I've only seen on TV—being "slain in the Spirit." Intermittently, people yelled unintelligible words—speaking in tongues. It's a scene not uncommon in Christianity, particularly in the Global South.

"He's not supposed to push them down," Jeff said to me, agitated. "He's pushing them down. Some of these pastors—they aren't doing the right thing. I don't agree with everything he's saying."

Jeff is a Pentecostal veteran. He loves prosperity preacher Benny Hinn and said he used to be in a deliverance ministry—a group that uses spiritual power to affect physical healing. Jeff told me he's kind of a rebel at the River at Tampa Bay. "He tried to [push me down] last week," Jeff said. "I didn't let him. I just stood there." I told him I wished I would have seen that.

On the night of my visit, everyone who was slain in the Spirit went down. While glossolalia has its origin in the New Testament, the apostle Paul suggests that speaking in tongues without interpretation is unhelpful. I didn't see any interpreters that night, only a strange, sickening sound emitting from all around the room. It is psychotic, unremitting, demented laughter, people lying on the ground, laughing without ceasing for minutes on end. This Holy Spirit laughter, I later find out, is said to have grown in prominence during the ministry of Howard-Browne, and it's one of his signatures. The crowd was beginning to spread out as more people made their way to the giant bonfire on the back porch, and others came forward for baptism. I never heard an official ending to the service, no closing hymn—just an eerie quiet in the worship space broken by *hahahahahaha*. I told Jeff I was going to try to find Pastor Allen. He asked me when my book would be coming out, and I told him.

"Oh, good," he replied. "That'll be before the Rapture." And there's the rub: in all of this, the necessity of impending doom keeps the fear and defensiveness of many Red State Christians at a fever pitch, which keeps them a captive audience and emotional prey for pastors like Allen or presidents like Trump.

Jeff told me he has three books he's writing, all of which he said are certain to be best-sellers. "Good luck!" I told him as we parted.

He looked at me with squinted eyes. "Don't say, 'Good luck.' That means you're referring to Lucifer. That's where 'Good luck' comes from."

We Need to Protect Our People

I stepped over the remaining laughers, being careful to avoid the chatting college students now back on their smartphones, impervious to the drama around them. Pastor Allen stood outside. By then, it was about 11:00 p.m. He was talking to another minister, dressed similarly to him, with a slightly too-tight button-up shirt. They both grudgingly acknowledged my presence. Gone was the fiery faith healer and preacher; Pastor Allen was just another guy you might nod at in the sports bar after work, ordering wings and a beer.

"Yeah, I grew up Catholic," he said when I asked about his background. "Heathen. But Catholic."

He told me he intended to go to the Naval Academy and then went to the University of Georgia. My later online searching shows he attended a few colleges but doesn't note him graduating from any of them. He told me he's a history professor now; apparently, the River Ministries has its own seminary. "I was going to be a lawyer," Allen continued. "Then I got saved," as if the two are mutually exclusive. I pressed on, asking Allen why he thought it was so important for the church to defend itself and advertise that the pastors carry guns. Pastor Allen defended the signs outside, saying that Howard-Browne has had death threats and that the church does "inner-city" ministry. "We aren't messing around," he said, when I asked about the measures the church had taken to defend itself. "We aren't looking for trouble. We do everything through the law. You notice we have a sheriff's deputy here."

Pastor Allen said my presence at the church was old news for them. They were inundated with reporters after the Sutherland Springs shooting. The *Washington Post* and other mainstream media outlets covered it, but Pastor Allen mentioned *Fox and Friends*. "I told them the same thing," he said. "Jesus would say if you don't have a sword, go get one. But he also blamed Peter for cutting off Malchus's ear. The issue is not a gun, but a heart."

It was the first mention I heard that evening of having a heart. I feel a certain kinship to Allen. Our kids are the same age; he has girls, and I have boys. He told me that he has been a youth pastor at the River for twelve years. "We've put ten thousand kids through our ministries," Allen continued. "Our kids don't even talk about guns. They want their friends to know about eternity."

Allen and the kids he referenced at the River fear an eternal hell much more than they fear a school shooting. Who wouldn't sacrifice personal safety to defend the right to a glorious eternity? Who wouldn't fight to defend their eternal salvation? But the River misses the point of grace, promised by Jesus on the cross and mocked by Pastor Allen. Lost at the River is the biblical idea that we aren't the ones who are called to earn or to defend our salvation. We are called instead to gratitude for life rather than ultimate fear of death, for Easter follows Good Friday, and eternal life follows death. But grace is unsatisfying in the winner-takes-all world of the River, so it must be subjugated to fear and zero-sum games. Winning means nothing if no one loses. Heaven doesn't matter without hell. Just ask Donald Trump. Pastor Allen told me he doesn't care about the criticism of Christians who support Trump. He said people don't get it. In the absence of a competing idea, he assumed I'm with him.

"I don't think anyone who isn't a conservative Christian can have an opinion on a conservative Christian. And look at the choices we had. Did you want Hillary? As a *Christian*?"

The idea of voting for Hillary, he assumes, is unimaginable for any Christian. He identifies the fatal Democratic mistake: misunderstanding and underestimating the Christian antipathy toward Hillary Clinton. More than guns, abortion, gay rights, small government—the Red State Christians I spoke to across the country were unified more in their hatred of Hillary than in any other way. More than the issues themselves, they were motivated by a hatred of Hillary that felt personal and, they assumed, mutual.

Allen casually turned the topic back to guns. He said he grew up around guns but not hunting. Guns are not for sport but for serious protection, needed in an age when Christians are under siege. "We need to protect our people," he said, then turned back toward the flames, his face transformed in the darkness.

Gun Ownership and Rural Christian Culture

The conservative Christianity I encountered at the River at Tampa Bay is not the dominant form of conservative Christianity in America. Most gun rights supporters don't rely on fundamentalist doctrine to back up their views about guns. Instead, in many American families, guns are tied to hunting, community, and rural culture. When I returned from Florida, I conducted interviews with more mainstream conservative Christian gun rights supporters, Christian leaders living in communities where conservative Christianity is tied to owning guns and supporting gun rights. Former US Marine Greg Yeager, now a Lutheran copastor with his wife in rural North Carolina, told me that he usually goes to look at people's guns during pastoral care visits. Across the street from his house, a man had a sign on his mailbox: ATTENTION LIBERALS: YOU WON'T TAKE MY GUN. Yeager just laughed. "I told him if he finds a liberal around here, let me know."

Yeager's community is on the edge of Appalachia and still influenced by Appalachian roots. Up in the hills, people worship at small mountain Baptist churches, and the county was dry until 2016. Guns are everywhere, and they're sometimes necessary for shooting animals. People believe they have to defend themselves—almost a Wild West mentality. Though Yeager does not currently own guns, he said he knows some people carry guns during his Sunday worship services. "Probably three to four people who are law enforcement, including the sheriff," Yeager said. "And probably three to four people who are not law enforcement. . . . To a certain extent, it's a fear thing and a control thing. When you have [a gun] in the building, it's just one less thing to worry about. People do not storm into people's houses here. It doesn't happen. Generally speaking, people obey the code."

Yeager, who grew up outside Seattle and not surrounded by gun culture, says even he is sometimes surprised by the way guns are just a part of life in his community. "A group of young women asked me if I'd take a class with them one Sunday," he said. "I figured it was yoga or maybe pottery. They wanted to do a concealed-carry class." Yeager has his concealed-carry permit, as do most people in the church. He said it's like going through the PreCheck line in the airport and makes it easier to buy a handgun.

A pastor in a liberal denomination serving a conservative community, Yeager sees both sides. He said sometimes his liberal pastoral colleagues misunderstand his community. "They think everything boils down to race, but it really doesn't," Yeager said. "The people in my community are all into law and order, and Trump appealed to that. It's mostly because they know police officers. They *are* police officers."

Yeager said some in his community admitted that during the Great Recession, many people laid off from their manufacturing jobs got jobs as police officers even though some of them "had no business packing a weapon." People in his community understand the unfairness and inequality faced by people of color, Yeager said, and they voted for Trump primarily because they see their community's economy dying. "They've battled NAFTA for twenty-five years," Yeager said of the furniture manufacturers in his area. "NAFTA has been pretty decent for most of the country. It's been pretty crappy for this crew."

For Appalachian Christians, Yeager suggests, gun ownership was tangential to support of Trump. And anyway, Democrats didn't even bother campaigning in his community.

For many Americans, gun culture begins at a young age. Willie Rosin, a pastor in rural northwest Iowa, started squirrel hunting when he was six years old. "You didn't play with toy guns; you learned how to use real guns," he said, noting that even his mom hunted deer and antelope, carrying around little Willie in the child carrier backpack at age two during hunting trips. Rosin's experience of gun support in his church community runs closest to the rural ideal of sport hunting culture, where guns are a part of recreation and even sustenance. He still owns fifteen guns, though he said he'll never own a pistol for self-defense, and he owns a concealed-carry permit just to carry guns in his car for hunting.

Rosin said what troubles him as a gun-rights-supporting pastor is the allure of power and mystique in gun ownership, suggesting that people want guns for power rather than for practical reasons and hunting for sport. He senses the fear even in his own sanctuary, where some of his parishioners carry concealed guns to worship. "It doesn't make me afraid, but it deeply saddens me that a place that literally means safety does not have that vital purpose anymore. Sanctuary is not sanctuary anymore," Rosin said.

Rosin said that in his rural, conservative community, people voted for Trump primarily because they are pro-life or they hoped Trump would lower their taxes as small-business owners. "The overwhelming reason was change," Rosin said. "They were tired of feeling like they were being oppressed. The biggest Trump supporter I know voted for Obama twice."

On the Iron Range of Minnesota, hundreds of miles from Rosin, in a county that has long been one of the few Democratic rural strongholds in America, another small-town pastor has learned the importance of guns to her community. Pastor Beth Pottratz worked in a high-crime area as a high-school teacher prior to becoming a

Lutheran pastor. Many of the kids she taught were involved in gangs, and after she left the school, a former student of hers was shot and killed due to gang violence. She now serves in a community where guns are central to rural hunting culture. In just thirty minutes, driving from her rural northeastern Minnesota home into town and back, she saw four notices for events about guns or hunting, and she received a graduation party invitation featuring a senior photo with a boy holding his rifle.

Raised in suburban Minneapolis, Pottratz had little experience with guns. Despite her experiences with gun violence at the urban high school, she has come to appreciate the role guns and hunting play in her rural community. She even attended a friend's wedding reception at a gun range, where they made sure that no one who was drunk got to shoot. Pottratz said that when she started her job as pastor at the church, a parishioner quickly reassured her, "Don't worry about anything; there's enough of us around here with guns if anything happens."

Pottratz told me she has come to appreciate the gesture, living in a world that would be unfamiliar to many of us who live in metro areas. People are more isolated in rural communities, from Appalachia to Iowa to the Northwoods, and they feel more responsible for their own meting out of justice and sustenance. Guns play a role in that, but they aren't as mythologized for power and control, and they aren't a part of existential doomsday fears, as they are at the River at Tampa Bay.

Pottratz's community is historically Democratic, due to long-standing union ties in the mines of the Iron Range. But northeastern Minnesota swung to Trump in 2016, something Pottratz attributes to Trump's promises to miners and manufacturers, along with the idea that the Democratic Party was moving away from labor union representation and into identity politics. She said people didn't talk much about guns; instead, they hoped Trump would bring glory, or at least opportunity, back to their communities and otherwise leave them to their social values.

From the apocalyptic, gun-toting pastors at the River in Tampa Bay, to the more familiar rural Christian hunters who attend mainstream churches and voted for Trump, enduring conclusions are hard to draw when it comes to gun culture and Red State Christians. Separating a healthy culture of hunting and measured support for gun ownership from a fear-based Christianity that is desperate to protect its own is essential to understanding Red State Christians and their guns. While they are not the majority of American gun owners, we need to pay attention to the vocal minority of Red State Christians like the ones I met at the River at Tampa Bay, whose commitment to gun rights is based in fear, isolation, and an impending American Armageddon.

CHAPTER 4

Bibles and Boob Jobs:
The Money and Influence of
Orange County Christians

I'd lived in Orange County, California, for less than a year when I first started to realize how much the area set the tone for and reflected Red State Christian culture. It was early 2016, and I was checking out an exercise group called Fit4Mom: Stroller Strides on a sunny Friday morning in North Orange County. Jacob, my oldest, was in preschool, and one of the moms from my church was an instructor for the group and invited me to join. So I joined the circle of moms next to the park with my youngest, Joshua, in the stroller—Lululemon stretchy yoga pants for the win.

I was excited to connect with my fellow moms. Even though most of the moms I knew said they didn't work full time, being a mom in Orange County functioned like a full-time job. In a conservative atmosphere that valued traditional family roles, some people had a prejudice against moms who worked full-time, though no one would say it out loud. Moms needed to manage complex households and a wide array of children's activities, all of which were half day or less. I'd recently heard about a semi-scandal from a few years ago at the church I worked at, when the preschool considered offering a full-day option. "We lost families," a longtime church staff member told me. "The stay-at-home moms were worried about their children interacting with full-day kids."

Gulp.

I was working full-time as pastor of community life and discipleship in a large Lutheran church in Yorba Linda, California, neighbor to Anaheim and Brea in North Orange County—also known as the hometown of Richard Nixon. Nixon might have been forced to resign under shady circumstances decades ago, but he's still Yorba Linda's favorite son. The highway my husband took to work was named after Nixon, and my church was a block away from the Nixon Presidential Library, where lots of locals host weddings and marriage receptions in the opulent gardens.

While a few dads stood in line for preschool drop-off, the stars of the show were indisputably my fellow moms, carrying in Pinterest-worthy art creations for child birthday treats and dressed to the nines in athleisure. Most women, while they didn't work full-time in a traditional sense, were nonetheless constantly working a variety of jobs and side hustles. Some of them were bakers and clothiers and fitness instructors; others were models and bloggers and even lawyers who worked from home most of the time.

When I first came to Orange County, a friend told me that the high rate of divorce in Orange County (about thirty-three people in Orange County initiate divorce proceedings every single day) related to this intense pressure to have a traditional family structure in one of the most expensive places to live in the United States.[1] While women were expected to look sexy, they were also expected to be present most of the time with their children. In places like San Francisco or New York City, the bulk of child care or housework would be outsourced to nannies and housekeepers. But Orange County maintained a do-it-yourself, traditional family American ethos, despite its wealth and glamour. My friend told me that men in the county felt the pressure, too, to make enough money so that their wives could have enough time to maintain the appearance of the perfect American family and be home with the kids. Many men subsequently traveled a great deal for work or worked a lot of hours. You'd hear cases of marital affairs: men with their female coworkers, women with local firefighters or police officers. It seemed the divorce rate was related not to weaker marriages or to a more liberal view of marriage but instead to a pressure-cooker environment for families and a cost and style of living that required husbands and wives to spend a lot of time apart.

During my family's time in Orange County, I was fascinated by the blend of traditional American and Christian values and by the way those values included a certain sense of materialism, money, and focus on appearance. Nowhere else in America does this particular blend of Christian conservatism coexist so prevalently with ostentatious displays of wealth. Nowhere else in the country are women expected to toe the line between Madonna and whore so effortlessly. And it must be said, nowhere else in the country was I loved and taught to love as I was in Orange County. I'd been raised with a certain level of Midwest suspicion and reserve. Growing up in Minnesota, I heard people say "Minnesota nice," which means you might say hello to a stranger or push their car out of a snowbank, but you certainly wouldn't hug them or ask them to be your friend. So I came into social situations holding myself back a bit, waiting to see if I could trust you, waiting to see how you might burn me. In Orange

County, people entered social situations with arms open wide, and they welcomed my family in the same way.

Sure, as the rare woman pastor in the community, I was frequently asked, "Oh, you mean you're the children's pastor?" And one unforgettable time, a visitor to our preschool Christmas concert told me, "Your husband did such a wonderful job!" She was referring to my colleague, the senior pastor, who was nearly thirty years older than me.

Still, the love and hospitality my family and I experienced in Orange County made it feel like home. Having spent some of our lives in blue states where religion was often suspect and the church irrelevant, Orange County loomed as a nostalgic Christendom Disneyland with a church on every corner and a large proportion of children attending Christian schools. Most churches were packed on Sunday mornings, and pastors were afforded a measure of respect and moral authority unrecognizable in many other parts of America.

When I pulled up to Stroller Strides that bright Orange County morning, Donald Trump had not yet been elected president, though he would win in a few months' time. The 2016 election was historic because Orange County went for Clinton, its first time to back a Democratic presidential candidate since 1936. (And in the 2018 midterms, Republicans were swept out of office in every Orange County congressional race.) Data would show that much of the county was still red, particularly majority-white districts in wealthy South Orange County and in North Orange County, where we lived. What turned Orange County blue in 2016 were areas that had become predominately Hispanic, such as county seat Santa Ana, pockets of Anaheim, and other areas of Orange County that were majority minority, including places with high numbers of Asian immigrants from China or Vietnam—those areas and women voters, who voted overwhelmingly Democratic in 2016 and 2018.

When I told friends across the country that we were moving to Orange County, our conservative Christian friends in the Midwest often regarded Southern California as some sort of liberal, hippie oasis, with no morals, values, or religious compass. To dispel those myths, I knew I had to tell the stories of Orange County Christianity, and after Trump's election, I knew I also had to write about Orange County Christianity because I could see the way that trends in this conservative enclave of Southern California were influencing Red State Christians across America.

I doubt whether Trump could have won Evangelical voters if not for the influence of celebrity Christians, including the churches and pastors of Orange County. The University of Southern California's Center for Religion and Civic Culture published a study in January 2018 about how California megachurches changed Christian culture, making much the same contention.[2] The report notes that in California, there are more than two hundred Protestant, theologically conservative churches with at least two thousand weekly attendees—more than any other state, including Texas.[3] Scholar Richard Flory says that the most significant characteristic of these megachurches in California is their ability to "appropriate elements from the larger culture, be it popular music, performances or even dress styles."[4] Prior to celebrity pastors and large California megachurches, fundamentalist and conservative Christians tended to stay out of the spotlight and live at the margins of culture. But California megachurches, beginning in 1955 with the Crystal Cathedral of Garden Grove, Orange County, made Christianity cool and glitzy.

With its proximity to Hollywood and its abundance of fat wallets, the OC was the perfect place to figure out how to market fame and conservative Christianity. I twice attended conferences (in 2012 and 2016) at one of Orange County's largest churches, Mariners of Irvine, and I was amazed by the way conservative Evangelicals—many with Southern Baptist roots—could transport themselves into a California-cool environment.

Trump, with his own combination of bombast and celebrity, would not have appealed to conservative American Christians had they not first been warmed up to the idea by conservative celebrity preachers, many of whom had their genesis in Orange County and Southern California. Suddenly churches decided it was OK to be in the spotlight, it was OK to use elements of culture that were previously considered immoral or unethical, in order to reach a larger goal. It's not surprising that American Evangelicals, thus desensitized, were willing to sacrifice purity for popularity. They'd already done so in their largest and most profitable and influential churches.

Still, Trump's election changed Orange County Christianity, dividing its entrenched centers of Christian power and influence, and forcing pastors and church leaders to take political sides. As the county and its churches grew increasingly diverse, with more women in leadership roles and more people of color in influential staff and pastoral positions, it seemed obvious that the county's politics would change as well. Yet this process would not come without requisite pain. I spoke with African American mothers whose children were tormented at their local high schools the day after Trump was elected. I witnessed churches, my own included, that were rife with division and heartbroken over politics. I spoke to pastors who were shocked at the level of support for Trump within their pews, pastors who wondered if their advocacy for antipoverty efforts and lifting up of Jesus's voice for the marginalized had been utterly ignored as inconsequential.

I saw people on both sides, Republicans and Democrats, who weren't sure what to do in the face of such open discord. The OC is known for its emphasis on pristine appearances, and churches in which all had been well, both financially and socially, for so many years weren't sure how to deal with open conflict. After the election, the waters would calm, but then would come the onslaught of sexual-abuse scandals at large Evangelical churches, the #MeToo movement, and the confrontation of older, more conservative leadership at OC megachurches with younger churchgoers and their support for gay rights and other progressive causes. This aspect of OC Christianity gave me hope that even the pain of open conflict and political discord within congregations would result in a new, stronger, and more honest Christianity, with a leadership that looked more like the demography of its churches. I hoped that in the same way Orange County Christianity had influenced American Christianity to appropriate music and celebrity culture, now it would lead the way in forcing American Evangelical churches to have hard conversations about important topics: immigration, poverty, gay rights, racism, women's rights, sexual abuse. And I hoped that out of these hard conversations would come a newly won focus on the gospel, which would survive it all and emerge stronger.

Almost two years after Election Day 2016, I returned to Orange County, having left my church there in May 2017 with sadness but also a fresh drive to go back to writing and to family in the Midwest. I needed to return to the place where I had learned to love without reservation, the place that had taught me the vulnerability of the American church, and I needed to see what Jesus was up to in Orange County, regardless of Trump and American politics.

Back to Cali

The first place I went after landing at John Wayne Airport in Irvine, following the requisite stop at In-N-Out Burger, was Saddleback

Church, home to mega-famous pastor Rick Warren. A native Californian and best-selling author of *The Purpose-Driven Church* and *The Purpose-Driven Life*, Warren is the son of a Baptist pastor in San Jose. He attended conservative Southwestern Baptist Seminary in Fort Worth, Texas, before beginning his ministry. The most successful leader of the 1980s church growth movement, Warren started Saddleback in the theater at Laguna Hills High School on Easter Sunday 1980. Today the church boasts more than twenty-two thousand in attendance each weekend, with campuses around Orange County and throughout the world.

Warren is something of an enigmatic figure among conservative Christian leaders. While he has publicly opposed same-sex marriage and criticized President Obama for his record on religious freedom, Warren remains friendly with Obama and gave the invocation at Obama's inauguration. For doing this, he encountered opposition from the right and left: from the right, for allying with a Democrat; from the left, for his opposition to same-sex marriage and other progressive causes. Five years later, Warren faced personal tragedy when his youngest son, Matthew, died by suicide after years of battling mental illness. Warren later spoke out about the church's failure to help people dealing with mental illness.

Prior to my visit, Warren had been dealing with health issues and was giving most of his sermons via video. Of all the megachurch pastors I attempted to interview, Warren was the least accessible. Reaching him required weaving through myriad loops of PR handlers and church staff. Finally, I was told I was welcome to attend church services but was asked to please respect a request not to seek to speak to staff, members, or attendees regarding my book. Saddleback prides itself on being "seeker sensitive," so I was surprised by this unwelcoming response. I told Saddleback as much, and Warren's secretary informed me that Warren received hundreds of thousands of emails and letters yearly from around the world, and he was simply unable to meet with everyone who asked. Warren's inaccessibility revealed a limiting factor of the megachurch model: religion and Christianity had been commodified at Saddleback, and Warren was a weary CEO.

Having been told that Warren was ill and preaching via video, I was in for a surprise when I arrived at the Saddleback campus in Lake Forest, about thirteen miles inland from world-famous Laguna Beach, in opulent South Orange County. I parked in one of the many available lots, walked around cones, and made my way up sets of stairs toward what I assumed must be the worship center. From the entrance road, Saddleback Church had its own name built into brick, much like the signs marking the gated communities that line the streets of this part of Orange County. Even amidst the Southern California August drought, the campus was verdant, filled with plants, palm trees, and fountains. Contemporary Christian music played through speakers hidden in the shrubbery, and banners proclaimed the weekend's baptism celebration.

Saddleback claims to be the first church in history to have baptized fifty thousand people, and they had decided to celebrate that weekend with an explosion of baptisms. The Christian tradition of baptism involves casting off evil and the devil and being born again to new life in Jesus, by the Father, Son, and Holy Spirit. Saddleback's baptisms had a more California feel. Various pools were set up around campus, each with a decorative photo backdrop fit for Instagramming your baptism, complete with flowery font and relevant biblical text. All those preparing for baptism were given identical gray T-shirts, while nearby tiki-type huts sported "Baptism Sign-Up" signs. Baptizees queued up to fill out information cards.

"THIS IS MY NEW LIFE!" the T-shirts read, though Saddleback must find it tough to follow up and create authentic new life and deep community with each of the people baptized in the weekend's bonanza. I spent about ninety minutes at the church myself without speaking to another human being, but maybe that wasn't the point. These baptisms, and the church itself, betray an individualist, West Coast ideal as much as a biblical tradition. The baptisms were about you starting over for *your own* new life, not about joining a Christian community or welcoming in the kingdom of God.

Still, I was shocked to notice, while looking for the worship center, that standing waist-deep before me in one of the baptismal pools was Warren himself! Despite his health problems, he baptized person after person, each one clearly delighted for the intimate moment with the famous pastor. Warren raised his hand, recited a few words, and then supported the back of each baptizee as he lowered them into the pool, often brushing the cheek of young women and girls, and then going in for hugs after the act was completed. The whole thing was live-streamed to screens around the campus and around the world. At the end of each baptism, the crowd standing nearby applauded softly, with occasional cheers from family and friends.

In line with Warren's Southern Baptist roots, Saddleback practices believer's baptism, and I had to wonder how many of the people in the pool had been baptized as infants. I knew lots of mainline Christians and Catholics who were baptized as infants, only to have an Evangelical reawakening as young adults and be "rebaptized" in nondenominational churches—a practice that mainline and Catholic churches consider heterodox, if not heretical. Saddleback came across as disingenuous by bragging about baptism numbers when many people had likely already been baptized. Of course, Saddleback, like most Evangelical megachurches, does not consider infant baptism valid.

I noticed Warren's obvious fatigue. I watched a few more baptisms, at the rate of about one per minute, and then I went into the worship center, which I finally located across the path from Warren's baptismal pool. There he was again, this time on large screens in the front of the room, where a video showed him in a big leather armchair, giving that weekend's sermon via video, in which he also appeared tired and even ill. His eyes were half open, and his voice hoarse and strained, as though he couldn't breathe well through his nose. Maybe his fatigue came from the loss of his son, a tragedy that shook Warren hard. Matthew had tried so hard to fight against depression, and Warren's broken heart evidenced the deep love he had for his son and for his family. Maybe it was years of indefatigable church growth ministry. Maybe it was that even the greatest professional success could not make up for all the years of giving all of himself to the engine that was Saddleback and Purpose-Driven business/ministry.

Warren's sermon that day was milquetoast: self-help and positive thinking mixed with a little Bible trivia. Warren pioneered the use of bulletins with fill-in-the-blanks activities to keep people on track during the sermon, much as a children's menu keeps the kids occupied at a restaurant. He still uses them today, though at this point, it felt formulaic and tired.

Days before I'd come to Orange County, more allegations of sexual misconduct against Willow Creek's Bill Hybels—another famous megachurch pastor—had surfaced in the *New York Times*, and Willow's entire board of elders and new lead pastors had resigned over their mishandling of the situation. Warren has been scandal free, but the news about Hybels coupled with Warren's obvious exhaustion gave the appearance that the church growth and megachurch movement was giving up its last gasp. While hundreds of seats were still filled at Saddleback, the crowd was not exactly inspired, and most people filed out silently at the end of Warren's sermon, well before the band finished playing the final song. At a time of crumbling institutions and after the Great Recession, maybe people want more from their churches than a personal guide to being a better individual with a side of Jesus thrown in, all delivered via video.

To my eyes, Saddleback just felt gimmicky. True, Saddleback lacked the social conservatism and overt Christian Nationalism I experienced in Dallas; it did not attempt to manipulate believers by the power of a prosperity gospel. Instead, Saddleback felt vacant, notwithstanding the people in the worship center. To wit, I noticed the vacuity of Saddleback's famous Connection Card, copied by churches all over the country, placed in the back of the seat in front of me:

My Response to Today's Message:
Please check ALL that apply. . . .

Option 1: I made the decision to follow Jesus today. . . .

(Pick up your New Life gift at the Connection Center).

In the midst of the Trump presidency, as America grapples with political division and a diminishing role in the new global economy, with the American government separating families at the border, with conservatives worrying over unisex bathrooms and slip-sliding into total moral anarchy, maybe people no longer need a New Life gift. Isn't New Life gift enough?

The New OC Christianity: A Pastor's Wife and a Brown-Skinned Youth Pastor

Leaving Saddleback with my infant baptism intact, I went back to the hotel to rest up for Sunday. Sunday morning, I would attend an early service at my prior congregation, and then I'd head to worship at Influence Church in North Orange County, a relatively new church plant where the lead pastor was also an occasional online columnist for FOX News and a former apostle to young Hollywood. After a plan to paddleboard the Newport Dunes, I'd then attend youth service Sunday night at Mariners Church, the second-largest church in Orange County after Saddleback.

My return to my congregation overflowed with the hospitality, joy, and love I had experienced there first as a pregnant thirty-year-old pastor. The conservatives of old Yorba Linda who had chided me over my video of Obama singing "Amazing Grace" during a sermon years before were no less warm and loving than they had been upon my leaving. I was sometimes astounded that, in Orange County, often the seniors had the least qualms about a female pastor leading their church. They never said a word about it, never asked if I was the children's pastor or if my husband was a pastor, too. They just loved me because I loved them, and our time spent together in prayer and at hospital bedsides overcame any political differences.

The music and worship staff at my former church, both vocally and instrumentally, worked in the music and worship department at nearby Biola University (**B**ible **I**nstitute **of** **L**os **A**ngeles), a conservative Christian college in La Mirada, and one of our church worship staff members served as dean. After the 2016 election, even our church staff lost the ability to listen to each other helpfully across partisan divides. Difference in political opinions caused hurt feelings and misunderstandings. Coming back in 2018, I was grateful to see that upon my return, any misunderstandings had dissolved, and we could mutually give thanks for the ministry we'd done together. Here, in the local congregation, relationships had weathered the political storm, though we all bore scars.

The Influencers of Influence Church

If Saddleback and even my former congregation represented old-school, Orange County, contemporary-lite worship, then Influence was cutting edge, with the flavor of nearby LA. We worshiped in a free-flowing, unrestrained style for a long time, in a darkened room with lights flashing and a young, blond worship leader bouncing and dancing across the stage, tossing her hair in the air. Influence didn't use gimmicks or even glitzy gifts; instead, the music played to the senses, beats pounding against the walls as people—even the young couple and their infant next to me—bobbed their bodies to the music. Influence Church started in a theater, as megachurches do, in February 2012. In July 2013, the church bought part of the US Post Office Building off Santa Ana Canyon Road in Anaheim Hills, and worship began in the new space in December 2013.

When Influence started, most people knew of it because of Phil Hotsenpiller, a former teaching pastor at Yorba Linda Friends, a north Orange County megachurch with Quaker roots. A self-styled entrepreneur, Hotsenpiller is a man of many pursuits. Educated at Southwestern Baptist University in rural Missouri, he began to serve as a peripatetic Southern Baptist pastor in Louisiana, Missouri, Ohio, and Denver, where he went through a ministry and family crisis, took a sabbatical to Oxford, England, and then resurfaced at Jacksonville Chapel in Lincoln Park, New Jersey, outside of New York

City. Unaffiliated and somewhat ambiguous about its roots, the Chapel nonetheless embraces aspects of Pentecostalism that Phil and his wife, Tammy, hadn't encountered in their traditional Southern Baptist churches. Tammy said it was at Jacksonville that she learned about grace, and it was in Manhattan that, through a Jewish-Catholic friend, she gained confidence in her own vocational ministry. When the Hotsenpillers' children decided to move to Southern California (their daughter for college and their son for his own church plant), Phil and Tammy weren't far behind.

While working at the Quaker church in Yorba Linda, the couple also started a ministry called {la}God, meeting at the W Hotel in West Hollywood with young actors and musicians. In New York, Tammy had gotten her certification to be a life coach, and Phil had founded New York Executive Coaching Group. The two were inspired by the fame and glamour of working in Southern California, and Tammy didn't want to leave and give up her own work outside the church, including ventures in fashion with Nordstrom, Nickelodeon, and then-popular brand Ed Hardy. Still, Phil's flamboyance was a bit too much for the leadership at Yorba Linda Friends. Phil was asked to leave, and in a meeting in February 2012, he announced he'd been called to "birth" a new congregation. The whole thing had an air of Southern California prophecy about it, as the Vineyard Church movement, popular in Tammy's native Missouri, had begun just down the road at Canyon High School, and Vineyard founder John Wimber had supposedly given a prophecy that a new revival would not end until "it flows down the canyon." For Tammy, the fact that Influence Church was started at *Canyon* High School, where the Vineyard Church began, just off *Santa Ana Canyon Road*, was evidence of God's desire for the couple to influence the world and the fulfillment of Wimber's prophecy. Influence's genesis also spoke to the growing edge of American Pentecostalism, distinct from the more staid Southern Baptists, who had long led church growth across the United States. Pentecostalism is more egalitarian in its gender roles, more open to leaders of color and women, and without the historical baggage carried by Southern Baptists and American conservative politics.

Tammy later told me that the Hotsenpillers had met while both were involved with the hippie-ish Jesus People movement while in college at Southwestern Baptist in Missouri. Their early love of music and belief in baptism by the Holy Spirit carried them through to Influence Church and to their attached record label, Influence Music, whose opening album featured America's Got Talent's Michael Ketterer and hit number two on the Billboard chart. Phil also had a penchant for outrageous political sentiment. He had written a book about the end times called One Nation without Law, and he'd written online columns for FOX News in the aftermath of the Sutherland, Texas, church shooting and on the topic of California wildfires. (He rejects the science that wildfires are related to global warming.) Phil had been an early Trump booster, and I found interesting, if not disturbing, his own blend of spirituality, end-times prophecy, and celebrity. But I was more interested in hearing from Tammy, who had started a women's empowerment ministry as an arm of Influence Church: Women of Influence.

In my awe of Orange County women and their ability to toe the line between sexy Southern California and appropriately Christian and traditional stay-at-home church wife, Tammy was at the front of the line. I wanted to know her thoughts on the political divide of American Christianity, and she had transitioned from Southern Baptist pastor's wife to pastor in her own right, here in this deep-red corner of liberal California, where many a religious revival had been launched, maybe even my own.

Blondes and Bibles: A Powerful New Ministry

On an August morning that dawned hot and sultry in North Orange County, I drove up Santa Ana Canyon Road in Anaheim Hills to Influence Church headquarters. I opened the door of the church and walked into a flurry of motion. Tammy and four of her colleagues were meeting with a Hispanic woman from the local Boys and Girls Club. They were talking about single moms who were interested in Women of Influence, and Tammy suggested that Women of Influence could partner with a local pizza place to provide food for the club's gatherings; the woman had been purchasing food out of her own pocket.

"We can do that," Tammy insisted.

"I don't mind," the other woman said, shaking her head.

I saw a glamorous, powerful, determined, formidable group of women. As the meeting ended, Tammy welcomed me in. I realized that at all of the megachurches I had visited, the women pastors, despite their outwardly glamorous appearance, were the most down-to-earth and willing to sit for an in-person, on-the-record interview. While Tammy was fashionably dressed, with stylish blond hair and makeup that belied her sixty years, she moved and spoke with a surprising lack of pretense. Before she told me her story, she talked about an Orange County political operative she wanted to introduce me to. Her brain was moving a mile a minute. She was unstoppable now. All those years of standing in her husband's shadow, only to found her own ministry later in life, had combusted into explosive energy. Tammy wasn't holding back anymore.

The office space itself was on the ground floor, and the room held a large conference table without a prominent desk or fancy chairs. Tammy's coworkers, two pretty blond women who I figured were around my age, stayed in the office, working on their laptops while we talked. At times she'd say, "Oh, I don't think I've told my staff all this," but then she'd keep going anyway. Like many American success stories about West Coast people, Tammy's story began in the Midwest. When she was growing up, she attended a traditional Southern Baptist church in Saint Louis, Missouri, and as a young teenager, she went on a mission trip to Haiti. "My friend and I went together," Tammy said. "And of course, we were so naive. We took a suitcase full of matching outfits to Haiti. Well, I came back suitcase-less. Everything I had I gave," she said. "Something shifted in my life at that point."

The trip to Haiti marked her initial call into ministry, but as a Southern Baptist woman, Tammy knew she had three choices: global missions, organist, or pastor's wife. She wasn't all that musical, and she didn't want to live overseas, far from her family. So Tammy requested a meeting with her pastor's wife.

"I've been called into ministry," she said. "What does it take to be a good pastor's wife?"

Well, she was told, she couldn't use her passion for fashion or for athletics. Instead, she had to be FAT: Faithful And True to her husband. Tammy told me the acronym was well known among her Southern Baptist friends. So she did the best she could, leaning into her own call to ministry by trying to become a pastor's wife and pursuing a relationship with her pastor's son, who was likely to be a pastor himself.

A few years later, Tammy was engaged to her pastor's son, but it didn't last when she attended Southwestern Baptist University in Bolivar, Missouri. There she became involved with the Jesus Movement, filled with guitars, folk music, and talk of the miraculous and super-natural. "We were meeting with Vietnam veterans who had returned from war, messed up on LSD," she said. "We prayed over them and saw miraculous healing."

In the Jesus Movement at Southwestern Baptist, Tammy met Phil, who was "larger than life." He had become a believer during his first year of college and was involved in the Jesus Movement as well. The two married quickly and moved together for Phil's studies at New Orleans Baptist Theological Seminary. Tammy, then in her early twenties, quickly became a mother of two. She was still feeling the itch of her own call to ministry, without a good way to fulfill it. "I wanted to bring what I loved in the world into the church, but the church didn't embrace me," she said. "I was told to follow my husband. And that's been the rub all my life: how do I be me and do ministry?"

They moved to tiny, rural Wilson, Louisiana, which is located on the border with Mississippi and was still mired in segregation and racial tension. The racism she encountered bothered Tammy, whose mother, Sharleen, had friends and acquaintances of all different races and cultures. "There wasn't a holiday that passed [while I was growing up] that we didn't have someone from another culture at our table," Tammy said. The segregation of the Louisiana church stifled Tammy so much that she felt she had to hide her wedding photos every time a deacon from church came over to dinner. The reason? Her ring bearer, a five-year-old boy named Randy who had gone to Tammy's mother for childcare, was black.

Times weren't easy for Tammy as a young mom in Louisiana, but Phil's career as a Southern Baptist pastor took off quickly. They moved from a church in Saint Louis to a larger church in Columbus, Ohio, to an even larger church in Denver. Tammy thought Phil was moving closer to the inner ring of the Southern Baptist Convention, and she found herself deeply rooted in the subculture of the Southern Baptist church, which she found limiting. "We all get into the rut of whatever subculture we're in," she told me. "Now, I always ask, 'Do you have Christian convictions, or do you have the convictions of Christians?' I had convictions of Christians."

In Denver, Tammy said her marriage and their church suffered "an explosion," and Phil was asked to take a sabbatical to England, after which he went to work at the aforementioned Jacksonville Chapel outside New York City. It seems likely that the "explosion" involved an extramarital affair, but Tammy has never made that public. For a woman so open and unguarded, she still works and lives in a culture that is led predominately by men, and she is still a pastor's wife. Nevertheless, the time in England enhanced Tammy's own calling into ministry, which continued in New York City. She discovered a passion for fund-raising and for leadership training, and in the secular business world, Tammy found the acceptance and encouragement she had always longed for in the Southern Baptist church. Her fashion business ventures continued in Southern California, as Phil pastored at Yorba Linda Friends, and Tammy started a Pilates ministry that grew to more than two hundred women, raising thousands of dollars for new schools in India.

Still, in Tammy's words, "There wasn't room for me to do ministry at Friends." They already had a women's pastor, and she wasn't allowed to minister to mixed groups. So when Phil made the decision in 2012 to plant Influence Church, Tammy believed her time had come. Women of Influence started in 2012, with weekly meetings on Monday nights led by Tammy and others. As she had in her business ventures, Tammy worked her network, raising funds and building partnerships with female Christian leaders, musicians, authors, and speakers.

I first heard of Women of Influence in 2016, meeting with a woman who attended my church, a powerful attorney for children's rights. Danielle was the embodiment of the Orange County woman: a mother of four with cascading, curled blond hair, a toned physique, and an appearance much younger than her biological age. Like many of the women I knew and loved in Orange County, Danielle had much more to offer than her appearance. She had a powerful personal story: she'd lost her mother at a young age and had been abandoned by her father and later her stepfather. She was a star athlete who left her family home before graduating from high school, and she surmounted many obstacles to become an attorney. Later, she battled cancer and conflict in her marriage. Through it all, Danielle maintained a quality of grace and faith that increased, rather than decreased, even in the face of life's challenges. She had attempted to participate in women's ministry and small groups in our congregation, but she just couldn't find a good fit. As we met over coffee near her law office, which happened to be across the street from Influence Church, she told me about attending Women of Influence and hearing Tammy's story. She told me the program was all about helping women tell their own stories in light of the gospel. I was enthralled when I heard about this powerful gathering of women, raising their own voices to tell their own stories. I intended to visit Women of Influence, but our family moved back to Midwest in a matter of months. Instead, I finally ended up meeting Tammy, in the heart of Women of Influence headquarters, more than a year later.

As Tammy told me her story, she concluded with the powerful role that Women of Influence had played in her own journey toward claiming her ministry and telling her story. She told me the story of a trip to South Africa with Phil, early in their journey with Influence Church. She had asked him to go for a walk with her, after she had spent the day, as she had for many years, trailing behind him from conversation to conversation with various Christian luminaries, always supporting him, always nodding and smiling when she was supposed to. She felt exhausted, jet-lagged when they'd arrived, but had never thought to say no when Phil asked for her support. Responding to Phil's needs was, she had been told for many years, her godly duty and ministry. At that point, she just wanted her husband to come with her on a walk.

"No," he said. "I'm just too tired." For Tammy, it felt like a final straw. *Why won't you just do one thing for me?* So she left to walk alone, listening to a song they often sang at church, Kim Walker's "Holy Spirit." The words echoed in Tammy's brain. The Holy Spirit was calling *her* into ministry of her own, not just to support Phil. Tammy said that day she saw a puzzle that was her ministry. She realized God wasn't asking her to put the puzzle together, only to gather up the pieces (she now wears a puzzle piece around her neck), and then she knew, finally, that she was loved by God simply for herself, not for who her husband was.

"I thought I was supposed to walk with my husband," she said. "But I learned I was supposed to walk with God and step out of my husband's shadow." As we wrapped up our interview, Tammy's next appointment was waiting outside, and I wondered how she squared her own ministerial awakening, her goal to empower women, with her husband's conservative political advocacy and vocal support of Trump, thrice married and widely decried as a misogynist. At first, Tammy backed up her husband, telling me that she was "definitely" a Trump supporter, and she believed he was a person of faith. Then, she began to backtrack, naming Trump as having a "personal struggle with his sexual side," for which he "needed help."

"If we had another candidate," she said, "maybe it would be a different story. I—will—probably—vote for him again." When asked about Obama, Tammy initially said she believed, as her husband did, that he was a Muslim. Then again, she backtracked. "I shouldn't have said that. Maybe he wasn't a Muslim."

She looked genuinely torn. She mentioned watching (and loving) *Madame Secretary* on TV but hating Hollywood's liberal agenda. At sixty years old, a product of the baby boomer generation, a graduate of the Jesus Movement, and a beneficiary of the Southern Baptist church growth movement and traditional Evangelical culture, Tammy stands at a precipice. She has benefited from Evangelical culture as she also tests its boundaries. How much ministry can a woman do? How can a woman leader in the church look and act? As I looked at the young women in the room with Tammy, I saw how she had expanded the boundaries to make room for them. And I wondered how Orange County Evangelical women like them might change the rules for Evangelical women to come, as political truths once held sacred by Evangelicals could be challenged and changed. The Evangelical embrace of Trump may be precursor to something more revolutionary and less patriarchal.

This Brown-Skinned Youth Pastor Is Not Your Barista

The final stop on my OC worship tour was Mariners Church, one of the most beautiful church campuses in the country, located just miles from Newport Coast and some of America's costliest real estate. I first came to Mariners in 2012; I was an intern pastor in Vegas, and I attended the Catalyst West Conference, put on by Andy Stanley's North Point megachurch in Atlanta and hosted by Mariners each year on the West Coast. If Saddleback was the nineties-era megachurch, Mariners represented a hipper blend of Hillsong and Hollywood. When I attended Catalyst West again in 2016, I was surprised to hear some anti-Trump jokes from the presenters. This was the Westmont College, wealthy and educated Evangelical crowd—the Evangelical intelligentsia—a crowd initially resistant to Trump, since he was not considered a true conservative. But while the speakers on stage joked about Trump, most people in the four-thousand-seat worship center weren't laughing. The rank-and-file Evangelicals embraced Trump more quickly than their pastors did. Nevertheless, as the tax cuts for the wealthy were passed and pro-life justices appointed, even the leadership at Mariners fell in line.

I wasn't sure what to expect at Mariners when I arrived for Sunday-night youth worship. I wandered around the massive campus for several minutes, trying to figure out where to go. The worship center was quiet and dark, so I poked my head into other buildings and found them full of people attending support groups. Finally, I walked up some stairs and into a room full of college students. A handsome young man with broad shoulders and black hair stood in the front of the room, pacing a bit but speaking in an even tone about wisdom.

"Remember Proverbs 29:23," Wes Tameifuna said. "'Pride ends in humiliation, while humility brings honor.' Pride and wisdom will always be in conflict with each other. The mark of being wise is knowing what you don't know. Humility is always acutely aware that it needs someone. . . . Wisdom is never the product of a self-made person. And I know that hurts you to your core as Westerners, but there is no such thing as a self-made person. Jesus's call is always to the humble. It's not really about if you have it; it's about whether you're going to step up and create it for others. Our isolation is lying to us, and it's costing us the very thing it's promising us."

The fifth sermon I'd heard in forty-eight hours was the first one to grab my attention. All weekend, I'd heard the gospel of self-improvement, the glory of the individual, the start of *your new life,* but here was a preacher in the glitziest Southern California megachurch trumpeting the value of humility.

Tameifuna unleashed a countercultural message for an America obsessed with mirror selfies and a president who couldn't think of anything for which he had to ask forgiveness, a countercultural message for an Evangelical movement that had come to worship winning, the gospel of the self-made man, pulled up by his own bootstraps to "make something of himself." Tameifuna reminded people that God's forgiveness and acceptance of us is, in a sense, an undeserved handout. It's an aspect of the Christian message that doesn't always resonate in an America where everything must be earned.

Tameifuna preached on about humility and integrity and community and legacy. Then he told his listeners to consider being prayed for, and as the night wound down, the service ended in song, and the mostly twenty-somethings drifted off into the hazy Orange County evening. In spite of a line of people hoping to speak to him, Tameifuna accepted my request for an interview, and we stepped out onto the Mariners back deck. Tameifuna, age twenty-eight, told me he lived far from Mariners in Corona, California, across the Orange County line in Riverside County. Thirty-five miles from most places in Orange County, Corona is often the only affordable place for a young family to purchase a home in Southern California, especially on a pastor's salary. I found it somewhat galling that a multimillion-dollar operation like Mariners couldn't afford to pay its young-adults pastor a living wage in the community where he worked, but such is the reality in Orange County.

Tameifuna told me his ethnic background is Tongan (Pacific Islander) and Mexican, and he hadn't grown up in the church. He came to faith at megachurch Crossroads Christian in Corona. He'd worked at Mariners for four years after playing football at Fullerton

College. He attended Vanguard University in Costa Mesa, majoring in biblical studies. Early in his ministry career and without a seminary degree, Tameifuna was nonetheless a big draw at Mariners. When he spoke, he had magnetism—a certain ineffable quality of connecting to people, which can't be taught. But he chafed at the limits of the megachurch culture, noting that while he'd finally had the opportunity to preach at the main worship center the previous weekend, he'd gotten negative feedback about the tattoos on his arms.

"But some people," Tameifuna said, shaking his head. "People like me, who didn't grow up in the church, maybe that's the thing that makes them connect." He was frustrated at the confines of the conservative Evangelical world, even here in laid-back Southern California. The nearly two years since Trump's election had been trying ones as he watched his fellow Evangelicals fall into line with what he considered a presidency corrupted by racism and sexism.

I asked Tameifuna about the recent allegations of sexual misconduct in megachurches, and he told me about one of Mariners' campus pastors, who had said his divorce was due to some problems watching pornography but turned out to involve a whole host of extramarital affairs. Tameifuna said his wife, Taylor, who also works for Mariners, had been active in the #MeToo movement and had gone to Women's Marches, and she had changed the way he thought about accusations of sexual misconduct, especially in churches. "I feel like the culture can really vilify women," Tameifuna said. "No one will really say it out loud, but they sort of act like [the accusation] is just an inconvenience for the men who've been accused. I don't agree with that. I get that it's an inconvenience for you, but what these women have gone through is not even comparable."

Tameifuna talked about the elevated tensions in Orange County church staffs following the 2016 election, particularly between ministers of color and white pastors and church laypeople on elder boards. "In these large megachurches, you'll often have outreach positions that are filled with people of color. There was a definite tension and friction on church staffs during the election, because one side had theological reasons for supporting Trump, and the other side was saying, 'But this affects my daily life and the well-being of my family.'"

Tameifuna remembered emotions running high at Mariners and in other Orange County megachurches on Election Day 2016. "You had some people in their offices crying, and some people were ready to celebrate. And some people sort of tried to police the reactions of people who were crying—trying to say they shouldn't cry, and it wasn't a bad thing." Those who were upset were told to "stop crying," and their coworkers didn't understand why Trump's election felt so personal for people of color on Orange County megachurch staffs, Tameifuna told me. "Some people did try to explain why they were upset and talk about it, but the hard part is that the burden is always placed on minorities to speak up and explain why you should care about me. That gets really emotionally taxing—always having to explain to people why they should care about what happens to you."

I was surprised at Tameifuna's openness. Working at a megachurch, for a conservative Evangelical organization, often entails a virtual vow of silence, acquiescence to the more troubling aspects of the organization in return for its positive fruits, like global mission trips and preaching to thousands every weekend. But the last two years had been exhausting, and Tameifuna was grateful to finally explain what had happened to him in this place.

"I'm Tongan and Mexican, and we have a predominately white staff," Tameifuna said. "I've been mistaken for the server at the cafe lots of times. I can't tell you how many times someone has asked me to fix the sprinklers in the lawn." As a pastor of color at a megachurch, he told me, "You do feel like being here, you hit your head on the ceiling. It's hard. It's hard to decide what can we be advocates for without being considered political. You can feed people and work on poverty, but anything that is remotely considered social justice is off-limits."

Tameifuna said that when he preached at the main campus, he had people come up to him afterward and express surprise that he was giving the sermon at Mariners. "We're used to brown people being in a story from a mission trip," they told him. "We're not used to hearing you tell the story. We're not used to hearing from brown people from here, instead of from a third-world country." In spite of his thriving young-adult ministry and platform at the nation's seventeenth-largest church, Tameifuna was discouraged. He mentioned that his mentor at Mariners, another outreach pastor who was a person of color, had left Mariners to start his own church in Santa Ana.

"I am unsure of the future of the megachurch itself. I'm not sure what I think about pastors being brands. It's hard to find a pastor who is just a good person and committed to the local church," Tameifuna said. "After Obama left, and the morning after Election Day, I didn't feel hopeless, but I did feel betrayed. There were all the morality issues in the election and problems with Trump with women and people of color, and they still voted for him."

CHAPTER 5

Young, Free-Thinking, and Pro-Trump: Young Midwestern Farm Families in Rural Missouri

Trump's Red State Christian support is concentrated in the center of the country, in rural and suburban counties far from either coast. I was particularly interested in the stories of Red State Christians from Missouri, where my mom grew up, I attended college, and my husband's family still lives. Missouri used to be called the Bellwether State because it had voted for the winner in all but three presidential elections from 1904 to 2016. Missouri used to be fairly balanced between Democrats and Republicans, and many of the people we knew there had supported Bill Clinton, a native of nearby Arkansas, despite holding conservative political beliefs.

Missouri changed, though, between Bill Clinton to Barack Obama, and the Show-Me State grew much more conservative. Missouri voted for Republicans McCain and Romney in 2008 and 2012, and people in the state moved significantly to the right during Obama's presidency. While Missouri used to be dominated by its two "blue coasts" of Kansas City and Saint Louis, its urban share of the population has decreased while its rural population has increased. The state, which has always been torn between its Confederate roots and its status as part of the agrarian, prairie Midwest, has often been at the heart of the nation's racial fault lines.

Missouri offered me an opportunity to look into the rural, midwestern soul of America in the time of Trump. It's one thing to look at Trump supporters from a distance and to draw national trends; it's something else to look at the faces of close friends and family whom you've known for years and to understand their strong support for such a divisive president.

Driving down I-35 into America's Heart

Unlike my other trips, my research into young, rural Missourians began in the car with my husband and two little boys, driving that familiar route down I-35 from Minnesota through the entire state of Iowa, passing cornfields and Ames and Des Moines, leaning west into the broad, grand state of Missouri, the crossroads of the nation, and cresting finally past the Royals' Kauffman Stadium on I-70 down a chapel road to my husband's parents' home. Missouri runs through my blood. My mom grew up here in Kansas City, attending inner-city Center High School and sitting in the front row for civil rights and Vietnam War tensions while her dad pastored a Lutheran congregation near the state line separating Missouri and Kansas—the same state line that once separated the Union from the Confederacy. My husband's hometown, the same town where my mom's sister raised her girls, is rumored to be named after a Confederate leader, though the stories are conflicting. (Some people say it's named after a local dentist.) This trip was mostly about family. We'd swim in the neighborhood pool, eat homemade cinnamon rolls for breakfast, and then drive down to the small farming community where my husband's dad had grown up. There we'd have a big family reunion at the local Missouri Synod Lutheran church, involving as many of the seven siblings and their families as possible.

I'd arranged to meet with some local farm families after the reunion, attend the Evangelical Lutheran Church in America (ELCA) church, and interview some high-school students for my book. But I knew that in the background of their stories were the stories of my married family and of my best girlfriends from college, most of whom grew up in farming communities not far from Cole Camp. Their stories would have a piece of me in them, too. When my mom was born, her parents lived in a trailer home on the Wartburg Seminary campus in rural Iowa. The story is that her parents put her in a cardboard box between them on the front seat, wedged between the seat back and the dashboard of their car, and drove across these same rural roads and highways to my grandpa's first church in rural western Nebraska, where he'd stay for a decade until traveling back east to Kansas City, where West meets East and North meets South.

I've talked to many people and families who have felt torn apart by politics and religion. The love I have for my conservative Missouri family and friends I carried with me across the country as I spoke to Red State Christians. Now, in Missouri, I'd come closer to telling the stories that were closest to my heart.

Young Farmers, Pastors, Wine, and Antiques in Cole Camp, Missouri

The national rhetoric tends to go like this: Small towns are dying, and entrepreneurship is clustered in big, expensive cities like New York and San Francisco. All the young people are moving out of rural America; nothing is left but abandoned homes and factories and opioid-addled young adults. In some ways, this narrative rang true in my travels to central Pennsylvania and Appalachian small towns and churches. There I sensed a powerful tug of despair, and I heard about "all the kids" who'd long ago left town for larger cities. Cole Camp, however, was different. Here I found the youth, hopefulness, and work ethic that Americans had always romanticized in the small-town Midwest.

On Saturday afternoon after our family reunion, we drove out to Uncle Doug's farm, to the house where my father-in-law and his six siblings had once lived, a house built by their father's own hands. Today the barn and the farm equipment still stand, but it's mostly unused. Uncle Doug is in his seventies and can't get around the way he used to. The farm held the promise and memories of the past, as well as the uncertainty of the future of the proud Denker name in Cole Camp. The Denkers were known for always winning the pull-up contest at the Cole Camp Fair and for outrunning all the other boys in area cross-country races. My father-in-law hadn't lived there since he was drafted into the Vietnam War in 1968, but for our family, it would somehow always be partially home. I remembered the first time I had come here—a college girlfriend of twenty, falling in love with my husband-to-be even more when a few of his uncles pulled out fiddles and started singing as we sat around the crowded farmhouse living room.

On our visit to research this book, we spent some time on the farm, and then my family headed back to Kansas City in my in-laws' car, dropping me off with our car about twenty miles up State Highway U in Sedalia, at Hotel Bothwell, where Harry Truman once stayed. I took a few minutes to get settled before hopping back into my car and back onto Highway U, down the road to Cole Camp and a little place called Wine, Antiques and More, just off Main Street in downtown Cole Camp. They offer local Missouri wines, locally made sausage and cheese, and yes, nachos and beer. I settled into a chair at an upstairs table that had been set aside by my friends, Pastors Kimberly Knowle-Zeller and Stephen Zeller, both Lutheran pastors, though Kim was taking a break from ministry to stay home with their kids and advance her own writing career. Stephen was the pastor of the other Lutheran church in town, St. Paul's, an ELCA congregation.

An identifying feature of Cole Camp is its staunch German Lutheran-ness. Both the Missouri Synod and ELCA churches are packed full on Sunday mornings throughout the year, not just with seniors but with families and young children. Kim even told me that the two churches had booths opposite each other at the annual fair, selling exactly the same food: a rotating assortment of pies, hot dogs, brats, chili dogs, grilled burgers, and what they call "juicy burgers," similar to sloppy joes. (If that's not a metaphor for the ways denominationalism divides American Christians despite all we share in common, then I don't know what is!)

Nonetheless, as things tend to go in small towns, the group gathered tonight at Wine, Antiques and More crossed denominational lines. My ELCA pastor friends had invited some of their friends from town and church: Eric Kullman, age thirty-five, had grown up going to the Missouri Synod church but switched over when he was older and married Emily (née Oelrichs), thirty-three. The two had been married twelve years and had three children. Also joining us was Emily's sister, Erin Oelrichs, thirty-two, who came back to the Cole

Camp area after college at Missouri State. Erin works in a bank, but true to the entrepreneurial spirit I found in Cole Camp, she's also a cake decorator on the side.

All three were Cole Camp natives from farming families: Erin and Emily's dad is on a national board for dairy farmers, and their family operates one of the area's largest dairy farms. Emily went on to earn a master's in radiology after undergrad, and she works locally as a radiology technician. Eric, like his wife and sister-in-law, shatters a myth of small-town sameness; he is a former drummer who once played in what he calls a red-dirt-road country band called Renegade Rail. The group played and toured for years, mostly in Texas, and Eric said he probably could still be touring today, though he wouldn't still be married. "It wasn't the kind of life for a husband and dad," he said.

Fresh off the success of his group's best-known hit, "Fat Girls and Weed," Eric came back home to Cole Camp and reunited with childhood pal Emily at the Cole Camp Fair. "It's kind of funny because our moms were friends," Emily said. "We used to hang out as kids, but of course we don't remember it."

The three thirtysomethings represent an interesting cross-section of small-town tradition and millennial optimism. Like their urban counterparts, Eric, Emily, and Erin each have a variety of side hustles. Eric works as a bricklayer and owns a farm, where he grows row crops and raises some beef cattle. They joked about inviting Pastor Stephen, a native of western Maryland, to come with them to bale hay.

Eric said he decided to give up touring when he remembered a piece of advice from his pastor at the Missouri Synod church growing up: "Give a man until he's twenty-five," the pastor told Eric. "If he's still running around after twenty-five, he'll probably never stop." When Eric returned to Cole Camp, his family ultimately helped him with funds to start farming, and he learned a trade in bricklaying on the side, which brought him into contact with the few remaining Labor Democrats in Missouri.

"They're not liberals," Eric said, noting that he didn't really know any liberals in Cole Camp. "They're blue-collar Democrats. I think forty or fifty years ago, I would've been a Democrat. I'm a union guy. But now our union is so corrupt, I basically just have it for the health insurance."

All three Cole Camp natives had voted for Trump, though none was an early adopter. "I'll be honest, it was mostly baby boomers who got it first," Eric said. "Right away, my dad was like, 'Trump, he's my guy!' And I said, 'I don't know.' I was more, 'Anyone but Hillary.' But when Trump won the primary, I was in. I thought, 'That's exactly what we need.'"

What Eric, Emily, and Erin found attractive in Trump was his independence—the idea that he could not be bought or influenced by any political party—and that he promised to run the country like a business. Where conservative Christian voters in the deeper South or from more Evangelical or Baptist traditions tended to emphasize the Supreme Court or Trump's position on social issues, these young midwestern voters were focused more on lines like "draining the swamp" and "America first." While many in America have watched Trump's presidency as one scandal or gaffe after another, these voters saw an underlying flow of economic boons and conservative governance. They weren't concerned with Trump's tweets or egregious comments, and if they were watching Fox News, they probably weren't seeing in-depth coverage of the Mueller investigation or Trump's various court entanglements.

"I don't care about the rude comments. I couldn't care less about the social issues," Eric said. I recognized in Eric, Emily, and Erin something I'd seen among other midwestern and rural Red State

Christians: fatigue. They had felt chastised by President Obama and by Democrats. They did not want to be called racist, but they hesitated to confront past instances of racism and injustice. In Cole Camp, I didn't see any plantations or hear stories about long-ago slave-owning families, despite the fact that Missouri was a slave state. The rural midwestern Americans I met carried a mix of pride and a sense of shame, a hesitation to admit America's original sins because their identity was tied so strongly to being an American and the pride that went along with that.

For a state that stood at the border of the Union and the Confederacy, race always lies just under the surface in Missouri. Just what role did racism play as the Show-Me State moved decisively to the right just as America's first black president took office as a Democrat?

When I asked Eric what bothered him most about Obama, his answer was revealing. Eric didn't dislike Obama because of his policies or the way he governed or anything about Obama himself. Instead, Eric keyed in on something Obama had said that made many rural Americans feel ashamed, at least the way Obama's words were clipped for conservative campaign ads. "The 'you didn't build it,'" Eric said without hesitation. "The idea that we couldn't be proud of what we had."

Eric was quoting an oft-replayed clip used by presidential candidate Mitt Romney in 2012, showing Obama speaking at a campaign appearance in Virginia. In context, Obama said:

> If you were successful, somebody along the line gave you some help. There was a great teacher somewhere in your life. Somebody helped to create this unbelievable American system that we have that allowed you to thrive. Somebody invested in roads and bridges. If you've got a business—you didn't build

that. Somebody else made that happen. The internet didn't get invented on its own. Government research created the internet so that all the companies could make money off the internet.[1]

Obama's larger point was that Americans needed to recognize our interdependence. He concluded by saying,

> So we say to ourselves, ever since the founding of this country, "You know what, there are some things we do better together." That's how we funded the GI Bill. That's how we created the middle class. That's how we built the Golden Gate Bridge or the Hoover Dam. That's how we invented the internet. That's how we sent a man to the moon. We rise or fall together as one nation and as one people, and that's the reason I'm running for president—because I still believe in that idea. You're not on your own; we're in this together.[2]

The different interpretations of Obama's comments on the right and left remind me of the very different ways Americans see America. The divides are not only partisan but also urban versus rural. Many of the Red State Christians who voted for Trump didn't see themselves as part of the "together" that Obama envisioned.

Was that because Obama was black? The suggestion of racism was also cited by Eric when he talked about his dislike of Obama. "And that you were racist if you didn't support him. That was an argument stopper. Someone says you're racist, the conversation is over," Eric continued.

White Americans have a difficult time talking about race. Among Red State Christians, such defensiveness makes conversation nearly impossible. Racism needs to be discussed in America, especially among conservative whites. It's frustrating to have conversations so easily shut down. Racism is a problem that requires a remedy among white Americans, especially as conservative Evangelicals continue to wrestle with the ways the Bible has been used in support of injustices against people of color, even in support of slavery. While Eric's words about how the accusation of racism can shut down conversation are important for liberals to hear, conservatives also need to realize that defensiveness about racism is only stopping conversations that could begin to heal America's racial wounds. As Obama's presidency showed, America's racial wrongs cannot be righted without the participation of white Americans, across party lines, without the defensiveness that comes when people are afraid to admit their own racist tendencies. Today, Trump only exacerbates the problem among white Americans with his accusations of racism against people of color. Racism needs to be understood not as an insult or an epithet to be tossed out but as a very real part of America's history, an original sin that not only plagues individuals but also is entrenched in the story of America itself.

A key difference I noticed here in rural Missouri, as opposed to other places where Red State Christians carried Trump to the presidency, is that the Christians here did not overwhelmingly see their faith leading them to vote for Trump. In fact, the Oelrichses told me that they sometimes still see Democrats as the ethical and generous party, the party your religion might influence you to vote for. When I asked Eric about how his religion influences his politics, he looked quickly at Pastor Stephen and then looked away. "I don't want my religion to influence my political beliefs," Eric said. "That makes it much more complicated. They say here if you're young and you're not liberal, you don't have a heart, and if you're old and you're not conservative, you don't have a brain."

According to these rural midwesterners, you become more conservative as you get older, meaning that the projections of liberal millennials growing up and voting Democratic as they get older and vote more often could turn out to be wrong in rural midwestern states like Missouri, especially if Democrats abandon rural midwestern communities for the foreseeable future. Still, remember that these rural midwestern voters are very different from the more socially conservative voters across the American Bible Belt who attend Evangelical and Southern Baptist churches. While many Evangelical megachurch pastors have been Trump boosters and supporters, Eric says he doesn't want his pastor to talk about politics in church.

"I get squirmy," he said, revealing a conflict between his libertarian economic values and what he hears in church on Sunday. Much of Trump's support here, beyond the occasional Make America Great Again cap, is eminently practical, at least in theory. The voters I interviewed bought into Trump's positions on immigration, if tepidly, viewing them through a lens of law and order, tinged with distrust of the mainstream national news media. These voters allow that family separations are terrible, but they also value the Republican appeal to lawful and orderly immigration proceedings. Social-media postings of children in cages that turned out to be from the Obama era didn't help convince Emily.

Closer to home, Eric noted that he was frustrated by fines imposed by the Occupational Safety and Health Administration (OSHA) on primarily white construction work crews in Cole Camp. "They don't mess with the Mexican work crews, because they're going back to Mexico. [OSHA] knows they won't pay fines. But we live here, and we will pay. So they fine us," he said. True or not, the idea of Democrats as big government and regulation hungry hit home here in the rural Midwest. "Rural libertarianism is growing because it's just

'Stay the heck out and leave me alone. Or do something, but just don't tell me about it. Don't force anything down my throat,'" Eric said. He talked about seeing a Facebook post that showed the Iwo Jima Memorial depicted with soldiers carrying a rainbow flag. "That was disrespectful to me," Eric said. "I mean as far as gay marriage goes, you want equal rights, you got 'em, right?"

Before we're done talking, I mention the one example of government overreach that farmers have embraced: farm subsidies and crop insurance. Eric and Emily explain that most of it works as insurance for crops or grass for cattle farmers, subsidized by the federal government. "I'd be a hypocrite if I said I didn't take them," Eric said. "But I would be OK if we did away with all of it. The thing is that if in the first year of a farm, it was a drought year, I would lose it all. The subsidy would be the only thing that would save me." There's a practical way that these small-town families see the world. They can be theoretically opposed to subsidies, but they also do what's best for their families. Emily points out the hypocrisy of "Hollywood liberals," who oppose immigration restrictions but "aren't inviting unaccompanied children and families to swim in their pools." Young farmers must stare potential disaster in the eye most years, reliant only on their own hands and a small government subsidy to survive. Their relative closeness to the land and to practical survival forces different calculations politically than among young urban families.

Emily says this is connected to her Christian faith, as she remembered make-or-break years growing up on the farm. "As a farmer, you really have to put your whole trust in God each year. There's a lot you can't control. It really is about faith." This faithfulness has little to do with social issues and much to do with the sovereignty of God, which Red State Christians view as threatened by the progressive secular socialism espoused by many Democrats.

The Generation That Understands: Cole Camp High Schoolers

I learned more about the Christian faith of rural Missouri Red State Christians the next morning after church at St. Paul's Lutheran in Cole Camp by talking with three local high-school students. Camryn Schear, age seventeen, Carter Wienberg, seventeen, and Delaney Gerken, fifteen, all attend Cole Camp High School and St. Paul's Lutheran Church. They had all recently returned from attending the ELCA's National Youth Gathering in Houston, where they heard from mostly progressive speakers on a variety of controversial topics. They even heard from a mom and her ten-year-old transgender daughter. I was curious to learn how hearing these speakers influenced a group of conservative high schoolers in small-town Missouri.

I asked the Cole Camp students, who had been surrounded by high-school students from all over America, what misconceptions people had about them and about their town. "They might think we are racist, but most of the time, we just don't know any better," Wienberg said. "We don't have as much diversity."

I found Wienberg's comment revealing, not only because Gerken is multiracial, but also because it showed again the defensiveness and sense of shame among rural Americans when it comes to racism. They saw the sinfulness of racism, and because they knew how wrong racism is, they were unable to repent for their own culpability in it. Still, these young people were more earnest and willing to talk about it than the adults. "We don't know any better," Wienberg said, demonstrating an admirable mix of frankness and humility.

The three high-school students talked about life in a small town, about how being "bad" as a middle schooler could influence your reputation for life, about the vandalism and mischief created by kids who were basically bored and looking for something to do, about the division in the high school between "farmers," who wore jeans and cowboy boots, and "athletes," who wore sweatpants and tennis shoes. Even though Schear's parents farm, she was considered an athlete because of how she dressed. Wienberg, wanting to fit in with athletes Schear and Gerken, said he did both, but Schear insisted, "I'd call you a FuFa," slang for Future Farmers of America, and she noted that most of the "farmers" at her school would have nothing to do with her.

The students talked about jokes about Trump during the 2016 election and about a government teacher who supported Hillary Clinton and was vocally anti-Trump. "That upset some people," Wienberg said.

Gerken, whose mother is white and father is African American, was the only one to voice displeasure with Trump. "I didn't want either Trump or Hillary," she said. "And now I see on social media some people look up to him, and I don't think he should be doing and saying everything he does on social media. It influences young people a lot."

Like the adults the night before, the high-school students said politics and religion were separate in their minds. When asked about racism, Gerken was hesitant to share her experiences. She told me that her parents were not married, and her father had been involved with drugs and lived separately in Sedalia, though she was close to her uncle, his brother. "My grandparents own the grocery store here, and everyone knows me, so racism doesn't really affect me," she said. "People don't, like, think I'm in gangs or anything."

I felt sympathy for Gerken and the line she walked as a multiracial teenager in a mostly white rural town. She said she chose not to look at the Confederate flag symbols she occasionally sees in town as something negative. "I can't make a big deal over things like that, because then I'd always be making a big deal of stuff, and it would never end," she said. I recognized the tension here between the idea that the white majority had been shamed by Democrats and the idea that the black and multiracial minority had been swallowing their hurt for generations in rural midwestern America. We need to find a middle ground where people can repent and forgive one another without the halting effect of shame, so that everyone can heal. Gerken shouldn't have to carry the hurt of the Confederate flag and the bondage of African Americans it represents.

The Cole Camp high-school students shared the fears and struggles of their generation: worries about a school shooting and the possibility that it could happen in their small town; an attempted suicide by the high-school quarterback, who had been Wienberg's friend and mentor; and stories about self-harm and abuse but a hesitancy to go to therapy, which Wienberg said was "still not accepted."

The students also shared their generation's openness to same-sex relationships and sexual orientation. "I have changed what I think about gay people," Schear said. Noting that gay and lesbian students attend the high school, she added, "Around here, people think it's not OK to be gay, but I want to share and say, 'Hey this isn't that bad. It's OK.' [At the Youth Gathering in Houston], we covered all these topics, and it really changed my mind. We talked about it after, and Pastor Stephen said that there are a lot of rules in the Bible, rules against lying as well, and the most important commandment is to love each other as God loves us."

Wienberg pointed out that some students at the high school are history buffs and some people bring Confederate regalia to school, but "they don't mean anything by it, and the principal makes them take it down." The idea of a small-town Missouri high-school principal enforcing rules against Confederate flags might not seem revolutionary, but in the decade since I attended college at Mizzou, this is a big change. Confederate flag bumper stickers were pasted on cars and trucks all around campus, especially at the Farmhouse fraternity, and I'd never heard or seen anyone reprimanded for it.

While Cole Camp and Missouri are increasingly conservative, I also noticed a growing movement among the high-school students to listen to one another—a movement rooted in the deep, biblical faith of the farmers here and their children. The high-school students all noted the hatred that sometimes surfaces in their small town, but they also expressed hopefulness for the future. "I think our country is so divided now," Wienberg said. "We all want the same things: everybody wants to be happy, and everybody wants America to be the best. People don't want to open their minds to talk to both sides. That's something I want our generation to change."

"If we accomplish one thing," Schear added, "I hope that we are the understanding generation—the generation that wants to look to understand each other and not hate each other." Schear's words represent an admirable goal and a hopeful way for Americans, rural and urban alike, to find our way to common ground. Most of the Red State Christians I spoke with felt so desperately misunderstood that they didn't have the ability or the desire to understand Americans who are unlike them. Maybe it will take until Schear's generation reaches middle age for Americans to drop our defensiveness and listen to one another, especially on tough topics like race. Still, I saw signs of hope in rural Missouri, where Christian Nationalism was weaker in the churches and people still saw Jesus as champion of the lowly.

CHAPTER 6

Winners and Losers: Trump, Football, and Christianity

Wouldn't you love to see one of these NFL owners, when somebody disrespects our flag, to say, 'Get that son of a bitch off the field right now. Out. He's fired. He's fired!'"[1] Trump was rolling, riffing at a campaign rally in Alabama, combining colloquial language, expletives, patriotism, and the "You're fired!" epithet, which originated on his NBC reality TV show. His words marked a new front in Trump's war against American unity, a new dividing line between who stood with Trump (the "real" Americans) and who stood against Trump (the ones who would "disrespect" the flag). Trump's words, spoken on September 22, 2017, smashed headfirst into former San Francisco 49ers quarterback Colin Kaepernick's kneeling protest during the national anthem before NFL games. Trump incited national opinion against Kaepernick, who would never play in the NFL again.

The original reason for the protest was forever lost. Kaepernick and other protesting players said they wanted to draw more attention to police shootings of unarmed black men, police brutality, and unfair treatment by the police of African Americans. At the time, African Americans were twice as likely to be killed by a police officer as unarmed white Americans.

Kaepernick had protested quietly, his silent kneeling mostly kept off TV screens and not embraced by the league's biggest stars, until Trump's words in Alabama. Two days later, more than two hundred NFL players sat or kneeled—even New England Patriots quarterback Tom Brady, a onetime Trump supporter who kept a Make America Great Again hat in his locker. To those who say sports and politics should never mix, welcome to America. For decades, the NFL and football programs in general sought to be the "most American" of all sports, bleeding sporting references not only into politics but into Christianity as well. In the late twentieth and early twenty-first centuries, to be an American, especially in red states, meant to love God, honor the flag, and cheer for your football team. Somehow, American pride, Jesus, and pigskins got conflated, and the NFL came to represent all that is sacred about the America Trump was elected to represent. Notably, that America is also predominately white.

The ideal of American pride and American football being forever joined together was irreparably changed in 2017, as Kaepernick and his fellow players' kneeling protest gained unprecedented national attention. Sensing their unique power and influence, the mostly black players seized a moment when white America was watching, kneeling during the pregame national anthem. The racial disparity between NFL players, who are mostly black, and owners, who are predominately white, played a role in the protests' dividing lines.

While the NFL has come to represent conservative patriotism and the sort of "God and country" Christianity popular across southern and rural America, 70 percent of NFL players are black.[2]

The African American players—many born into less-affluent families, made millionaires by their athleticism—and the white team owners and executives—many born into wealth, made millionaires by a combination of family background and business savvy without ever playing sports themselves—coexisted somewhat uncomfortably for decades, even as the proportion of black players rose and the proportion of black owners and coaches stagnated. The status quo held, even as retired players began to speak out about the punishing long-term effects of professional football, including concussions, on the human body and about the poverty brought on by poor money management and greedy agents and handlers.

Many football players embraced the conservative Christianity of their coaches and became outspoken advocates for the pro-life movement. Matt Birk and Benjamin Watson, for example, spoke at events surrounding the 2018 March for Life. Other players avoided politics and went on to careers in broadcasting. Rarely had NFL players before Kaepernick been involved in political protests, and no US president prior to Trump deigned to use a political campaign rally to engage in a war of words with professional athletes.[3]

Trump likes to brag that he is "one of the best athletes," even as people tell stories about the "floating mulligans" he takes on the golf courses he owns to improve his score.[4] He likes to claim friendships with athletes, and he considers athleticism an essential part of being a successful American man. That said, video is available online of a much younger Trump playing tennis with Serena Williams, so you can be the judge of his claims to athletic greatness or even mediocrity. For Trump, calling for the firing of protesting athletes fits a pattern, a tendency to lash out when threatened, an angry response when anyone dares to expose Trump as weak, or goes against what he perceives as America's "natural order." He pivots quickly to rile up his base, spinning into aggression when it seems the America he has come to save is being saved by anyone but him.

For America, however, the confrontation between the wannabe athlete celebrity president and the protesting black NFL players brought to the fore a conflict that was not only about politics and sports but also about religion and about who has the final word on Christianity in America. Which Jesus would have the final say in American history? Which Jesus do American Christians worship? The Jesus who stands with his hand over his heart while the anthem plays or the Jesus who kneels before the flag as if in prayer, protesting silently against injustice? Both Jesuses are a vital part of the American experience. During the Trump presidency, the commitment of two strains of American Christianity, African American and white conservative, have been tested and tried over and over again, and both draw more people into the fold while also sending thousands of people running out the doors of the American church.

My Religious Sportswriting Experience

We attended church regularly, as well as church camp and church choir, but sports were the axis around which my family's world spun. I grew up with a dad who played college football and a maternal grandpa who had joined the ministry only after an ill-fated tryout for Major League Baseball. I was the firstborn and my dad's "boy," so I learned to throw a spiral at age four and was pitching baseball at five, bringing my trusty glove and bat to elementary school, and listening to my transistor radio under the covers each night for Minnesota Twins games. My mom was born just a year or two too early for Title IX, but she nonetheless competed as a diver, as a gymnast, and briefly in track and field. She would later teach aerobics and a variety of fitness classes, and my childhood consisted primarily of being perpetually in motion, from soccer to T-ball to dance to swimming to volleyball to basketball. I played traveling everything; summers were softball tournaments, and winters were basketball tournaments. I wanted to earn a varsity letter in three sports at my large suburban high school, and I did so in volleyball, basketball, and track (though I later quit the basketball team in a pointless feud with the coaching staff).

As a writer on the high-school newspaper, I was the first female sports editor. In college at the University of Missouri's Journalism School, I was assigned the sports beat at the Columbia *Missourian*, where I quickly rose through the ranks to cover minor Big 12 conference athletics, traveling to Big 12 basketball tournaments in Dallas and Saint Louis when I was just twenty years old for the rival Columbia *Daily Tribune*.

Intending to double-major in political science and magazine journalism, I instead fell in love with a pickup basketball all-star named Ben, whom I called Basketball Boy before I knew his name. I found out he could dunk, and that was the end of it; our high fives at the drinking fountain in the Campus Recreation Center would turn to exchanging wedding rings seven long years later, and I instead followed my heart into sportswriting, graduating early and moving to Kansas City with Ben. I'd later take a sportswriting job in Naples, Florida, and then after almost three years covering minor-league hockey (in addition to the NFL, the Super Bowl, high-school football, and other Southwest Florida sports), I followed a long-ignored call to attend seminary and become a Lutheran pastor. No matter my profession, though, a part of my heart would always be left at the gym and in the softball field. Sweat was to me as incense to a priest, comforting me and bringing me closer to the holy presence.

My pastoral presence in congregations was usually preceded by this interesting factoid: she was formerly a sportswriter! Suddenly, people wanted to talk to me. Sports, for me and for much of the world, have always been the ultimate bridge builder, creating conversation and commonality among diverse groups of people who could unite in their shared love of the Chicago Cubs or their shared hatred of the New York Yankees. People are always surprised that I know many sportswriters who are people of faith, and I even know a few other sportswriters-turned-pastors. Both professions are made for storytellers, and no one loves a redemption story more than a sports fan or a Christian.

The Faith of the Football Coaches

While sportswriting in the red Gulf Coast counties of Southwest Florida, I first witnessed the power of the connection between conservative Christianity and big-time sports. Naples was home to some of the best high-school football teams in the state. Naples High won the state championship in 2001, 2003, and 2007. I heard that the coach, Bill Kramer, hosted a Bible study for area coaches. Marooned far from family and friends, temporarily broken up or in long-distance limbo with my future husband, I was seeking a bit of stability and a return to faith. I happened to be working on a longer-form profile piece on Coach Kramer for the special section on the upcoming football season, and I used a little time at the end of our interview to ask Kramer about his faith. He was quiet and not at all pushy, and he recommended I attend First Baptist of Naples, where he said most of the other area coaches went. Leaving the parking lot after practice, I ran into one of the other football coaches, a guy closer to my age named Bronze. He, too, was a devoted Christian and recommended First

Baptist. He'd been a former player for Kramer not many years ago and attested to the presence of Christian-based coaching not just at Naples but at many of the high schools in the area. Southwest Florida is a microcosm of the centrality of conservative Christian faith among coaches, particularly football coaches, across America. In a profession that can rise and fall with that year's quarterback, coaches need a grounding center in their lives, and amid living and dying on the fortunes of teenage boys, coaches need a reminder of the presence of eternity in their lives.

Football and conservative Christianity were overlapping worlds, I found out, and while occasionally coaches were challenged by public school districts or secular groups or students of non-Christian faiths, in essence sports were an anachronism in American public education. God might have been kicked out of schools, as conservatives like to phrase the 1962 *Engel v. Vitale* Supreme Court decision that eliminated public prayer from public schools, but God is still alive and kicking, and throwing, and running, and maybe even tackling on American high-school football fields—a lively Christian faith borne on the gridiron and ministered to by coaches, not pastors.

Coach Kramer Talks Football, Faith, and Trump

Naples High coach Kramer knows a thing or two about blending sports and religion. Kramer is not your stereotypical high-school football coach, the one you see in the movies grabbing kids' helmets and screaming in their face. He is quieter, if no less intense, and while Kramer is certainly a conservative, he has a diverse background: a master's degree in guidance and counseling, as well as a master's degree in computer science, in addition to health and physical education degrees from Liberty University.

I came back to Naples in March 2018, nine years after I had left. I stood in the humid air of Southwest Florida and felt it rush back—the memory of the time I had tried to attend First Baptist of Naples, months before the 2008 presidential election, when they included a voter's guide, misspelling the Democratic candidate's name B-A-R-R-A-C-K, and had us all kneel and pray to end abortion. I attended the young-adult group at First Baptist afterward anyway, desperate for young-adult companionship that didn't involve alcohol—which I ended up finding in beach volleyball instead. I didn't fault Kramer for his conservative church or for the way First Baptist reminded me of the stereotypical Southern Baptist megachurch. Its glittering white buildings represented all the wealth of Naples and little of the poverty experienced by so many of the football players who would bring fame to Naples High, among them NFL players Spencer Adkins and Carlos Hyde. I could see, too, that conservative Christianity had done much good in the world of football and in the lives of football players and coaches.

Kramer related to his players, the vast majority of whom didn't grow up with their birth parents, because Kramer didn't grow up with both of his birth parents either. He was born about as far from Naples as you can get—on Northern California's coast, just outside San Jose, before it was Silicon Valley, with four older sisters and a mom whose strength would foreshadow Kramer's own. When he was ten months old, Kramer's world shifted on its axis. "Mom left Dad, basically running for her life," Kramer remembered. His dad hated the desert, so Mom took the family south of Tucson, Arizona. Kramer doesn't know much about his birth dad, except that he wasn't a good father or husband. He's not sure where he got his football prowess from; he only knows one thing he has in common with his dad. "I hate the desert, too," Kramer says, pausing uncomfortably. "I never thought about that before. I guess that's one thing he gave me."

Kramer's mom met his stepdad, who would bring a younger half-sister and half-brother into the family, at a small conservative Evangelical church in Arizona. There Kramer saw the ugly side of Evangelical Christianity, which he says "soured" his two older sisters on church. His stepdad was active in the church and hid his violence, which was instead inflicted on Kramer, his mom, and his sisters at home. "No one in church knew how violent he was," Kramer said. "That's when I first saw the hypocrisy of it."

Nevertheless, Kramer was a church kid. He wasn't allowed to do much in high school except go to church, so he was in youth choir and Royal Ambassadors. The family home didn't have air conditioning, so in the hot desert summers, Kramer said his family was "pretty much at church or the library anytime the doors opened."

A standout wide receiver in high school, Kramer wanted to be anywhere but home for college. He decided to play football at Western Yuma College in Arizona. "I pretty much went buck wild the first year," Kramer said. "At the end of the first semester, I was not in a good place." And that could have been it—another poor college football player, whose life peaks on the gridiron, only to fizzle under newfound freedom and lack of family or institutional support. Despite the hypocrisy he experienced at church, Kramer chose a different path. He says he repented after that first year, deciding he wanted to serve God, and he didn't care if he played football or not. Like thousands of Americans at the time, Kramer would be saved by the *Hour of Power* with Rev. Robert Schuller of the Crystal Cathedral. His grandma, whom the family called a prayer warrior, saw a commercial for Liberty University, established in 1971 by conservative culture warrior and Baptist pastor Jerry Falwell.

"Bill," Grandma said. "It's a Christian school, and they have football there." She called the admissions office, which, remarkably, offered Kramer a chance to attend Liberty and walk onto the football team.

"I got on a bus with thirty dollars in my pocket and a one-way ticket," Kramer said. "I had no safety net. Luckily, I got a full scholarship after the first semester." At Liberty, he left partying behind, saying simply, "It was time for me to do what I needed to do." That matter-of-factness would manifest itself later in Kramer's coaching style: plainspoken, firm but not angry, with high expectations for his players to follow a straight path. From Liberty on, Christianity was always the centering force in his life as he met his wife, Susan, his junior year and followed her to Florida and as he endured teasing from his fellow coaches at his first coaching job, an assistant at American High School in Miami.

When asked about his Bible studies, Kramer at first hesitates. "I mean, we're not holding hands and singing 'Kumbaya,'" he says. "I'm a football coach." Football and Christianity, while often mixed, are sometimes an odd pair: a sport that insists upon violence and a religion that insists upon nonviolence. Yet Kramer embodies the idea that while violence is necessary to survive in the tough world his players know, Christianity and Jesus serve as a counterweight to the self-centered violence exalted on the football field.

Naples is known for its wealthy retirees, but the city also has its poorer pockets, where lots of kids who attend Naples High live. The city and county have a large population of Haitian refugees, and neighborhoods far from the ocean look much different from the estates lining Naples's beaches. As in much of America, majority-minority neighborhoods in Naples are less well off than majority-white neighborhoods, though plenty of younger white area residents lost their homes and their security during the mid-2000s recession and housing crash, which hit Southwest Florida hard. As it does across America, poverty in Naples coexists with opulent wealth.

Football, long the bastion of conservative Christian and American values, is also one of the few places in American culture where racism has been subsumed by team unity and a focus on the individual. In Kramer's first job, his Miami high school was evenly split, one-third white, one-third black, and one-third Latino, as was the coaching staff. They didn't know what to make of the no-cursing, square, white guy from Liberty. He says the rest of the coaching staff didn't even talk to him for a year, telling others to "tell Jerry's kid . . ." referring to Falwell. Kramer was singled out because of his background and his faith, and maybe even for his comparative gentleness as a coach on an "old school" staff. He just let it go, focusing on his other job as head coach of the successful girls track team and also on his marriage and kids. Kramer and his wife went on to have four girls over a period of eighteen years.

When he was first offered the head coaching job at Naples, Kramer hesitated. The program had a putrid past: only one winning season in sixteen years, and five coaches in nine years. "When we started, I had no health insurance, and we had three little kids," Kramer said. He took the job anyway. Nineteen years and fourteen district championships later, he was inducted into the Florida High School Athletic Association Hall of Fame.

Throughout his tenure, he was known as a Christian and as a conservative, though never political, and with moderate opinions on things like women's rights and preventing abortions while caring for unwed mothers. Surrounded by sisters and daughters, how could Kramer not temper his football side with some flexibility, even as he gained a reputation as a faith leader among Southwest Florida coaches?

There's a story in Naples that as the local Tea Party gained strength in area Republican politics, its members approached Kramer to run for US Senate with their support. Kramer turned them down, citing a weird vibe and an inability to lead in the same way at Naples High, especially with so many players of color, if he were a member of such an overtly conservative, white group.

Speaking seventeen months after the 2016 presidential election, Kramer was still conflicted about his vote. "It's such a conundrum," he said to me, suggesting that the media propped up Trump because they thought he was the only Republican candidate Hillary Clinton could beat. "He's a clown. As a Christian, I cannot defend that guy." Further reflecting on the election, Kramer continued, "He was the best choice at the time. Florida was a big deal, and it was a swing state. Maybe if I wasn't in a swing state, I could've not voted, but I don't know, when you're in a state that matters—"

He spoke in a certain regretful phraseology that I'd heard from a number of Red State Christians, yet Kramer also experienced the election in a unique way because of his position as football coach and his affinity for so many players and coaches of color, many of whom were opposed to Trump's positions and rhetoric. Christian athletes and coaches during the Trump presidency have existed in a uniquely diverse world that had been shaped and supported by the same structures of patriotism and conservative Christian values that led to Trump's election. Trump loves the idea of owning a football team, but you can't imagine him playing football, in much the same way Trump loves the idea of American Christianity, but you can't really imagine him raising his arms in praise and worship or going up for an altar call.

"Football," Kramer said with a reverential air, "is the only sport where you have people who don't touch the ball. The offensive line—all they do is serve. We talk about that. Football is all about the team." While noting the rise in concussions and head trauma among football players, Kramer suggested that football is nonetheless essential in the lives of America's young men. "You're gonna have these guys who are risk takers, and they want to be more physical and violent, and if they don't have football, what are they gonna do?" Kramer said. "Because those guys are always gonna be there. And I know the risks of playing football. I know all the dangers. But what are these guys gonna do?" Kramer sees himself as a guide of sorts for these violent and misguided young men. His story is not all that different from their stories, and he said that has long been a point of connection with his players.

As for the institutional church, remembering the hypocrisy he witnessed at a young age, Kramer was somewhat dismissive. "The divorce rate among churchgoing couples is only two ticks lower than the national average," Kramer says. "The divorce rate among couples who pray together is 2 percent. So I said in my counseling class, why don't we just pray together?"

In a conservative Christian world and an athletic world rocked by stories of domestic violence, Kramer said he is on the same side as the #MeToo movement, though he says he is often misunderstood when he uses biblical language such as women being "vessels." "I really think I'm on the same page with women's rights activists," says the man who has lived his family life surrounded by women. "I'm not questioning women's toughness. I've been a women's track coach. Women are unbelievably strong and tough. I believe, too, there is a biblical way to treat women that is unique to how we treat men."

Kramer's way of framing his ideas on gender identity might open conversation between feminists and Red State Christians more effectively than the ways the positions of pro-life and pro-choice activists are often framed in national media. Kramer respects women; it's evident in his comments about his track athletes and about his family. A divided America under President Donald Trump needs conversations that begin with mutual respect, and for Red State Christians, sports are a place to find that mutual respect that crosses dividing lines.

You Can Be the Water Fountain, or You Can Be the Drain

Kramer is emblematic of the ways American politics leave out voices that could lead to consensus. As a Liberty alumnus, Kramer said he felt betrayed when Jerry Falwell Jr. came out early for Trump, before the Republican primaries even ended. "I thought, 'Why are we using our influence for that sorry guy?'" Kramer said. "Where is the accountability in the church? What about divorce?" But those who raise this critique often go unheard in prominent Christian and Republican circles. So Kramer has focused on coaching.

"We say, 'Be great day to day,'" he said, a rebuke to Trump's grand slogan to Make America Great Again. "I haven't watched the news for nearly a year. I'm focused on my players. All I know is, if I'm going to have impact in their lives, I'm gonna love them first. And football is a great tool for producing leaders. I've yet to see something better, especially for harnessing the talents of dudes who still exist who will break into cars and do things for a rush." Kramer is well known in the world of Christian football coaches, a brotherhood vast and spanning the ranks from high school to the NFL. He spends time with like-minded coaches at camps for the Fellowship of Christian Athletes and at Black Mountain Coaches Camp, convened by NFL legend and prominent Christian Tony Dungy.

Kramer told me that Americans outside of football, Americans who don't follow sports and don't consider themselves conservative

Christians, have the wrong idea about football coaches and about Christians. "I've yet to see something [from Hollywood] that doesn't make us out to be total buffoons," he said. "They think that we're self-serving egomaniacs—not that there aren't those people out there. But for me, football is just a vehicle."

While Kramer would be the last to say that he's a gentle disciple or that winning doesn't matter, he centers himself on coaching the whole person, not just the football athlete. He counts among his proudest achievements the players who came to know Jesus and the players who came from tough family situations to finish college and succeed as fathers and husbands in their own rights. Kramer sums up his life philosophy this way: "When we get a drink at the water fountain after practice in the Southwest Florida heat, it is like the best thing ever. You can be that for others. You can be the water fountain, or you can be the drain."

"There's a bed pan, too," Kramer added. He seems to be suggesting that maybe the bed pan is Trump.

College Coach Turned Christian Leader

Charlie Weatherbie is tall and confident, and he walks with the air of a man who was once all-state in football, basketball, and track, all at once, in Kansas. He has the look of a classic American football player—a quarterback at Oklahoma State who went on to play for the Canadian Football League and become head football coach at Utah State, Navy, and Louisiana Monroe. Weatherbie achieved the erstwhile American dream to be paid to play and coach football, to achieve a certain level of fame and wealth, and to do it all without forever sacrificing his body and mind. He still carries a chip on his shoulder, however, about what might have been.

We shook hands outside a Southwest Florida restaurant on his way to a meeting for the Fellowship of Christian Athletes, the regional group of which he is the area director. He still has the manners and language patterns of Kansas, and he was generous with his time, though he was irritated at the restaurant employees' lack of English.

Weatherbie was once one of those young men referenced by Kramer, the ones who were prone to risk taking and even violence, and who found their place and future on the football field. He told me he was kicked out of the lunchroom in elementary school and had to dig ditches in the playground. A middle-school teacher told him he was headed to juvenile delinquency and jail, with no chance to graduate from high school, despite his prowess in football.

"You're not leaving this office until you make a decision about where you're headed," the teacher told a twelve-year-old Weatherbie. That same year, Weatherbie was baptized. The pastor told the churchgoers where they'd spend eternity, and what heaven and hell looked like, and where they'd want to go. "I sat there shooting spit wads into the offering basket, but then I went forward," Weatherbie said. "From that day on, I went 180 degrees different, though still fighting sometimes."

The youngest child in his family, he has determined that some of his misbehavior stemmed from academic difficulty. "I didn't know how to communicate," Weatherbie explained. "I had trouble reading. I had to take special classes; I had dyslexia. I had special teachers, and I'd get teased. I didn't know how to defend myself with words, only with fists. It was tough." Sports were his outlet, eventually giving Weatherbie tools and social skills to thrive not just on a team but in society. He said being a quarterback showed him the value of taking responsibility and giving credit to others, a trait that would carry on into his coaching career.

His best year as a coach was in 1996, when his second-year Navy Midshipmen went 9–3 and won the Aloha Bowl. The next season would be his last winning record as a coach, and Weatherbie left Navy in 2001 after a winless season, then hired on at Louisiana Monroe in 2003, where his Warhawks won the conference in 2005 but didn't qualify for a bowl in seven years. Disappointed by his fall from head-coaching splendor, Weatherbie leaned into his faith, taking a role at First Baptist Orlando, working as a fund-raiser for local missions, and then moving on to lead the Fellowship of Christian Athletes in Southwest Florida in 2016. "I miss the glamour of coaching," Weatherbie admitted. "Things you shouldn't really miss. I miss people calling me back right away. My wife said people won't call you back like they used to; you aren't a head coach anymore."

More overtly conservative than Kramer, Weatherbie is also refreshingly honest about the highs and lows of American sports, and he backs up his talk about his Christian faith by recounting actions, saying his first coaching job came after doing a twenty-one-day Daniel fast, a commitment to partial fasting and prayer that alludes to the fast of the Old Testament prophet Daniel and was created by Rick Warren. From the front pages of the sports page to losing season after losing season, Weatherbie has seen the highs and lows of athletics and Christianity. "When following God, you have to surrender," he said to me. "You have to be broken down. And we don't want to surrender."

For Weatherbie, sports brought him to places he had never imagined going to when he was growing up in small-town Kansas; through sports, he made connections with people from all over the country and the world. "There's nothing like breaking huddles with somebody," Weatherbie remembered. "It doesn't matter what color or what socioeconomic status you are. All that stuff is set aside. When you win together, when you lose together, there is a spiritual bond."

He told me the story of a former Division I college player he was working with in Orlando, a player who had become homeless and addicted to oxycodone. He'd been to three rehabs, and after Weatherbie got him into a fourth, it finally seemed to take. The player was reconnecting with his wife and daughters; he was clean for six years. Then everything fell apart. He called Weatherbie, asking for help again, but Weatherbie feared he was enabling the bad behavior. He said he ultimately had to turn the situation over to God, but it still ate at him. That's not Weatherbie's only experience with addiction; his oldest son struggled with drugs and alcohol. While Weatherbie's coaching career soared at Navy, his son was dropping out of high school and trying to get a GED. The tough-love, no-excuses parenting that Weatherbie practiced only pushed his son further away.

Of his son, Weatherbie said, "I guess he felt he wasn't living up to our, I guess my, standards." While he coached and made headlines, Weatherbie struggled not to feel a failure as a father. He discovered his own addiction to food and battled obesity. Ultimately, his son, Lance, found solace at a Pentecostal rehab in Texas. Weatherbie told me that Lance has been clean for over a decade. Like his son, Weatherbie found his redemption in church. He tells a life story of roughness and moments of gentleness, of high highs and low lows, of being misunderstood and of going from feeling on top of the world to being rejected by the only game and job he'd ever loved. Maybe that's why Weatherbie relates to Trump.

"I love Trump," he said. "He's a reactor, rather than a responder. But a lot of people, that's why they voted for him." A victim of negative media coverage himself, Weatherbie relates to Trump's media battles. But he says that Trump's Christianity isn't all for show—that a friend of his is a retired caddy who golfs with Trump once a month. "He says that Trump every morning has a phone call with his pastor [Orlando pastor Paula White], and they pray together," Weatherbie's friend told him. "If he doesn't start his day that way, he's all off for the day. He really wants to do the right thing."

"We've just gotta give him grace," Weatherbie says.

African American Christian Witness in Sports

In spite of their candor, both Weatherbie and Kramer were reluctant to address the NFL kneeling controversy and Trump's response, and both downplayed the issue. Kramer said that his players of color didn't relate to Kaepernick, and Weatherbie said that while he recognized that "there are black-white issues," Kaepernick's choice of protest did not solve those issues. Neither coach wanted to talk much about Trump's words either, sensing that the idea of a sitting president battling NFL players would not be good for their sport, their religion, or their country. Nonetheless, avoiding discussion about Trump's words or Kaepernick's protest is a luxury afforded only to white players and coaches, who do not have the expectation of their communities to use their positions of power and privilege to address societal ills and inequalities.

This difference also extends to the way that faith functions in sports. For white Christian athletes and coaches, the focus of faith tends to be a personal one, about dedicating one's life to God, making different decisions about partying and one's standing as an athlete or role model, and possibly participating in dialogue and raising awareness about conservative social issues, such as abortion.

For black Christian athletes and coaches, many of the same attributes of faith stand, particularly as most athletes and sports teams are influenced primarily by conservative Southern Baptist–leaning coaches and organizations. Uniquely, though, for black Christian athletes, they inherit a proud African American Christian history of protest and community organizing. African American churches and pastors drove the civil rights movement. Black athletes have often been expected to demonstrate their commitment to social justice and racial equality, whether it's Muhammad Ali's refusal to go to Vietnam or Kareem Abdul Jabbar (then Lew Alcindor) refusing to play in the 1968 Olympics after the 1964 death of fifteen-year-old black youth James Powell, shot by off-duty police lieutenant Thomas Gilligan.

Thus, just as Kramer's and Weatherbie's commitments to conservative Christian faith and values track with a long history in football of hewing to the conservative political and Christian tradition, so, too, does Colin Kaepernick's kneeling protest against police violence toward African Americans hew to a long history of African American athletes using their platform to lift up racial inequities and injustice, and a history of African American Christian protest, led by African American pastors and churches.

The third Southwest Florida football coach I spoke with was Stanley Bryant, an assistant principal for attendance and discipline at Naples High School and an assistant coach on Kramer's staff. Years ago, when Kramer first came to Naples, Bryant was an African American teenager trying to find his way, playing football but also getting into trouble. His dad had been in and out of his life since Stanley was a boy born in Arcadia, Florida, a small farming community northwest of Naples where 34 percent of children grow up in poverty.

While his dad was in and out of jail, the family moved to Naples when Stanley was three. He said his mom made them attend the African Methodist Episcopal church when he was young, but "as soon as I was of age to not go, I stopped going." Then, in 1998, Kramer's first year as coach and Bryant's junior season, tragedy struck. Rusty Larabell, a sixteen-year-old player on the junior varsity, collapsed unconscious after the JV game against Naples's crosstown rival. He was rushed to the hospital for emergency brain surgery and remained in a coma for ten days, until his family made the decision to remove life support. Bryant, having "disconnected and gotten into mischief, doing things that were not in line with Christian values," attended the memorial service with his teammates at a local church. The pastor made an altar call, and Bryant, in the midst of his teenage grief, confusion, and sadness at the trauma in his own family life, heard the voice of God speaking to him that day.

"I remember sitting in the pew, thinking, 'I'm not going up there.'" He and his teammates all poked each other. None of them would go up. Then something shifted. "I felt like something was calling me. I said I'm getting up no matter what these other guys think of me." The same conservative Christianity that sometimes papers over the racism of Trump and other white leaders changed Stanley Bryant's life. He became active in the Fellowship of Christian Athletes. He started a Bible study at his house.

"You knew everyone was watching you after you got saved," he recounted to me. "They wanted you to mess up." Instead, Bryant led a revival of sorts in his family. His sister and other family members recommitted to their faith. Bryant attended Christian summer camp and went on a mission trip to South Africa with Athletes in Action, and he earned a college scholarship to Southern Illinois.

His dreams of playing professional football were crushed with a tragic car crash while Bryant was working for UPS over Christmas break in Naples. He had multiple shoulder surgeries during his junior year of college. Still, Bryant persevered and dreamed of eventually coaching football. He went on to earn degrees in health education and history. He eventually returned to Naples High and Coach Kramer, where today he is assistant principal and an assistant coach, bringing the perspective of a former student and football player, as well as being one of the school's only African American administrators and coaches.

While Bryant is a product of the same conservative Christianity that led Weatherbie and Kramer to vote for Trump, Bryant is also a product of the African American Christian history of protest and social justice, so he views the NFL kneeling protest, and Trump's response to it, with different eyes than other coaches. Talking about Trump's remarks to protesting NFL players, Bryant shakes his head, sad and defeated. "Has anyone ever done the things he has done?" Bryant asked me. "I was very offended by [Trump's] comments—not just as a football player but as an African American human being."

In his role at Naples High, Bryant has seen a change in racial relations and the way people talk about race since Trump's election. "I've seen a difference in boldness and willingness of people to openly express racist views," he said. "It has happened to me at school with parents. And it's because of Trump making the statements that he makes."

Bryant and Kramer stand together in the breach, staunching the flood of racist hatred as together they coach boys without fathers in their lives, boys looking to unleash their strength and energy on the football field instead of breaking the law, praying together not as blacks and whites but as people together working toward one goal, in which no one is more essential than the other.

If the hopelessness of the end of Kaepernick's protests, commodified the next year by a Nike ad; the quashing of dissent by Trump's vice president, who left an NFL game after the anthem played; and the silencing of athletes by NFL owners who sometimes seem to see themselves as slaveholders represent the hopelessness and defeat of the divisive Trump era brought to light through sports in an age when Christianity is used as a pawn to serve patriotism and entrenched wealth and power, then the hope*ful*ness too found in sports cannot be forgotten. This is the same hopefulness that brought Cubs fans back to beat the curse and the same hopefulness that brought Bill Kramer, abandoned by his violent dad and disillusioned by his hypocritical Christian stepdad, to the football field to believe anyway in players who were once like himself. He coached them to believe that football is a tool not for wealth but for love, a love that would sweep up Stanley Bryant at a funeral altar call and lead him onto the field and eventually into a place where he would be a voice as a school administrator for students like himself because of football.

Football doesn't have to lead to faux-patriotism or quashing of dissent, as it did with Trump and Kaepernick. Rather, football can lead to relationships that give hope to America, like Bryant and Kramer's. Their voices should be privileged among Red State Christians, rather than voices of hatred and dismissiveness, like those of Trump and too many NFL owners.

CHAPTER 7

The Evangelical Intelligentsia: What about "Establishment" Christians?

I was sitting at a well-appointed table at quintessential Washington, DC, lunch spot Acadiana, on New York Avenue between 10th Street and K Street. The restaurant was lobbyist-chic, old-money DC with white tablecloths and political operatives at every table, serving up Cajun-style fare to southern legislators and their lobbyists from both sides of the aisle. Everyone could go for a little blackened oyster with their lunch now and then. I'd just arrived that morning from Minneapolis, covered in January bleak and blizzard, only to arrive in dazzling midwinter DC, with a brilliant sun lighting up the mall ahead of tomorrow's March for Life, a sort of Evangelical who's-who delegation, with school buses of Catholics driven in from across the nation to celebrate the man who'd recently been called "the most pro-life president in history."[1]

Trump was anything but the genteel, white-glove president evoked by this old-school DC scene, and I wondered how the more mannered, and moneyed, set of conservatives and Evangelicals were coping with this bombastic president. If they prided themselves on their sobriety, their temperance, and their fidelity, Trump was the antithesis of the Republican moneyed and educated elite. Yet he was their champion of the moment.

Maybe my lunch partners would shed some light on the situation. Republican political operative and coauthor of *The Great Revolt*, a 2018 book on Trump voters in the Rust Belt, Brad Todd had suggested we meet at Acadiana, and he proudly ordered up a round of oysters. Todd was appearing on MSNBC with Chuck Todd (no relation) after our lunch, and he represented the kind of conservative DC power player who had been initially hesitant to embrace Trump but later came around to appreciate the force of the Trumpian movement and its overtake of the GOP. We shared a similar journalistic past, both having earned degrees in journalism at the University of Missouri before journalists were considered the "enemy of the state." Todd had since started a political advertising firm, OnMessage, which became the lead consultant for the 2010 Republican takeover of the United States House. At the time of our lunch, he was finishing up his book with *New York Post* writer Salena Zito and was full of research and facts he'd discovered while traveling and interviewing people in counties that had flipped from Obama to Trump in 2016. An Appalachia native himself, of East Tennessee, Todd represented an interesting amalgam of things making up a window into conservative power and influence at the time of Trump. He was also a devout Christian—a regular attendee of Aldersgate United Methodist Church in Alexandria, Virginia, which former Trump chief of staff and RNC chairman Reince Priebus was known to occasionally attend.

Todd's religious background makes an interesting point as we study the "Evangelical Intelligentsia." Todd and other conservatives like him do not fit as neatly into the Evangelical boxes checked by many other Christian Trump voters. At Aldersgate, unlike at the Southern Baptist churches attended by many Red State Christians, two of the pastors and preachers are women. They even preach about social justice or poverty from time to time, though Todd jokingly says, "Sometimes they got a lot of angry emails from me." Todd, like many of the Red State Christians I spoke with, held more complex ideas about gender and theology than headlines about Red State Christians might lead you to believe. He told me he grew up Southern Baptist but left because it became too theologically conservative for him.

"When they said women couldn't be pastors and they had to stay home, I got up and walked out," he said, adding, "If you are conservative socially but not theologically, it is hard to find a church home." I noticed as we were talking that this sort of theological and religious nuance was lacking in most political debates about Christian voters and Donald Trump. As his campaign romped through America, inciting rallies and protests all over the country, Trump's supporters were painted as backward, racist, and generally intolerant. Certainly, some of them were. But there were others like Todd who didn't fit neatly into the categories the media sometimes drew for Trump voters. Todd has a sister who is a Presbyterian pastor in Houston. You wouldn't hear him shouting, "Lock her up!" at a rally or branding himself "deplorable." He had earned a master's degree and was financially well-off. Rather than fitting the Trump voter mold, Todd basically represented the longtime conservative Republican voters who, though initially hesitant, came to support Trump for the same reasons they'd supported conservative candidates in the past. Stories like Todd's, rather than the Never Trump stories so prominently bandied about in the media, represent a truer picture of the mainstream Republican and Evangelical Intelligentsia response to Trump's candidacy and presidency.

Todd, like many in DC that week, had the Supreme Court front of mind as he began to talk about the 2016 election. He suggested that the sudden February 2016 death of Supreme Court Justice Antonin Scalia, in particular, motivated Red State Christians to embrace Trump, coupled with Trump's support for the Religious Freedom Restoration Acts, designed to allow religious organizations more latitude in areas like health insurance and contraceptive coverage, and to allow doctors to refuse doing surgeries that went against their religious beliefs.

Todd didn't talk like a man enamored with Trump; he mentioned Trump's marriages and the ways Trump speaks about women. Instead, what came forward most was Todd's ruthless pragmatism, an element overlooked in studying the Republican and Evangelical embrace of Trump. "I buy the King Cyrus thing," Todd said. "People wanted to win. People were afraid of losing." Red State Christians were more afraid of losing than they were afraid of Trump. For a besieged populace losing the culture wars, losing the media, and losing the millennials, fear of losing and utter defeat was palpable. Fear of Trump paled in comparison especially to fear of Hillary Clinton. Speaking again about the average American Trump voter, Todd mentioned the media portrayals of the opioid epidemic ravaging Appalachia and many of the places in the Rust Belt that turned the election for Trump after voting twice for Obama. Todd suggested that the narrative that Trump voters were dumb and drug addicted is wrong. Those weren't the people voting for Trump in Appalachia, he said. Instead, people who were slightly more well-off, living in towns and owning businesses in places ravaged by opioid addiction—they were the Trump voters. People who were watching Fox News, paying attention to the Supreme Court, and hoping for a change to turn around their towns—they were Trump voters.

Still, Todd acknowledged that there is a sort of circus following around Trump, made up of his voters and of the American media, for whom Trump's name has been a boon. "I think Trump has become really good at commanding the circus," Todd said, suggesting that the alt-right was a fringe movement not relevant to mainstream Republicanism or to Trump's win. Certainly, thousands of alt-righters would disagree with Todd, and the other hordes of people who subscribe to racist and anti-Semitic, anti-women ideas online would also disagree. But it's important nonetheless to note that alongside their support of Trump is Todd's support of Trump—and the uncomfortable accommodation of mainstream Republicanism with Trumpism, which has blown up the once-genteel and politely conservative Republican Party. Truly, the seeds were sown for this type of split long before Trump, with the Tea Party and the conservative dominance of the 2010 midterms, in which Todd was instrumental. On the topic of race itself and the not-so-silent elephant in the room that was Trump's dismal performance among voters of color, even Evangelicals of color, Todd was regretful and a little defensive. He noted the Republicanism of military veterans of color and recalled George W. Bush's outreach to African American Evangelical pastors with "little to show for it."

Todd told me a story about his son recently asking, "Why don't brown people go to church? They're in school with me. They're in the park with me. Why aren't they at church?" Despite the relative liberalism of the American mainline church, including Todd's home congregation, which is Methodist, Sunday morning remains the most segregated hour in America. Todd said it is among his regrets that church remains so segregated. He said it is a failing of the church, and he talked about the disappointment of Obama voters in the Rust Belt who switched to Trump in 2016. "They voted for Obama, hoping for racial reconciliation, that we can finally beat this thing," Todd said. "When it didn't happen, they were disillusioned, hopeless."

If Trump's nativist rhetoric was disconcerting for more traditional conservatives like Todd, it's unsurprising that Todd reserves the most ire for former Trump adviser and Breitbart News chairman Steve Bannon. "My father would call him a flimflammer," Todd said, and the ousting of Bannon later that month by Trump would be a victory for these traditional Republicans who were not always at home in the Trumpian takeover of their party.

From Todd's traditional conservative perspective, racist incidents during Trump's presidency are the result of a moral relativism overtaking American politics, culture, and religion. Todd sounded like a bona fide Evangelical pastor when he said, "The mainline church has gone into moral relativism. There has been an end to absolute standards. That's how you end up with Trump, but he's not the cause of it, he's the result of it."

Todd's words represent an argument alien to progressive ears, but it's an important one to consider when dissecting the role of American Christianity and Trump's election. Not all Trump voters were weaned on a steady diet of hell, brimstone, female subjugation, and racist invective. Some of them were expats from mainline churches that had become overwhelmingly concerned with social justice; so fuzzy had progressive theology become that anyone seeking an absolute moral authority found they could only locate one in conservatism.

Todd brought up another critique of mainline American Christianity: that it's an anachronism. America's most progressive churches are also its most traditional, with many pastors wearing full clerical garb each Sunday and organs playing hymns from hundreds of years ago, with churches using the same liturgical settings that were first developed in the 1960s. "So many churches are irrelevant," Todd said. "We teach people to do things the way we did them fifty years ago. When we have a church that is irrelevant, morality fails." He had a point about the decline of American mainline religion. Churches that are so progressive politically and so traditional practically have a limited audience, which is why the progressive religious torch has almost always been carried by Evangelicals of color, not by the American mainline church, which is mired in intra-church battles, clinging to its outmoded and overpriced institutions and institutional structures, bleeding money and parishioners daily until churches, seminaries, and ultimately denominations fold entirely.

I Am an Establishment Republican

At this moment in our conversation, Steve Larkin, a former Reagan appointee with dapper dress and moneyed southern tone, walked up to the table. "Well," he said gently and with good humor, "I am what you call an establishment Republican—which means I have no respect in this town anymore." Larkin carried with him a copy of a *Wall Street Journal* editorial he wanted to share with us. He spoke of compromise and "doing things the way you were supposed to do them," with bill cosponsors from the other party, when people used to get along and work together. Millions of men like Larkin exist in the Republican Party, though not all with his pedigreed past and political accomplishments. They share his calm manner and his genuine desire to make America great, but they are truly a dying breed.

Like Todd, Larkin downplayed the racist incidents surrounding Trump as primarily political theater, and he noted that after the carnage of the alt-right march in Charlottesville, Virginia, "No one talks about what happened after the policing results came in, and they fired the police chief." Rather than whipping up the country into a frenzy, à la Trump and his rallies, Larkin favors a more traditional southern Republicanism—supporting law and order, avoiding talk about unpleasant topics, and being fiscally responsible.

While some Trump supporters embraced the "deplorables" label, Todd and Larkin, like most of the Trump voters I spoke to for this book, do not consider themselves to be accurately portrayed by the media. Above all else, they do not want to be called racist for voting for Trump. Todd said that in Obama's presidency, the dream of racial reconciliation was replaced by a grand liberal experiment, involving Obamacare and the advancement of liberal social causes, such as gay marriage and unisex bathrooms. When discussing race, Larkin lowered his voice even further. He spoke about his own conservative American family, which is also multiracial. The Larkins have two adopted children; the eldest, Jessica, was adopted from Korea. "We were trying to teach her all about Korea, to make sure she knew all about her roots," Larkin said. "And I asked her, 'Do you want to go to Korea? We can take you.' She said, 'Dad, I am American.'"

Larkin's dream for his daughter has been upended in Trump's America and will never again be understood the same way. "When's the last time you heard someone say, 'I am American' with no hyphen?" Despite Trump's anger mongering, misspelled tweets, and chant-filled rallies, you can see here the appeal of his simple campaign, "Make America Great Again," and the ways it plays to a nostalgia for a simpler time, even if that time didn't exist in the way people remember it.

Todd lifted up a common conservative critique of President Obama: "Obama created the hyphen and embraced the hyphenated American instead of racial reconciliation. It's a rainbow, not a melting pot, and all the colors stay separate." Left unanswered and unasked is the question that came to me later: What else could Obama, himself a product of a mixed race marriage, have done to unite America? Still today called a usurper, his citizenship questioned, his Christian faith denied by many conservatives, Obama struggled to become the uniter that he began by hoping to be. It's always easy for the dominant group, white Americans, to want racial reconciliation without the difficult work of repentance and recognition of past wrongs. Trump was certainly not leading white Americans down that path. Still, Todd and Larkin were not wrong when they noted the liberal penchant for more government and the consequent conservative aggrievement.

Larkin recounted his work for an aluminum association and a proposed White House visit during Obama's presidency. "How many gay members do you have?" Larkin said he was asked by the White House. "Well I don't know. I'm sure we have some, but we work in aluminum. That's all I know," Larkin replied, befuddled. "You can't come unless you tell us how many gay members you have," Larkin said the reply came back. "Now that probably wasn't Obama," Larkin granted. "But that's what was happening in government. And that's the kind of perceptions that came out." The idea of liberalism run amuck, the fear of socialism on steroids under a President Hillary Clinton, probably did more to win over most Red State Christians than anything Trump did or said. And these concerns had more to do with pragmatism than any idea of Evangelical destiny and King Cyrus/Trump.

Still, lost within it all was an evaluation of the gospel of Jesus Christ, friend to the poor, liberator of the oppressed, savior of all, and an analysis of where that gospel played any kind of role in American politics—something for which Evangelical Christians had fought for decades. At best, for Todd and Larkin and many Red State Christians, Trump represents a mercenary fighter, a journeyman quarterback who happens to be wearing their jersey at the moment and thus deserves their cheers or at least the benefit of circumspection. When I asked if Trump really is as racist, authoritarian, and nativist as he comes across, Todd said this: "Trump sells condos. Every day. And he's willing to endure a lot of incendiary comments to do it. He doesn't have a long-term plan, and he has a short memory about the mistakes he makes." When I asked about conservative Christians' dedication to more outwardly liberal causes, like social justice or poverty movements, Larkin mentioned his church's work with Stop Hunger Now, and Todd said the problem for Red State Christians is that Democrats have "politicized social justice," and "you can't get people to get on board with it."

He went back to the divisive rhetoric of "calling your neighbor racist. That's become the litmus test. To create social justice, you have to call your neighbor racist. That's a big litmus test. That's tough." Maybe it's more important for white Christians to be able to call ourselves racist than it is to call our neighbor racist, and that is the nuance and depth and introspection that has been missing in the debates about the racism inherent in Trump's campaign and presidency, at least among white American Christians.

Another reminder is pertinent here, as I recall the end of my conversation with Larkin and Todd. Trump voters do not fit neatly into the boxes made for them by the extremes of Trump's electorate. Todd, for example, is as vehemently anti-death-penalty as he is pro-life. But, he said, because of the politicization of social justice on the Democratic side, it is hard to find conservatives to work with him on this consistent ethic of life. Larkin's lament ended our conversation, and I left it feeling saddened by the silencing of more moderate voices in American politics, the resultant cynicism and lack of political involvement by many young Americans, and the lack of religiosity and churchgoing among so many young Americans.

"We just talk all about what divides us," Larkin says. "There isn't one conversation about what we have in common." That's true of both Christians and Americans.

Southern Baptists Who Dared to Criticize Trump

Many leading Evangelicals, in the months before the 2016 presidential election, looked to Russell Moore for guidance. Moore was unrelentingly critical of Trump, even live-tweeting Trump's address at Evangelical Christian flagship Liberty University, with President Jerry Falwell Jr. Among Moore's tweets on January 18, 2016:

> This would be hilarious if it weren't so counter to the mission of the gospel of Jesus Christ. #TrumpatLiberty

> Trading in the gospel of Jesus Christ for political power is not liberty but slavery. #TrumpatLiberty

> Absolutely unbelievable. #TrumpatLiberty

> Politics driving the gospel rather than the other way around is the third temptation of Christ. He overcame it. Will we?

> Being faithful to the wife of one's youth is succeeding in real life.

With such vocal criticism coming from highly placed Evangelicals, many assumed Trump could never carry the Evangelical vote and thereby the presidency. Still, months later, on May 9, 2016, Trump responded, naming Moore on Twitter with this seminal tweet: "Russell Moore is truly a terrible representative of Evangelicals and all of the good they stand for. A nasty guy with no heart!" Trump and the Evangelical masses would have the last laugh.

The morning after the March for Life in Washington in January 2018, I visited the final day of the conference put on by Moore's group, the Ethics and Religious Liberty Commission of the Southern Baptist Convention. The atmosphere at the conference, then one year into Trump's presidency, was an uncomfortable collision between the forward-moving leaders of American Evangelicalism, the vanguards of its past (think Falwell Jr., Robert Jeffress, and Franklin Graham), and the everyday Christians and Evangelicals who handed Trump the presidency. After the conference, I spoke with Southern Baptist pastors Dean Inserra and Jeff Dodge of Ames, Iowa, who was interviewed regularly during the 2016 Iowa Caucuses. Neither voted for Trump, and neither for Clinton.

"The election affected me more than the presidency has," said Inserra, who is a Gen Xer. "I think it's affected my generation because of social media. We thought Twitter and Facebook were the real world. And when you're tweeting 'morality matters' and everyone is saying 'Amen,' you think people don't support Trump. And they did."

"Social media made us out of touch without realizing it," added Inserra. "We thought everyone felt the same way we did about Trump. That wasn't true of people in the pew. People came to me and said, 'I don't think it's a character issue.' They were truly offended [by me]."

Suddenly pastors, especially pastors of conservative churches, found themselves in the center of a world they didn't know they lived in. They recognized they might have been disconnected from their own churches. Meanwhile, some Evangelical leaders were embracing Trump wholeheartedly. They laid hands on him at the Oval Office. They said they saw him as God's anointed. Evangelicals *were* divided, though with 81 percent of white self-proclaimed Evangelicals voting for Trump, the rest of the country, particularly progressives, largely saw them as a monolith.[2] "People think there's only one kind [of Evangelical Christian]," said Inserra. "They think we're hateful. The same people who hate stereotypes put stereotypes on us. If you say you're for biblical marriage [alluding to gay marriage rights], they won't even talk to you. But Trump was such a polarizing candidate, it unleashed a lot of hate and anger on both sides."

Dodge, who said he comes from a liberal family, is teaching pastor of Cornerstone Church in Ames, Iowa. When he was interviewed during the Iowa caucuses, he often shared that he found Trump "morally repugnant." Dodge explained, "If asked my opinion, I gave it. And it was offensive to some. But I felt like the Republican Party was being hijacked. They were blindly going into this, or maybe they had blinded themselves to it." Dodge said a couple from his church who traveled with him to the conference are big activists for pro-life causes and also are pro-Trump. He said he often would go to them one-on-one to build bridges after the election, especially after finding out how pro-Trump his congregation was, in opposition to Dodge's own rhetoric. "I was sitting by [the couple] during the March for Life while President Trump addressed us," Dodge said. "And I knew we were having opposite reactions."

Despite his role as a leader in the Southern Baptist Convention, a denomination that Dodge said can be a turnoff for many in Ames, Dodge sees himself more as a bridge builder to liberal Christians than one who would damn them to hell. "My whole family are liberal Christians, and when someone like [Robert Jeffress] speaks for Evangelicals, it's awful," Dodge said. "People think that we are all narrow-minded, close-minded, and not willing to listen. I am really purposeful about constantly teaching people to listen. I want there to be a new tone set." Dodge told me that he meets regularly with one of his closest friends, the head of the Ames Progressives Association (which Dodge said is code for Atheist Club). They have engaging conversations, and it's hard for the Evangelical to hate the atheist, and vice versa, when the two are friends. Theirs is the kind of conversation and bridge building that is rarely seen in national media or among the prominent Evangelicals who surround Trump.

"It's hard," Dodge said. "Because you have two bold responses. One side is very pro-Trump. The other side, there is so much distance. They are so strong against Trump. It's tough to be a listening ear. I've encouraged more healthy dialogue." Dodge said he expects to be "increasingly more active and appropriately more political" for the 2020 caucuses. "It's time for the church to stand as the church. We need to let strong political views be marginalized. I want to help my church family to be more discerning and to think biblically."

But don't think that these Evangelicals are leaning so far from Trump that they're considering voting blue. "It'll have to be a third party," Dodge said.

Meanwhile, in Florida, Inserra too found himself having uncomfortable conversations with congregation members who voted for Trump and were offended by his outspokenness. "One person told me, 'I voted for Trump, and then I took a shower,'" Inserra said. "I think there are genuine people who went through that. Trump's Christian base has a loud voice. It's more powerful than we thought it was. It's closer to mainstream Republicanism than we thought, probably more than we are. I think this whole thing was a warning to the church not to get too close to politics. Because those people who have, it taints them."

Still, it's interesting to note the still-existent divide between progressive Christians and even the slightly more moderate wing of Evangelicals represented by the ERLC. "It's easy to criticize a Christian

Trump voter," Inserra said. "I don't think it's fair that Christian Hillary voters get a free pass. The progressive wing is there; it has some shoddy theology, but it's there." There it is again, that uncomfortable tendency to divide rather than unite, even among Southern Baptists looking outside themselves for Jesus's way ahead in a world that looks increasingly unfamiliar.

Moore has stepped back from some of his harshest criticisms of Trump and his supporters, likely because of the need for him to stay within the Evangelical fold after coming under harsh criticism from his fellow Southern Baptists. He has apologized publicly twice. "I stand by those convictions, but I did not separate categories of people well—such that I wounded some, including my closest friends . . . failing to distinguish between people who shouldn't have been in the same category with those who put politics over the gospel and for using words, particularly in social media, that were at times overly broad or unnecessarily harsh. That is a failure on my part," Moore wrote.[3]

As often is the case, even in the church, the Southern Baptist disagreement over Moore came to involve money. As of May 2018, according to *Christianity Today*, more than a hundred congregations threatened to hold back funding from the denomination's Cooperative Program, including $1 million from Prestonwood.[4] The SBC even started an investigation into the ERLC on behalf of those who had been critical of Moore.

So what can we make of this prevalence of ambivalent Trumpians within the Evangelical family? Is it significant that so many prominent Evangelicals have been critical of Trump yet were ignored by their congregations? And how about Todd and Larkin, representing the establishment and we'll say "nuanced" wing of Red State Christians, who may not consider themselves Evangelical?

One response is to put these voices into the same category as the vehement but ultimately powerless "Never Trump" Republicans. Well-funded, intellectual, and prominent members of the country's top editorial boards, Never Trump nonetheless never held any real influence within the Republican Party. Most Republicans and Red State Christians who did not enthusiastically support Trump instead went the way of former House speaker Paul Ryan, tepidly supporting Trump personally, while holding out hope that Trump would act as a sort of political fairy godmother with a dirty mouth, granting wishes of Evangelicals and conservatives right and left, while they ignored Trump's not-so-redeeming personal qualities. As David Roberts wrote for *Vox*, the problem with Never Trump was that it never had any constituents, only leaders. "Bret Stephens and Bari Weiss are a familiar type of glib contrarian. Their opposition to Trump has given them undue credibility among Washington lefties, whom they relentlessly (and boringly) troll. But whom are they speaking for? What has the Never Trump movement amounted to?"[5]

The same question could be asked of Inserra, or Dodge, or Moore, or Michael Gerson, Evangelical opinion writer for the *Washington Post* and author of the seminal piece on Evangelicals and Trump for *The Atlantic*, "The Last Temptation." Prominent Evangelical voices do speak against Trump, just as some establishment Republican political voices support Trump but do not fit into conservative religious categories as neatly as others (Larkin and Todd). The question is, Who are these voices speaking for? Do they have a following or, like the Never Trump political movement, are they more popular on the left than they are in their own camp?

Who are the anti-Trump Evangelical voices that matter, and to whom are they speaking? Most of these voices come from church leaders of color, many from the African American church. Today, in communities of color, it is still churches that serve as a beacon of hope, power, and organizing, providing assistance, mentoring, and a moral compass. Evangelicals looking for hope outside Trump would do well to look to Rev. William J. Barber II and his Poor People's Campaign, begun in May 2018 to continue a 1968 initiative planned by Rev. Dr. Martin Luther King Jr., to involve forty days of protests and direct actions to highlight the issues of systemic racism, poverty, ecological devastation, the war economy, and militarism.

"For too long, we've accepted this kind of moral narrative in America that has blamed poor people for their poverty and has pitted people against each other," Barber told the *Los Angeles Times*.[6] "We have seen this spread of the lie of scarcity—that we don't have enough. . . . We've got to have what we call moral dissent, moral resistance and a moral vision in this moment."[7] Barber's work with the Moral Monday movement in North Carolina has helped voting rights advocates win cases at the Supreme Court and prevent the reelection of North Carolina's Republican governor, Pat McCrory. Barber also spoke at the 2016 Democratic National Convention, grasping the podium like a pulpit and raising his voice to the timbres of all the black preachers who had come before him, summoning to the stage an energy not found elsewhere during Clinton's campaign.

Barber's presence at that convention limits his influence within Evangelical Christianity. Merely because he is tied to Democratic politicians and causes, many on the right in Evangelicalism refuse to work with him or join forces. It is further evidence of the devastating effects of the politicization of faith leaders in modern-day America and the uncrossable partisan lines that prevent working together even among Christians of common cause. In light of this bleakness, can we find hope among the latent resistance movement in the Southern Baptist Convention? Is anyone listening?

When asked about hope, Dodge talked about his work with students. He is the founder of the Salt Company student ministry, a mission to turn student ministries into local congregations, so that college becomes a time of faith development. "Working with students was the most refreshing part [during the 2016 election and Iowa caucuses]," Dodge said. "I think this next generation is less likely to line up under some banner ideologically. They are more nuanced. The idea that as a Christian, you have to be one way—I encourage students to learn to work through things biblically, to read writers who might be outside our faith community."

Similarly, Liberty University English professor Karen Swallow Prior spoke to National Public Radio about her students' turn from the Moral Majority politics of her own youth:

> I think the students at Liberty University really reflect what's happening with the millennial generation and in general, and that is simply that there is a sort of disillusionment and disengagement from the political process. I think some of that is born of disappointment and from the past election and just distrust of the political process in general. And I see that as probably a healthy counterbalance to the generation that I came up in. I was part of the Religious Right and part of the culture wars ethos from a few decades ago, where we probably did place too much faith in politics, and we're bearing the fruit of that now. And this is just a counterbalance that I see, and it's healthy and corrective and good.[8]

As Dodge and Prior find hope in the relative lack of partisanship of future Christians, Inserra offers an olive branch to progressive Christians: "I'd tell them that the first allegiance for Christians is

Scripture," Inserra said. "And we are trying to figure out what that means. We know what Jesus means. We are still trying to figure out what it means to live out our faith in our world and in our country. We have things we're still wrestling with. We're trying to wrestle with those questions and let Jesus be first."

The idea of an ongoing revelation within the Southern Baptist Convention—the idea that Scripture could reveal itself in a new way through the Holy Spirit even in a denomination that has resisted such development for generations—is a hopeful one indeed. As is the idea of Evangelical leaders being willing to admit they don't know everything already. Now if only Trump could admit that, he might be en route to an Evangelical awakening of his own.

CHAPTER 8

Evangelical Women and Donald Trump: Who's Grabbing Whom?

"And when you're a star, they let you do it."
"You can do anything."
"Grab them by the pussy."
"You can do anything."[1]

Those twenty-three words would have ended many a presidential campaign. They didn't end Donald Trump's, though. And maybe it wasn't so surprising. The same America that laughed at and pooh-poohed Monica Lewinsky's stained dress would rarely let a powerful man be brought down for mistreating or even abusing a woman. To many Americans, though they were loath to admit it, women weren't "people" at all. They were objects to be admired, kissed, grabbed—or, alternatively, scorned and mocked. Trump would finally prove that the Evangelical outrage about Clinton was based not on respect for women or for the institution of marriage but instead, as usual in America, on partisan allegiance over any kind of religious morality.

On October 8, 2016, though, I thought it was over. I believed there was no way Donald Trump could come back from this scandal, no way women could vote for a man who said this, particularly when he was running against a woman—the very woman whose husband had cheated on her. Female empowerment could not lose to male chauvinism in 2016. A day later, I watched with eighty-four million Americans as Hillary Clinton and Donald Trump participated in their third presidential debate. I expected Hillary to lean in, hard, to the woman vote. I expected her to lift up the beauty and dignity of being a woman and the ways that Trump had diminished women with his comments on the bus to Billy Bush about grabbing women and kissing them without their consent. I expected Hillary to address head-on what had happened in her marriage and why she chose to stay anyway. And I expected her to speak, emotionally, about what it meant as a woman to overcome stereotypes and be cast either as beautiful or brainy but never, ever both.

Instead, on the afternoon before the debate, Trump held a news conference with four women who had accused Bill Clinton of assaulting them. Then, during the debate, he lurked menacingly behind Hillary and never stopped driving the narrative. In response to a question about his comments on the bus with Billy Bush, Trump said, "No one has more respect for women than I do," and he quickly pivoted to the ways he would crush ISIS as president. Trump was sure of himself; he cast the "locker room talk" as being far in the past, and he effectively owned the narrative of the debate, a preview of election night. During his debate with Hillary, Trump stole the momentum. And Hillary, rather than using the debate as a chance to paint who she was as a woman, lamented the fact that this election was like none before it. But how could it be like any election before it, when America had a reality TV show celebrity facing up against the first female presidential nominee in US history? Hillary just kept hammering away at Trump's negatives. She never seized the narrative. She never revealed herself. She never embraced her own womanhood, but instead was swallowed up whole by her signature long suit jackets and pleated pants. Hillary was achingly but reluctantly embraced by a nation of women who never really understood her and by younger generations who had nothing in common with her—younger generations of liberal women whose pantsuit protest became a symbol of a contrived and out-of-touch Democratic Party.

For Evangelical women, the "pussy" comments weren't enough to overcome decades of right-wing media hatred of Hillary. Trump's comments on the bus were nothing compared with what Evangelical women had dealt with in the church for generations. As America would find out early in the years of the Trump presidency, Evangelical women had more to deal with when it came to male mistreatment of women than comments on a bus. And ironically, Trump's presidency would usher in a new era of female outspokenness about male aggression and the necessity of women's rights, even in the church.

Whose Character Matters?

Notably, Trump's comments about women failed to sway his male Evangelical pastor supporters, who were focused more on abortion, Planned Parenthood, and the Iran nuclear deal. A lonely voice of dissent, Russell Moore, tweeted, "If character matters, character matters." But character couldn't matter in this election. Hillary Clinton was incapable of claiming the moral high ground, and Red State

Christians wanted a win. They weren't about to squander their opportunity to dethrone Obama by throwing votes away on a third-party candidate, ushering in the victorious and vilified Clinton.

Still, Evangelical women's votes for a president who spoke this way about women were not the final word on women's rights among Red State Christians. A reckoning was coming, bringing America face-to-face with the problem of sexual abuse, a problem that would be revealed as endemic in the church itself. Just eight months before the presidential election, a film about sexual abuse in the Catholic Church had won Best Picture in the 2016 Academy Awards. *Spotlight* documented the sexual abuse and cover-up scandal involving Roman Catholic priests and church leaders.

Less than a year into the Trump presidency, actress Alyssa Milano brought sexual harassment and sexual abuse of women to the fore by starting an awareness campaign on the president's favorite medium, Twitter. "If all the women who have been sexually harassed or assaulted wrote, 'Me too,' as a status, we might give people a sense of the magnitude of the problem," Milano tweeted. I first saw the #MeToo hashtag pop up on my own Facebook feed a day or two later, posted by a female seminary professor. A few soul-searching moments later, I was typing it myself, reflecting on my own moments in the locker room as a sportswriter (though I never did hear anyone use the word *pussy*) and experiences I'd had in the church, where comments about my appearance, gender, clothing choices, and hair were at least as numerous as comments about my pastoral ability. Women across America were waking up at once to the incessant prevalence of sexual harassment. What many women had once felt they couldn't claim for one reason or another—"He didn't rape me," "I was drunk," "He was my friend," "I'm not pretty enough"—was now but one verse in a chorus of voices, a chorus heard only because of its ubiquity and its genesis among the elite women of Hollywood.

The first giant to be felled by #MeToo was Hollywood producer and mogul Harvey Weinstein. Two weeks after Milano first tweeted #MeToo, more than eighty women had made allegations of sexual abuse against Weinstein. He was dismissed from his company and expelled from the Academy of Motion Picture Arts and Sciences, his entire career now viewed with suspicion and his personal life in shambles as his wife announced in early October 2017 that she was leaving him. Women in America were finally beginning to see one another as allies rather than adversaries. President Trump kept a relatively low profile, huddling next to his third wife, Melania, as he watched powerful men around him in media and television fall. Even Trump booster and Fox News stalwart Bill O'Reilly wouldn't survive. He was terminated by Fox News in April 2017, a year after the resignation of Fox News CEO Roger Ailes. Ailes had gone on to work as a consultant for the Trump campaign and then died on May 18, 2017, due to complications of hemophilia. No one in America could staunch the bleeding when it came to the outpouring of allegations of sexual misconduct against powerful men.

In February 2017, three former gymnasts went on *60 Minutes* to accuse USA Gymnastics national medical coordinator Larry Nassar of sexual abuse. Three months later, gymnast Rachael Denhollander, one of the first to publicly accuse Nassar, testified in court that Nassar had abused her during five doctor visits in 2000, when she was just fifteen years old. Olympic gold medalist McKayla Maroney tweeted #MeToo about Nassar, saying he'd abused her since she was thirteen. Her teammates Gabby Douglas, Simone Biles, Aly Raisman, and Jordyn Wieber later added their own accounts of Nassar's abuse. Biles and

Douglas had been Olympic all-around champions in gymnastics, their lithe bodies and winsome smiles a reminder of all that is good, great, about America, in contrast to the wan athletes of China or eastern Europe. Now all that was tainted. Many Americans, grasping for some sense of solidity and normalcy in an ever-changing world, had elected Trump in hopes that all the ugliness uncovered in the Obama years, such as racism and homophobia, would be erased. But America's sins could never again be covered up, and, with Trump in office, the sins were only becoming more apparent. At Nassar's trial in January 2018, a voice would rise above the tumult, bringing the light of #MeToo to bear upon Red State Christians themselves and the church.

#ChurchToo

Rachael Denhollander could have been a poster child for American conservative Christianity. Like many Red State Christians, she had been homeschooled and dressed conservatively. Her hair was long, dark, and straight, reminiscent of the encouragement in many conservative Christian communities for women to let their hair grow long and avoid cutting it. Thus Denhollander cut a sympathetic, or at least familiar, figure to Red State Christians watching the coverage of the Nassar case. True to her conservative Christian background, Denhollander said she forgave Nassar—and then asked the judge to give him the maximum sentence. To Nassar himself, she said at his sentencing hearing, "I pray you experience the soul-crushing weight of guilt so you may someday experience true repentance and true forgiveness from God, which you need far more than forgiveness from me—though I extend that to you as well."[2] She was the final person to speak, and as she did, a long-held dam was broken, and the mighty waters of justice came crashing through. For Denhollander, a trained lawyer and married mother

of three who considers herself a conservative Christian, her outspokenness was costly. In her statement, she noted that speaking for sexual
assault victims had "cost me my church and our closest friends."

She told *Christianity Today* in January 2018 that Christians tend
to "gloss over the devastation of any kind of suffering but especially
sexual assault, with Christian platitudes like *God works for all things
together for good* or *God is sovereign*. Those are very good and glorious
biblical truths, but when they are misapplied in a way to dampen the
horror of evil, they ultimately dampen the goodness of God. Goodness and darkness exist as opposites. If we pretend that the darkness
isn't dark, it dampens the beauty of the light."[3] Denhollander had
shined a light into the sickly heart of American Evangelicalism and its
own cover-up of sexual abuse and oppression of women. As she told
Christianity Today, "Church is one of the least safe places to acknowl-
edge abuse because the way it is counseled is, more often than not,
damaging to the victim; there are very, very few who have ever found
true help in the church."[4]

Denhollander went on to say that the reason she'd lost her church
was her advocacy for other victims of sexual assault within the Evangelical community. She was referring to the Sovereign Grace Ministries scandal. In 2012, Sovereign Grace Ministries president C. J.
Mahaney and the ministry itself were accused of covering up sexual
abuse within the church network. The suit was dismissed in 2014,
though a former youth leader in the network was convicted of sexually
abusing three boys in a separate case. Denhollander drew an analogy
between the scandal at Sovereign Grace and the scandal of the abuse
she had suffered:

The ultimate reality that I live with is that if my abuser had
been [Sovereign Grace youth group leader] Nathaniel Morales

instead of Larry Nassar, if my enabler had been [a Sovereign Grace pastor] instead of [a gymnastics coach], if the organization I was speaking out against was Sovereign Grace under the leadership of [Mahaney] instead of [Michigan State], I would not only not have evangelical support, I would be actively vilified and lied about by every single evangelical leader out there. The only reason I am able to have the support of these leaders now is because I am speaking out against an organization not within their community. Had I been so unfortunate so as to have been victimized by someone in their community, someone in the Sovereign Grace network, I would not only not have their support, I would be massively shunned. That's the reality.[5]

Denhollander's words were all the more prophetic within the pages of America's most prominent magazine for conservative Evangelicals. For decades, women had been sublimated and objectified and silenced within American churches. But their liberation would never come from secular feminists. It would come from within the church itself, during the presidency of a man who bragged about grabbing women by the pussy. But the rise of women in Evangelical churches would not come easy. And many leaders would fall in its wake.

In 2018, Presbyterian pastor and author Carol Howard-Merritt found herself caught in the mix of surprising Evangelical support for Trump and Evangelical women's awakening about sexual harassment and misconduct brought forward by the #MeToo movement. Raised by conservative Christian parents who had left their Baptist church to attend a fringe charismatic church in the small Florida town where she grew up, Howard-Merritt left conservative Evangelical Moody Bible College to attend Austin Presbyterian Theological Seminary and seek ordination in the relatively liberal Presbyterian Church

USA. Writing two books geared toward the church's ministry to new generations, Howard-Merritt boldly stepped forward in her third book to write about abuse in the church and about helping people find ways to retain their faith in a loving God even after being hurt by the church. Her book, *Healing Spiritual Wounds*, was released just weeks after Trump's inauguration—and not long before Evangelical pastors' sexual misconduct and church scandals would come to light during Trump's presidency.

Before long, Howard-Merritt started to hear from Evangelical women who felt betrayed by Trump. "There seems to be a sense that they thought they were standing for something, and all of a sudden it all went away," she told me. "They realized it was all about power. And too many concessions had been made when they supported Trump."

As the #ChurchToo movement grew, Howard-Merritt noticed that she received more letters from women questioning their Evangelical faith. "There is a sense that Evangelicalism is a house of cards," she said. "If you start to question certain things, if you start saying maybe women should be treated with more respect, it starts unraveling."

Howard-Merritt told me that this sense of betrayal is related intensely to the investment of Evangelical women in purity culture. "They were told they needed to be morally pure, and there was so much pressure around that," she said. "To watch the same church who upheld purity culture so highly and so strongly just turn around when we have a president who has gone against so much of what purity culture stands for—it feels like betrayal."

I Am Damaged Goods

To understand the role of women in American conservative Christianity, in churches across America where the Trump vote was strongest, you first have to understand purity culture, a dominant more of American Christianity throughout the late twentieth and early twenty-first centuries. Popular Christian blogger Sarah Bessey wrote about purity culture in January 2013, in a post titled "I Am Damaged Goods."

In it, she writes, "I was nineteen years old and crazy in love with Jesus when that preacher told an auditorium that I was 'damaged goods' because of my sexual past. He was making every effort to encourage this crowd of young adults to 'stay pure for marriage.'"[6] Bessey recounts the pastor passing around a cup of water and asking everyone to spit into it, then holding the cup aloft and asking, "Who wants to drink this?" He was comparing that cup and its contents to a person who had had sex before marriage.[7] This demonstration on sexual purity is common in churches across America and in Canada, where Bessey experienced it. In her blog post, Bessey continues:

> Over the years the messages melded together into the common refrain, "Sarah, your virginity was a gift and you gave it away. You threw away your virtue for a moment of pleasure. You have twisted God's ideal of sex and love and marriage. You will never be free of your former partners, the boys of your past will haunt your marriage like soul-ties. Your virginity belonged to your future husband. You stole from him. If—if!—you ever get married, you'll have tremendous baggage to overcome in your marriage, you've ruined everything. No one honorable or godly wants to marry you. You are damaged goods, Sarah."[8]

Women, in the church medieval and the church American, and in traditional Islamic and Jewish cultures as well, are the keepers of the virtue of a family. Where that female virtue is sacrificed, so goes the purity myth, all are destroyed. Purity-based theology leads to honor killings in Afghanistan and oppression of women in conservative churches across America, forcing women to be traffic cops of their own bodies, silencing their own desires and urges, making them no more and no less than repositories for male fantasies and sinfulness.

At my public high school in Minnesota, we had the very public choice of two high-school health classes: abstinence only or abstinence based. I had no boyfriend and no intention of having sex, but something inside of me rebelled against the idea of a special class for me because of the lobbying of conservative Christian parents. Besides, I wanted to see the boys try to put a condom on a banana. I did, however, attend a special daylong retreat about sexuality, put on by a local church. My memory of the event is hazy, but I do remember being told of the importance of purity rings, given to us as girls to remind us not to have sex. That and the creepiness of the father-daughter dances were enough to dissuade me from fully committing to the conservative church youth group, though I still went for the guitars and the cute boys every Wednesday night.

In the early 2000s, Joshua Harris's book *I Kissed Dating Goodbye* was all the rage among my youth-group friends. Everyone knew somebody who was waiting until marriage to even kiss their boyfriend or girlfriend, and I even had a friend in college whose parents insisted upon old-fashioned "courting," rather than college-aged dating. Harris, a homeschooled Evangelical Christian, was young and earnest, like the type of guy I'd meet over and over again at Campus Crusades for Christ or Christian Campus House during undergrad at the University of Missouri. The Christian guys I met in college always knew what to say and what to do, at least according to the Bible or according to the conservative pastors we all listened to; they would hold open doors and ask for a first kiss if they were really bold. They were usually slightly nerdy and awkward, a bit unassured and unlikely to win a date in the non-Evangelical dating pool, but among the Evangelical students in college, they were the best of the bunch. Like some of these Christian guys I knew in college, Harris even wore a fedora on his book cover: fundamentalist-chic.

Again merely dipping my own toe into the Evangelical dating pool, I ended up leaving my Christian Campus House boyfriend for the slightly more assured engineer I met playing pickup basketball. My old flame ended up marrying a girl from our Bible study. I'm not sure if they kissed before they got married, but I did watch more than a few friends from that world marry young. Sometimes I wondered if they'd have done so if the sexual prohibition had not been quite so strong. I am resolutely pro-marriage, but getting married in order to be able to lose your virginity is not what God intended either.

The purity culture movement is a movement by, for, and in support of men. Women are vessels to be passed from father to husband, to be given away glowing in white on her wedding day. Women, unlike men, are not naturally sexual beings, the purity myth says. They are to be projected upon, not to project themselves. But the purity myth faded in American culture. As of 2016, Harris had recanted the advice he became known for in *I Kissed Dating Goodbye.* When confronted on Twitter by a woman who said the book was used against her as a weapon, Harris apologized. He told NPR, "Where my book was used as a rule book to say this is the only way to do it, I know that's not helpful. When we try to overly control our own lives or overly control other people's lives, I think we end up harming people. I think that that's part of the problem with my book."⁹

In a *Washington Post* article about purity culture, Lyz Lenz wrote:

Purity culture taught me that I ought to be passed down from father to husband, more an inheritance than a human. I was taught that men are my cover and my shield, when for the most part they have been the ones causing damage through molestation, rape and abuse. I was taught that my holy calling was to open my legs for one and only one and bear him children. Barring that, I was to keep them closed and never express desire or lust or fear or longing. So many women in my life cracked under the untenable pressure, often giving up on God all together. Others were forced into marriages with men who hit them and hid their abuse behind another message of the church borne from purity culture, that God hates divorce.[10]

Lenz mentioned a handout from her friend's pastor on making a happy home. Its number-one suggestion: "being available to your husband's needs."[11]

The wives and mothers who were the children of purity culture in the late 1990s and early 2000s were among the Red State Christians who delivered Donald Trump to the White House. For women reared in a world where their sexuality was to be hidden and "available" to men, "grab her by the pussy" was, of course, nothing out of the ordinary. Evangelicals had bigger problems than Trump's comments on a bus.

An Evangelical Reckoning

The 1980s saw the downfall of several televangelists, including Jim Bakker and Jimmy Swaggart, brought down by sex scandals. In the wake of the #MeToo movement, the first year of Trump's presidency would herald a similar reckoning. In late March 2018, Frank Page, the president and chief executive of the Southern Baptist Convention's executive committee, announced his resignation because of an "inappropriate relationship." Page was among the Evangelical leaders who met with and praised Trump in the Oval Office in September 2017. That same month, the *Chicago Tribune* published a series of allegations of sexual misconduct by Bill Hybels, founding pastor of Willow Creek, America's first megachurch. What makes the Hybels case unique is that Willow Creek had previously advocated for equality among women and men in Evangelicalism, and Hybels's wife, Lynne, had signed a statement of support for women who suffered sexual abuse in the church, called #SilenceIsNotSpiritual.[12]

After responding to the sexual misconduct allegations before his congregation, Hybels received a standing ovation—a response that was not unique. The same thing happened in January 2018, after teaching pastor Andy Savage admitted before Highpoint Church in Memphis that as a youth pastor at age twenty, he had fondled and forcibly initiated oral sex from a seventeen-year-old youth group member, Jules Woodson, who later came forward, inspired by the #MeToo movement and by the fact that Savage had not responded to her email seeking an apology. While Savage's church applauded, he told them that he hoped Woodson would receive the same "healing" that he had, insinuating the ripe old Evangelical trope that women are defiled by sexuality, even sexuality that is forced upon them by men, even by men who serve the church.[13]

The church not only fails women by covering up abuse of women in the church. In other cases, women who suffer spousal abuse are encouraged by pastors and priests to remain with their abusive spouses. Howard-Merritt said she gets letters about twice a month, sometimes more frequently, from women whose pastors told them to stay with their abusive spouses, something that happened to Howard-Merritt's mother as well. She said people outside conservative Christianity often underestimate the sexism and limited choices for women in patriarchal and theologically conservative households. Practices like homeschooling and mistrust of mainstream media set up conditions where sexism and abuse can flourish, she added.

"A lot of the bias against women I don't think is even conscious," Howard-Merritt said. "Many Evangelicals are very wary of women in leadership and could not vote for a woman as president." In such an environment, how could American Evangelical women challenge Trump on his comments about "pussy"? They were still fighting for the right to speak at all.

But in 2018, a sleeping giant was awakened. Evangelical women were finding their voices, not as a reaction to Trump per se, but as a ringing alarm bell about the ways American Evangelicalism has diminished women. Their awakening would not elect Hillary Clinton, not ever. But it could lift up another woman for president someday, and it could eventually doom Trump and his conservative Christian backers, who relied upon Evangelical women to win in 2016.

Beth Moore Speaks Out

Historically, American conservative Christianity has censored those who have threatened its sacred tenets, especially those who speak from under its own revival tent. In 2013, popular Christian blogger and TV personality Jen Hatmaker found herself sanctioned and her books removed from LifeWay Christian stores due to her public affirmation of same-sex relationships. LifeWay is the publishing division of the Southern Baptist Convention and one of America's largest providers of religious and Christian resources, though LifeWay closed all its brick-and-mortar stores due to declining sales in early 2019. But Hatmaker's sanctioning was during the presidency of Barack Obama, a time when Red State Christians considered themselves under siege, diminished, and threatened. Things were different under Trump in 2018. Red State Christians had a taste of power and access to the White House, and as an unintended consequence, dissenting voices had more room to be heard. Female voices would lead the way. Maybe the most unexpected dissenting voice was that of Beth Moore.

I knew Moore for most of my life as my mom's favorite Bible study writer and the default for any church that wanted to start a women's group. I viewed her as an inoffensive, blond voice for Jesus with whom I didn't necessarily disagree but whom I also didn't feel compelled to read or study. As an ordained pastor and seminary graduate, I spoke derisively about Moore, considering her a theological lightweight or, in the vein of Joyce Meyer, a Bible study sellout who only wanted to be rich and write boring books for women. Notably, Moore founded Living Proof Ministries, which does much of its work with LifeWay.

As a sign of the changing American Evangelical church, Moore was not banned by LifeWay, despite being vocal about her disagreements with much of Evangelicalism when it came to treatment of women. Moore broke her self-imposed political silence the day after Trump's "pussy" videotape aired. She broke her silence on Twitter, tweeting, "Wake up, Sleepers, to what women have dealt with all along in environments of gross entitlement and power. Are we sickened? Yes. Surprised? NO . . . Try to absorb how acceptable the disesteem and objectifying of women has been when some Christian leaders don't think it's that big a deal. I'm one among many women sexually abused, misused, stared down, heckled, talked naughty to. Like we liked it. We didn't. We're tired of it. 'Keep your mouth shut or something worse will happen.' Yes. I'm familiar with the concept. Sometimes it's terrifyingly true. Still we speak."

Moore's voice would be most clarifying, though, against church leaders who mistreated women. One of the most significant Christian leaders to fall because of his words and treatment of women was Paige Patterson, former president of the Southern Baptist Convention and president of Southwestern Baptist Theological Seminary when Trump was elected president. Patterson came to lead the Southern Baptists after playing a prominent role in the SBC conservative resurgence, beginning with the election of Adrian Rogers as convention president in 1979. Fearing that the SBC had drifted away from inerrancy of Scripture, Patterson and others convinced tens of thousands of people and churches to upend the annual Southern Baptist Convention, shifting the direction of the church and American Christianity in general for decades to come.

Patterson had spoken for years about the submissiveness required from Christian women, even in the face of spousal abuse, with little scrutiny from his church, his denomination, or American society at large. In a 2000 interview that was audio-recorded and resurfaced in 2018, Patterson recounted that he had told a woman who had been beaten by her husband to stay with her husband, submit to him, and pray for him. Patterson said the woman later came to him with two black eyes and said, "I hope you're happy." He recalled that he replied, "Yes, I'm very happy," noting that her husband had come to church and been saved the next day. Initially, Patterson was unrepentant when the story resurfaced. He told jokes and wore a cowboy hat at the seminary where he served as president, and he initiated the dismissal of a PhD student who tweeted a critical article about him. At the time, Christian blogger Ed Stetzer predicted Patterson would receive a standing ovation that summer at the Southern Baptists' annual convention, where he was scheduled to preach the main sermon.

Again, in light of prescriptions for abused women to "stay home and pray" instead of fleeing spousal abuse, Trump's comments to Billy Bush on that bus sound almost childlike. Red State Christians had other problems, and before conservative Evangelical women would rise up as a political force, they needed to confront the corrosive theology and pastors who had silenced them for generations.

Beth Moore was up to the task. As allegations mounted against Patterson, Moore wrote a blog titled "A Letter to My Brothers," stating that she previously hadn't planned to share her mistreatment as a female in the conservative Evangelical world, because she would "get fried like a chicken."[14] But, Moore wrote, "After recent events [Patterson, etc.] following on the heels of a harrowing eighteen months [of Trump's presidency], I've decided fried chicken doesn't sound so bad." She continued by recounting the times she wore flats instead of heels so that she wouldn't be taller than the men she worked with, of riding elevators with pastors and church leaders who didn't speak to her, of riding in cars with other pastors who didn't utter a word to her, and of team meetings where she was ignored or made fun of. "I know good fun when I'm having it, and I also know when I'm being dismissed and ridiculed," she said.[15] Moore explained that she had desired to get trained in the seminary, but after "reading the environment and coming to the realization of what my opportunities would and would not be, I took a different route."[16]

Moore wrote that she had originally accepted the limitations placed upon women in the conservative Christian church—not to lead or teach men or to preach—because she believed those attitudes came from Bible passages. Then, she continued, "early October 2016 [the bus video] surfaced attitudes among some key Christian leaders that smacked of misogyny, objectification and astonishing disesteem of women and it spread like wildfire. It was just the beginning. I came face to face with one of the most demoralizing realizations of my adult life: Scripture was not the reason for the colossal disregard and disrespect of women among many of these men. It was only the excuse. Sin was the reason. Ungodliness." She ended her letter by sharing a story about a theologian she admired. Upon meeting him, he told her, "You are better looking than [another woman Bible teacher]."[17]

As Moore ended her letter with a call for male leaders in the church to end acceptance of misogyny and lift up the women leaders championed by Jesus and the apostle Paul in the Bible, I was reminded of the challenges faced even by a titan like Moore in the conservative American church. When she tweeted out her letter, one of the first messages of support came from Evangelical megachurch pastor Matt Chandler, whose church practices complementarianism, the belief in different prescribed roles for men and women in the church. At Chandler's church, despite his purported support of Moore, she could never preach in the pulpit.

Still, challenges like these noted, it's clear that Trump's presidency awakened a new spirit of critique and outspokenness among Evangelical female leaders. From Rachael Denhollander to Jen Hatmaker to Beth Moore, change was afoot even in America's most conservative churches. This change could have political implications, because churches and pastors had to change before Evangelical women would ever consider supporting a candidate other than Donald Trump, particularly a liberal Democrat.

Despite Trump's record of marital infidelity, three marriages, and brutish, objectifying talk about women, Trump has been relatively progressive when it comes to his view of women and women's roles. He grew up nominally Presbyterian, born in New York City, not the Bible Belt, and he was not a Southern Baptist. Compared with many male Evangelical leaders, Trump did a lot to support women. He championed his daughter Ivanka, giving her a special position in the White House, and Ivanka vocally supported working women, ran her own company, and appeared anything but the submissive wife of churchly lore. Trump's campaign manager, former pollster Kellyanne Conway, was the first woman to successfully run a presidential campaign. She has remained among the closest of Trump's advisers and has proudly said she was raised by a single mother, grandmother, and two unmarried aunts. And as his press secretary, Trump hired Sarah Huckabee Sanders, who juggles that demanding position with the role of mother.

While these examples may fall into the awkward category of female leaders who make things more difficult for the women they lead (see Conway's diminishing of women who accused Trump of sexual misconduct; see Huckabee Sanders's defense of immigration policies that separated migrant mothers from their children), it's nonetheless obvious that Trump had few qualms about hiring powerful women and in some cases preferred to work more closely with women than with men. In contrast to staunchly traditional Evangelical vice president Mike Pence, who was known to practice the "Billy Graham rule" (not eating meals with women who weren't his wife and refusing to attend events without his wife when alcohol was served), Trump was positively progressive in his view of women's roles.

Trump's Female Pastor

You can find no more fascinating person in Trump's orbit than the woman he calls his pastor, former televangelist Paula White, so I went to visit her at her church in Florida in early 2018. Long before she gave the invocation at Trump's inauguration in 2017, White was a teen mom in Maryland who married the baby's father after a rocky childhood in Mississippi and Memphis. That marriage quickly ended, around the same time that White converted to Christianity at a predominately black Pentecostal church at age eighteen. Six years later, she married pastor Randy White, with whom she'd found Without Walls International Church. The Tampa church soared to more than twenty thousand members, making it the seventh-largest church in America in 2004. By 2007, Randy White had a prescription-drug addiction, the couple's ministry was crumbling, and they divorced. Paula White briefly took over Without Walls, and then in 2011, she became senior pastor of New Destiny Christian Center, a predominately black congregation outside Orlando. In 2015, she married former Journey keyboardist Jonathan Cain, who now plays backup music while White preaches.

During the rockiness of her ministry and her marriage, White also became a televangelist, broadcast on nine TV networks and particularly popular on Black Entertainment Television. White told the *Washington Post* that Trump first called her in 2001 or early 2002, telling her, "You're fantastic; you've got the 'it' factor."[18] With her blond hair, long fake eyelashes, and stylish outfits, White fit Trump's typecast look for a female leader. Still, she likely wouldn't have been the first choice of Trump's male Southern Baptist supporters, so Trump remains an enigmatic figure among Red State Christians. He governs like a traditional conservative, but his voters do not fit neatly into the boxes that once held conservative Republicans and Red State Christians. White and the congregation she pastors are an example of his out-of-the-ordinary allies.

Driving to White's church, I anticipated the glitz and glamour I associated with the megachurches I'd attended in the past. So you can imagine my surprise when I came upon the humble New Destiny Christian Center, down a rural road in inland Florida outside Orlando, the kind of place that determines national elections but rarely gets a voice on the national stage. New Destiny's sign, located across from an open field past several run-down neighborhoods, is so nondescript I missed it the first time. When I U-turned and pulled back in, I entered a dusty, unpaved parking lot and was warmly welcomed by the two African American men serving as attendants. Pastor Norm, a jovial, middle-aged black man, led me all the way to the sanctuary, and I stopped for a drink at the drinking fountain, but it was out of order. New Destiny had no cafe serving Christian versions of Starbucks, no ark for children's ministry, just warm welcomes and padded chairs and a relatively unfancy stage with unsophisticated graphics. White told me later that while she had to learn in televangelism how to raise money and teach people about tithing, she denounced the prosperity gospel and the idea that people come to her church to hear a pastor tell them if they follow Jesus, they'll get rich.

I saw her training at work during the service, as people were told to give seven hugs after turning in their "love envelope," but honestly, the charisma and love didn't feel contrived, it felt genuine, and the community felt more important than the money. Before the sermon, White introduced a local African American man who was running for Apopka City Council. The position was nonpartisan, but Alexander Smith (an associate pastor of a nearby church) said he was campaigning to bring a YMCA and a swimming pool to the city. The Apopka high-school swim team doesn't have a pool, even here in sunny Florida. Smith wanted affordable housing, too; he said he grew up in a shotgun house where you could see the back door from the front door, and his family fed chickens inside the house. It all felt distinctly non-Trumpish and a great deal more authentic and grounded than any other megachurch I've attended. In fact, I'm not even sure New Destiny is a megachurch. The worship space wasn't overly large, and the congregation was midsize.

When White stood to preach, the contrast was almost unfathomable. Here in this nondescript room in rural Florida, full of African American men and women, the majority of whom were middle class and many of whom had experienced poverty, up stood a glamorous white woman in a black leather jacket and stiletto heels, with the White House on speed dial and the former keyboardist of Journey playing background music. White began by lifting up the church's food ministry, its prison ministry, and "salvations" in the youth group. She spoke with a down-home accent and often said things like "turn to your neighbor and tell them . . ."

White's sermon started with a long journey through the Bible from Jezebel (literally a witch, said White) to Jacob, Leah, Rachel, and Paul (who White said was divorced, quoting "most theologians"). While her theological training and biblical knowledge were lacking and she repeated tired tropes about men having authority and women having influence, White was genuine. She spoke about her personal story, about her mom and her mom's three graduate degrees, about her mom and her son being Democrats, about her stepdad's abandonment of her, about the millions of people "won to the Lord through Paula White Ministries." Near the end of the sermon, White mentioned that she would be turning fifty-two next month. As I noticed when I spoke with her after church, a part of White is too tired to keep up the old televangelism charade. What she has left, however, is a genuine love of Jesus and a childlike hope that she can share his gospel even with Donald Trump. She lifted up her joy in teaching prayer school, her sadness in rejection of herself, her struggle to follow Jesus's command to love God and love others, and as the sermon ended, she moved into the Vision Offering. I prepared to roll my eyes. Here it comes—the prosperity gospel. The real Trump pastor comes out.

Instead, White invited Pastor Norm from the parking lot, now standing in back of the worship space, forward to talk about the Vision Offering. "My wife, Julie, had a vision for a mural in the nursery," he said. "We need some money, but we mostly need people to volunteer to watch the kids. It's not even about the money. We want people to teach the kids the Lord's Prayer—to say when they grow up, 'I poured into this one!'" I felt chastened. His words were innocent. Genuine. They just wanted someone to help out in the nursery.

I wanted to understand how this place could exist. Like so many Red State Christians and Trump voters I'd met, Paula White and New Destiny Christian Center defied explanation. The pastor to Donald Trump, a candidate abhorred by most African American voters and prominent African American leaders, led a church comprising predominately African American Christians. The reality TV president, whose home is plated in gold, listens to a pastor who used to be on TV but now preaches to a relatively humble congregation in rural Florida. The president who cheats on his wives and speaks derisively about women on videotape puts most of his faith in a female pastor, despite being lifted up by conservative men in whose churches women are not allowed to preach. In this uniquely American—and Trumpian—paradox, I found an unexpected source of hope. White, scarred from the public demise of her marriage and ministry in the early 2000s, now rarely grants interviews, but she agreed to speak with me for a few minutes after the service, surrounded by church staff, volunteers, and her husband.

Her shame and anger at being called a prosperity preacher was the first thing White wanted to make clear. "Put this in the book," she said. "TV ministry kills you. You have to do the telethons. I had to do them, but you'll never hear prosperity gospel here. Not ever."

Early in her ministry, White faced many of the challenges shared by conservative Christian women who sense a call to ministry. She was belittled, underestimated, and seen through a narrow lens as only a pastor's wife. White recounted that when she first started preaching, she was told to preach from the pulpit on the floor instead of up on stage. "They didn't think women could preach," she said.

Despite her fame and friendship with Trump, White insisted she is down-to-earth and "simplistic." She recounted her stepdaughter's death from cancer and her son's many "challenges," likely a reference to his struggles with drug addiction. She mentioned regret for some of the things she did in her twenties and thirties, but she said she remains convinced that "God gave me an assignment to show [Donald Trump] Jesus." When asked about some of Trump's critical statements about women and African Americans, White acknowledged, "There have been tough times, relationships do get tested, but it's been nothing about me and all about Christ." White feels called to a specific mission to pastor Trump. And maybe if he has a pastor, White is a better choice for Evangelical women than most pastors who consort with Trump. She promised she would "never not do my pastoral duty" to call out Trump for his sins.

I wonder, still, if White is taking advantage of her congregation to make money. Most of New Destiny's members come from modest financial backgrounds in central Florida. While White denied engaging in prosperity gospel preaching, she still makes videos suggesting people earn rewards for giving money to her church and will suffer consequences if they don't. Her language, while standard in most charismatic churches, especially predominately nonwhite charismatic churches, borders on manipulative. Those old televangelist tendencies die hard. White isn't the only one to use these techniques, and she's far from the worst. Still, they limit her credibility.

Curious about her predominately black congregation's view of White's support of Trump, I turned to Karen Stair, White's longtime hairstylist and a volunteer at NDCC. "It's all about love," Stair said in response to a question about how they could have a pastor who is so close to Trump. "I've worked with a lot of pastors before Paula, and most of them were African Americans. On my worst day, Paula showed me more love than any of them. People don't know her heart. She's very down-to-earth, and she cares about you."

"She's not up there saying, 'Trump, Trump, Trump,'" Stair continued. "She's there to lead him to Jesus." And therein lies the uniqueness of White among Trump's Evangelical Advisory Board. Maybe the hope for American conservative Christian women in an age of Trump comes from an unlikely place: a former televangelist who was once BET-famous and wears fake eyelashes and a leather jacket to preach. The choice of White as Trump's personal pastor, much like his choice of the other high-profile women in his orbit, says something about Trump, too. He probably would not be a good or even mediocre husband. He would not be your choice to speak about body positivity or empowering women. He objectifies women and critiques them physically. He is unfaithful in his marriages and is an absent father. His political positions compromise women's rights and destroy families in poverty. But unlike so many of his Evangelical pastor counterparts, Trump does appreciate a strong, smart woman. At least in that one way, he is more Christlike than many of them.

CHAPTER 9

Less Conservative, More Consequential: Rural Rust Belt Red State Christians in Appalachia and Central Pennsylvania

The headline from WTAJ, central Pennsylvania's CBS News affiliate, said it all: "President Obama's 2008 Altoona Gutter Ball."[1] Obama went to Altoona, like so many politicians before him, seeking the ever-elusive and consequential votes of the poverty-stricken rural Rust Belt mixed with northern Appalachia in central Pennsylvania. He knew he probably wouldn't win these counties. A Democratic candidate for president hasn't won Altoona's Blair County or the counties surrounding it since 1964. Still, Obama visited. Pennsylvania has long been decisive, and if Democrats pick up just enough votes in the middle and piece together a "blue wall" of sorts in Philadelphia, Pittsburgh, and Harrisburg, they can win Pennsylvania's electoral votes and maybe the presidency, just as Obama did in 2008 and 2012.

Obama went to Altoona, and he bowled at Pleasant Valley Recreational Center, which years later had four and a half stars and four reviews on Yelp, none of which mention the former president, whose photos languish at the end of the twenty-four pictures included with the listing. Around here, Obama's presence might not be a selling point.

"Nobody around here liked him much," muttered Steve Bacza, ten years later, after church on Sunday morning in nearby Bellwood, Pennsylvania.

"Outsourcing everything," added Steve's wife, Evie Bacza. "That was one thing Obama did that people really didn't like. Although he did come bowl here. But he came and left." They remember the bowling, Obama's suit and tie, the relatively empty rec center, and an air of discomfort. Still, Obama won Pennsylvania and the nation less than a month later, and he garnered a respectable 37 percent of the vote in deep-red Blair County in 2008.[2] Hillary Clinton didn't come to Altoona. Maybe she didn't want to read a headline about her gutter ball. Maybe she didn't think the red counties mattered—that she needed to focus on the suburbs and the cities, where she'd run up huge margins against Donald Trump. It wouldn't make a difference.

Eight years after Obama's visit, Trump went to Altoona, campaigning for the general election. He packed two thousand people into the main room at the Blair County Convention Center, with another thousand in an overflow room, cheering and jeering and carrying on. Obama's bowling score was long since forgotten. Trump pointed his finger and gestured with his hand, up and down, up and down, as he declared:

When a company wants to leave our country to go to another country and think they're gonna make their product, and because our politicians are weak, stupid, taken care of by lobbyists, special interests. Hillary doesn't know what to do. She has no clue—Crooked Hillary. And by the way, even if she did, she couldn't do it anyway, because her donors don't want to do it. I spent less and won [the Republican primary] in a landslide. Other people spent much, much more—three, four, or five times more—and they came in seventh. Who the hell do you wanna have as your president?[3]

His rhetoric might not have been eloquent, but it wasn't meant to be. Here in these hills, where the green trees climb to the sky and ridges rise gracefully out of the holler, what they wanted was someone who knew who they were, someone who could speak their language. Trump did. All that stuff about conservative social issues, the traditional Republican conservative and Christian lines, well, they didn't really fly here, not in the same way. The language of the moment in Appalachia, in the Rust Belt, in central Pennsylvania, and in the states that would decide the presidency was anger, cynicism, and power. For generations in America, the people of this region—the coal miners, the soldiers, the football players—had been the engine. Now these hills are overrun by the opioid epidemic, and mines and quarries are closing. Kids are leaving home and not returning, legions of people are on federal disability, although many of them are young and able-bodied.

They still speak the language of faith here; they talk of baptism and Jesus and prayer in schools. But Red State Christians in central Pennsylvania are distinct from those in the South or in Orange

County. They are grittier, hardened, less socially conservative, more independent, more wary of outsiders, more cynical, and more drawn to Trump because of what they see as a shared identity with him, rather than specific policy items or ideologies.

These Trump voters, contrary to popular liberal myth, are not the layabouts, the desperate, unemployed drug addicts who fill the ranks of the disability claims across Appalachia and the Rust Belt. Rather, these Trump voters are their neighbors, their parents and grandparents—the ones who managed to keep their jobs despite the recession and the outsourcing, the ones who held their cities together but just barely, and the ones who wanted to win for the first time in a long time. Trump rallied in Altoona on August 12, 2016. He won a single-event record for the Blair County Convention Center, and he suggested that the only way he'd lose Pennsylvania was widespread voter fraud. "On Election Day, Pennsylvania is going to be won here in central and western Pennsylvania," said US Rep. Bill Shuster, R-Everett, to the Johnstown, Pennsylvania, *Tribune Democrat*, "because these people are going to get out and vote."[4]

Twenty-eight days later, at the LGBT for Hillary Gala in New York City, 285 miles and what felt like light-years away from rural, quaint, aggrieved Altoona, Hillary Clinton called Trump's supporters racist, sexist, homophobic, xenophobic, Islamaphobic, you name it. "You know, just to be grossly generalistic, you could put half of Trump's supporters into what I call the basket of deplorables," she said.[5] Trump immediately seized on the line, calling it evidence of Clinton's "true contempt for everyday Americans." Altoona was listening. Two months later, Trump got seven thousand more votes in Blair County than John McCain had received in 2008. And Clinton got nearly five thousand fewer votes in Blair County than Obama had received in 2008. With the statewide race decided by fewer than seventy thousand votes, this difference was consequential. Spread out over a few more rural Pennsylvanian counties, you had the difference in the race and the presidency.

The Christians and Hillbillies of Central Pennsylvania

More than any other group of Trump voters, rural Rust Belt and Appalachian voters have been studied ad nauseam. After the election, liberals ran out to buy J. D. Vance's memoir, *Hillbilly Elegy*, in droves, hoping to understand a culture that was alien to many Democratic voters on the coasts. *Elegy* soothed liberals' wounds, with Vance, a Trump critic and Appalachia native himself, writing about his home, family, and community, and suggesting that much of the white working class's grievances and problems were self-inflicted. Almost a year after the election, outlets like the *Washington Post* were still publishing think pieces about *Elegy*, such as Democratic congressional candidate and Rust Belt native who grew up in poverty Betsy Rader's take that "*Hillbilly Elegy* doesn't speak for me," recognizing the ways that government aid had supported and needed to continue supporting families in Appalachia and the Rust Belt.[6]

Despite all of this navel-gazing by the national media and even quick-hit profiles and man-on-the-street interviews from small towns across the Rust Belt and Appalachia, something was missing. First, writers and reporters were always skimming the surface, writing quirky asides about "everyday" people in rural America and coming up with pithy names to describe voter groups. I also noticed that, in dissecting the election of Donald Trump, few people were talking about the role of churches and Christianity in the decisive Rust Belt and central Pennsylvania Appalachian counties. With this task in mind, I decided it was time to make a trip of my own to meet the distinct Red State Christians of the Rust Belt and central Pennsylvania.

Driving past the Steel City on a June summer day, I was struck immediately by its beauty. I paused across the river from PNC Park, in the Strip District at the original location of Primanti Brothers, where Joe Primanti first sold lunch sandwiches filled with fried potatoes to workers during the Depression. The sun was blazing, and crowds lined up around the side of the restaurant, some having traveled from across the state to attend the Pirates game that would be starting in a few hours. I ate (almost) my whole sandwich, then headed east.

I was surprised when, not a half hour into my drive, the interstate turned to a winding mountain road. Stunning Appalachian vistas towered on either side of the road. I slowed down, then sped up, climbed, then sank into a valley and out again. I'd rarely seen such green mountains, such verdant country, such gently rolling hills as far as the eye could see. These mountains had been somehow civilized, but the people living within them were fiercely independent, dismissed by politicians and pundits as the "forgotten people." Yet their votes carried many times the weight of voters in California, New York, Texas, or Illinois. Pulling into my hotel, I locked eyes with a little girl and a little boy, staring bleakly out their hotel room window at about three in the afternoon. A woman with scattered gray hair framing her face stood in the parking lot with a loaf of bread, feeding the birds. Inside, men and women scurried to prepare the main room for a high-school reunion. I had the feeling of going back in time and also going to a place I'd never been to before.

That night, I drove to Hollidaysburg, known locally as the "posh" town. I drove past stately mansions along the road from Altoona, down to the downtown area and Zion Evangelical Lutheran Church, established in 1853. The light poles in Hollidaysburg were festooned with banners and pictures of "Hometown Heroes"; the nearest to the courthouse was for a US Navy veteran who had served in Vietnam.

The military felt close here, and even the cost of the Civil War weighed heavily in the summer air. Back in Altoona after church, I pulled into Eat 'n Park, known as "the place for smiles," with a 1990s-style red-and-green marquee. Pastors Amanda and Drew McCaffery were getting out of the car next to me.

Proud to Be Appalachian

"We wanted to take you somewhere local," said Amanda with a smile, and soon we were friends. The McCafferys were different from most of the pastors I'd spoken with during my travels. Other than Trump confidant Paula White, I'd generally been speaking to male Southern Baptist pastors, and Amanda and Drew were a married clergy couple in a mainline denomination. Both came from relatively conservative Appalachian roots, but both had become more liberal in recent years.

Drew was the pastor of Bethany Lutheran in Altoona, one of seven Lutheran congregations in a city of fewer than fifty thousand people. The number of congregations was a relic of a time when Lutherans settled central Pennsylvania and established tiny neighborhood congregations, many of which used German as their language for worship. Amanda, who had just finished seminary that spring, was serving as a supply preacher at Grace Lutheran in tiny Bellwood while awaiting her first job. The McCafferys explained that many congregations in their central Pennsylvania synod lacked pastors simply because they couldn't afford to hire one. Many churches had trouble paying even $100 a week for a supply preacher. Theirs was a calling not especially easy for a young couple looking to start and support a family, but like so many here in the Rust Belt and Appalachia, the McCafferys were made of strong, determined stuff. The Lord had called them, here they were, and here they would serve.

Amanda and Drew told me about their lives before ministry. Drew, from the western corner of Appalachia, grew up in Ironton, right at the bottom tip of Ohio, where West Virginia, Kentucky, and Ohio meet. Ironton was once one of the largest producers of iron in the world and was known for having four daily newspapers, a racetrack, numerous saloons, brothels, and chapels offering "quick" marriages. By the time Drew was growing up, though, most major industry had left Ironton. As of the 2000 census, the per capita income in Ironton was just $15,391, and about 23 percent of the population lived in poverty. Drew was born to a single mom and never really knew his dad, whom his mom said was a "hot date." Later, his mom married his stepdad and birthed Drew's ten-years-younger brother. The marriage didn't last, though. Drew's stepdad was one of the "last to go" at the local factory when it closed. "He never could get another job," Drew said, and the resulting financial stress contributed to marital problems, leading to divorce. Drew's family attended the local Baptist church, but Drew was "asking too many questions," and he was asked to leave.

Amanda grew up in Hagerstown, Maryland, which she said is right on the eastern border of Appalachia. "I'm proud to be Appalachian," she said with a smile. Amanda had grown up, in her words, "spiritual, but not overly religious." Like many Americans, her family first returned to Sunday worship after the September 11, 2001, terrorist attacks in New York City. Amanda graduated college in 2009, during the heart of the Great Recession, and jobs for religion majors in the Rust Belt weren't plentiful. So, like many millennials at the time, she returned home, to Hagerstown, ninety minutes away from Baltimore and Washington, DC, but a world away and steeped in Appalachian and Rust Belt culture. She got the only jobs available to college graduates at the time in Hagerstown, working "full-time in fast food and part-time at the gas station." After a while, Amanda's mom was able to get her a government job, and she wound up working as a management aide for public housing, about twelve miles northeast, over the border in Waynesboro, Pennsylvania.

Softhearted and with a preference for the poor, Amanda found her own stereotypes challenged and affirmed during her work in public housing. Her father, a corrections officer, had always warned her about his work at the jail, and now she was working in her own governmental field with struggling people. She found herself spending hours listening to stories and trying to find a way—any way—to help families and individuals out of poverty. "I realized I was becoming more of a counselor to the people I worked with, so I decided to go to seminary," Amanda said. She carries with her the memory of working in government assistance—its shortcomings and also its good intentions and the people in need it can help. "I keep telling people it really is the minority who play the system," said Amanda, whose parishioners in central Pennsylvania are often against government assistance, at least in theory. "Most people are trying to do the best they can."

Appalachian Trump Voters and Social Issues in the 2016 Election

After meeting during college at Capital University, Amanda and Drew were reunited at Trinity Lutheran Seminary, where they studied together and got married. Drew graduated first and was fifteen months into his pastoral job in Altoona when Donald Trump was elected. At that time, Amanda was a pastoral intern at a nearby congregation. Most of the people they knew at their churches and locally were big fans of Trump because of his supposed business savvy, his promises about coal, his vocal support of the military, and his conservative stance on social issues such as gay marriage.

Drew remembered one night, shortly after the election, when he hosted a Bible study at a local bar. Someone asked him what he thought about gay marriage. "Well, I'm in favor of it," Drew said. "I think it's hard to tell people who have been together thirty years that they don't qualify for the same benefits that Amanda and I have." He had given a pragmatic, sensible, nonreligious answer, and within it, I recognized how Trump supporters in Appalachia and the Rust Belt differ from Trump supporters in more traditional conservative Christian areas. Here, Red State Christian voters tend to attend mainline churches or not attend worship at all, and their primary concerns are not conservative social issues but rather the economy, political corruption and mistrust, and a more amorphous understanding of the country's identity and who would best maintain that identity.

These voters wouldn't call themselves Evangelicals, Amanda said. I ask her if it's because the term is too political. "No," she laughed. "I think it's just too fancy of a word."

I was struck by the closeness of these social issues and the different ways they play out personally and theoretically in the lives of Amanda and Drew, who have family members who are gay and transgender, and others in the region. People would have one opinion in general and another one in particular. This happens often in families, particularly across areas like the Rust Belt and Appalachia, where overt racism, sexism, and homophobia are prevalent but families can have a preponderance of diverse members who may be of another race or come out as gay. These inconsistencies were confusing to an outsider, but they also fit with the pragmatic and non-doctrinal atmosphere of Appalachia.

The region is post-Christian in a way that much else of Red State America is not. Churchgoing rates have declined precipitously in

Appalachia, and while most people still attend mainline churches or Catholic churches, if they go at all, the churches here are becoming more elderly, and the pews more empty. Unlike in the rest of America, Southern Baptist churches and nondenominational churches have not rushed in to fill the void in Appalachia.

Christians in this region weren't particularly listening for Trump's promises on the Supreme Court or his economic philosophy. Instead, they were interested in his identity and the way his identity might restore national pride and patriotism, particularly in a region with a high rate of military service. Appalachians resonated with Trump's condemnation of kneeling NFL players, ignoring its racial overtones and focusing on the idea of Trump as the paragon of national pride. In an area that has had its pride kicked one too many times, they were grateful for a champion. Trump even managed to trump some Appalachians' Pittsburgh Steelers fandom. Amanda said, "I know a woman who was a huge Steelers fan, really die-hard, and when they stayed in the locker room for the anthem [after Trump condemned kneeling players], she burned her Steelers jerseys. She hasn't watched an NFL game since."

The Parishioners of Tiny Bellwood Lutheran

Grace Lutheran listed "A Time for Children" in its worship bulletin, and one participant came forward: an eight-year-old boy. I found out later that he'd been adopted by a family in the congregation from a local mom who had lost custody due to struggles with opioid addiction. Despite his tough family background, this boy was the light of the service. Amanda told me later that he'd even helped her lead when she was sick, and he had proudly shared with her that he'd recently won a black belt in tae kwon do.

I didn't know who would want to talk to me, an outsider, but with Amanda's introduction, the congregation was prepared. I knew almost instantly I'd love to chat with Steve, one of the church ushers. He had a garrulous, joking manner and imposing frame, wearing suspenders and a T-shirt. Amanda had told me that her congregation was older, but I noticed that the people in the pews were actually younger than at many other mainline churches across the United States. Most of them were still working, and while hard work and life had weathered their features, many weren't senior citizens yet, and I didn't see any wheelchairs.

After service, I sat down on a folding chair behind the sanctuary with Steve and Evie Bacza, who had met through their cousins when their families both had farms a few miles up the road from the church. "My dad even got Evie's parents together," said Steve, with a twinkle in his eye. "He got milk for them." Evie remembered the first time Steve walked up her family's driveway—the way her fifteen-year-old heart fluttered. Her whole family was excited. Three years later, Steve proposed on prom night. "I was being attentive," he said, meaning tentative, and waiting to propose and get married. After prom, Steve and Evie got married and later had one son, Steve Jr., whom they call Stevie. "Steve plus Evie," he explained. "Get it?"

They love dancing, their dogs, and the home they've made their own in the picturesque, rolling green hills of central Pennsylvania. At first blush, theirs is the rural Appalachian story ripped from the headlines and brought to life, though it is considerably more complex than the initial headlines. Steve told me he has worked at the stone quarry for twenty-six years; he builds material for highways and enjoys providing for his family and spending time with others. He proudly shared a photo of himself as Santa Claus. Still, Steve wakes up every morning in severe pain, which he attributes both to the manual labor of his quarry job and to old injuries from motorcycle accidents. He has had back surgery and knee surgery, and he said he takes eleven or twelve pain pills just to get out of bed and eight to go to sleep at night.

"One morning at church, my friend looked at me and said, 'Steve, you aren't looking so good!'" Steve remembered. "I was falling asleep all morning at church. Then I realized I hadn't taken my pain pills that day." The hard work and pain have worn down Steve's body, but at age fifty-four, he said he needs to work eleven more years. Evie also works, driving a school van for kids with special needs, many of whom are living with grandparents because their parents are unable to care for them. Her job is another difference from many conservative Christian communities. In the Rust Belt and Appalachia, women are needed and expected to work outside the home, and the lines of gender difference are not drawn as sharply. "It takes both to work here," Evie said.

This more progressive understanding of men and women's roles is also evidenced by the number of women pastors working in Appalachia. While deeply conservative in many ways, Steve and Evie have loved their female pastors. They speak fondly of former Pastor TM, an older white woman with short gray hair who presided over their twenty-fifth wedding anniversary vow renewal and had a fatal heart attack shortly after leaving her job at the church. Steve and Evie were previously Catholic, coming from Polish American families, but they were turned away by the moral scandals in the Catholic Church, as well as a perceived focus on money. "I think the priests should be able to get married," blurted Steve, in a moment of unbridled liberalism. "And Catholics are always about the money. I heard the floor at the parish cost ten thousand dollars. I never really felt comfortable up there." Now Steve is president of the church council at Bellwood Lutheran, which has struggled to maintain a budget large enough to employ even a part-time pastor.

Eventually, Steve and Evie began to open up about Trump and the appeal of the gold-plated, flashy millionaire to the plainspoken, hardworking people of central Pennsylvania. Evie said her uncle likes to curse at the TV when the news comes on. "The guys at work talk politics," Steve said. "They're die-hard Republicans." The reddening of labor is an interesting feature of Rust Belt and Appalachian politics. Blue-collar workers were once heavily unionized and heavily Democratic, but those trends have changed in recent decades, with the Democratic Party's focus moving to social issues and identity politics, away from traditional labor-friendly initiatives.

"Trump is trying to get rid of a lot of troublemakers," Steve finally said in support. I asked if there was a big immigration problem in Bellwood, but Evie said their concern lay elsewhere: "When my grandma came here from Poland, she had to have a sponsor." Steve and Evie see Trump as lifting up the America that they want to live in, and like Trump, they're defensive of all those who might seek to challenge or change the America they see as threatened. "Like those football players," said Evie. "If they want to be here, they should show that respect." I heard a certain racial undertone in her remark and the earlier comments about immigration—a sense that nonwhite Americans are privileged to be in the country and are not "real" Americans in the way that white Americans are. It's a line of reasoning that Trump often flirts with, and it finds a home here in rural Pennsylvania, even among families that, as mentioned earlier, are often of diverse racial and ethnic makeup themselves.

"They're just whiners," Evie continued, talking about NFL players who knelt. "They have all this money, and they're whiners." Steve added, "I work harder than them, and I will never have that money." I heard it again—the sense of aggrieved resentment against perceived winners in a country that has betrayed its past. Their words were right

out of Trump's playbook and play well in a region that has been mistreated by generations of American politicians. Even though there's
no proof or sense that Trump will be any different from past politicians, beyond some tweaked policies on coal production, the people
here trust him anyway. What Trump does effectively is twist their
resentment away from rich white men like himself and onto other
figures, such as nonwhite athletes or Hollywood stars. Trump does it
by making a claim of shared identity—that despite the gilded walls of
Trump Tower in Manhattan, Trump is more like them than nonwhite
athletes are, although many of those athletes grew up in poverty similar to that which exists in Appalachia.

"Buy American. Build American," Steve said. "He's trying to do
that." While the Appalachian Christians I met weren't moved by
Trump's socially conservative policies, they were adherents to a sort of
civic religion that aligned with Trump's patriotic and nostalgic sense
for a long-gone America. It reminded me of the Christian nationalism
I heard in Dallas, though it was not as theologically rooted.

"He's always praying," Evie said. "He is not afraid to talk about
God. He's always praying. He's the first one in a while that has been
like that. And when he gets out of the plane, he salutes the servicemen." This was an allusion to a popular, though debunked, right-wing
meme that President Obama did not properly salute servicemen when
exiting Air Force One. Evie's words about it are an example of the
ways that stories with false information and manipulated images have
greatly influenced voters in America's heartland.

"[Trump] always has flags out everywhere," Steve said. "You see
that in Bellwood, too." But the Baczas know that Trump is not really
like them, not exactly.

"He knows how to make money, just like the guys who own the
quarry know how to make money," Steve said. "The owner used to come

in and work with us. But now his son sold it to an investment group. It's all about money. It's not local anymore. Our checks don't come from the local bank; they come from New Jersey. It's all been outsourced. There's cameras everywhere at the quarry now. The owners aren't there. We had to cease production because of oversupply for the first time ever. It's just big business anymore." Trump, in Steve's view, is akin to the local quarry owner. He's still a rich guy, but at least he's our rich guy.

In a world full of work injuries and war veterans coming home with missing limbs and PTSD, part of what Appalachia wanted in 2016 was to be comforted by someone who said, "I alone can fix it." Steve has a friend who returned from Afghanistan to work cleaning tank trucks locally. "It's a dangerous job," Evie said. "One of the tanks exploded because it wasn't cleaned properly after leaving the war zone." Imagine leaving a war zone halfway across the world to come home to an equally dangerous environment, this time with little support. In some ways it's unsurprising that many in Appalachia end up preferring the familiar to the new, even if the familiar may let them down, too.

Still, their thinking is pragmatic and flexible, and the local, if available, will always outweigh the foreign. Steve talks about a friend of his who came out as a lesbian. "She has two kids, and now she is happy," he said. "It's opened up more here. If they're gonna be that way, it's fine. Just don't push it on us. We have a gay couple that are friends of ours; they're the nicest guys we know. We just don't broadcast it."

The Young Female Lawyer Who Has Hope for Appalachia

If Steve and Evie represent the old guard of Appalachia and its Christian support of Trump, I wanted to also dig into the sometimes surprising future of Appalachia, represented by its population of young, educated working women. After church at Bellwood, I headed back to Altoona, to Drew's church, Bethany Lutheran, in the East End, full of decrepit rowhouses, American flags, and children running up and down the streets, some without shirts. Here I met attorney Traci Naugle, age thirty-eight. Traci grew up in Altoona, raised mostly by her grandmother, Martavene, with whom Traci lived most of her life. I asked Traci about her grandma's unique name. "She was the eighth of nine kids, so she told me her mom was basically just running out of names," Traci said with a grin. Traci also lived with her mom, who struggles with mental health, and her Uncle Terrence, who was a high-school counselor and one of the first in the family to go to college. The Sunday we met, Traci was attending church with Terrence; she and her uncle still live together in the same house where Traci grew up. Terrence served as a father figure for Traci, whose parents divorced when she was a baby. Terrence offered a glimpse of stability in a sometimes chaotic life.

"I wanted to be a lawyer since ninth-grade civics," she said, recounting a friend who came from a rural mountain town outside Altoona and told Traci she didn't think women could be lawyers. "My grandma was very poor growing up; she worked retail jobs. Most women work in Appalachia. My grandma's family was mostly girls, and it didn't matter. If there was a job to be done, they did it. I didn't have that concept of gender roles growing up. It never occurred to me that women couldn't be lawyers."

A quiet, "terribly shy" teenager, Traci persevered through high school and majored in political science at Penn State, forty-five miles up I-99. Thriving in college, Traci briefly considered going away to law school. Then her grandma had a stroke. Traci immediately moved back to Altoona at age twenty-two. It never occurred to her to do otherwise.

"Just recently, we had to put her into a home," said Traci, sixteen years later. "She has a hard time remembering who I am, but she does sometimes." While caring for her grandma, Traci completed law school at Penn State. Today, she's a partner in the Altoona law firm Forr, Stokan, Huff, Kormanski & Naugle and the vice president of the Blair County Bar Association, as well as president of her church council. She said her high-school classmates were shocked when she returned for the ten-year reunion as a lawyer. "It's hard to get jobs, and it's expensive, so a lot of people don't go to college," Traci explained. "They think, 'I have to start working immediately.'"

As a young, single, female lawyer in central Pennsylvania, Traci is an anomaly. She focuses on estates, real estate law, and disability and Social Security. "You would not believe the number of people my age who apply for disability," she said. "It's mostly back pain or mental health. I don't have the statistics on it, but they start taking pain pills and they feel good, and they start to not be able to tell what is pain and what is not being on pills. They think, 'I can't work; I have this pain.'"

Working as a lawyer in a small town means Traci has long known many of her clients, their families, and her fellow attorneys. Sometimes she comes face-to-face with the class distinctions of Appalachia, and she even catches herself thinking, "Why does the girl from the rich family in high school want to hang out with me now?" She spoke to me about the area's longtime wealthy families, most of whom live in the big houses along the main road in Hollidaysburg. "The culture is very split according to place. Sometimes the big-name families will do charity work, and people will say, 'Oh, he is my friend,'" she said. "But they really aren't friends." That behavior pattern is reminiscent of the ways Trump has managed to connect with many of Appalachia's poor without making any meaningful commitments to them.

Election season was rough for Traci, who was outnumbered as a Democrat in her law office. She said the road to Trump was paved by area hatred of Obama. "In 2012, it was really bad," she said. "The N word, things you see on TV—you'd hear all of those horrible things. People weren't just saying, 'I disagree with [Obama's] position on the issues.' They were saying, 'I dislike *him*. Oh, and I also disagree with his position.'" A friend of Traci's recently ran for mayor of Altoona and received just 30 percent of the vote, a sign Traci sees that the area has become more Republican.

While there isn't much talk of conservative Christian social issues, Traci said the messaging is starker: "God is telling you to vote Republican," and voting Republican becomes another item on the checklist to be a "real" American, along with honor the flag, own guns, buy American, and pray. Sometimes, as often happens in Appalachia, ideology and practical truth differ. Many of the Social Security disability applications that Traci works on are from people she says are very pro-Trump. "I'm thinking, 'You know, this is the guy who wants to get rid of government benefits.' This is a government benefit!" she said. "There is a lot of resentment, and there are a lot of people who don't want to work."

Still, Traci is well known and loved in Altoona and central Pennsylvania. She was on the *Altoona Mirror's* list of twenty people under forty to watch. She doesn't need to advertise her law services, because she gets so many business referrals.

On the topic of immigration, Traci said racial and ethnic diversity is next to none in Altoona. Still, she said, a lot of people remember a triple homicide at a nearby nightclub in 2000. One of the people who was killed was a well-loved teacher at the high school. The killer was a Mexican national living in the United States illegally. "People don't forget that," Traci said. "But I don't understand: How can you hate your neighbor and be a Christian? How can you judge people and be a Christian? How can you deny people basic human rights? How can you destroy the environment? But no matter what I say, the other lawyers won't listen to me, so I pick my battles."

Instead, she argued about partnership structure at the firm, and she won, becoming a named partner. As her grandma's health worsens, Traci doesn't foresee leaving Appalachia. She sees signs of hope in Altoona, as some businesses return and families settle nearby. "My hope for Appalachia is that we can start rebuilding and bringing young families back. I'd like to see more life again," she said. "There is a sadness in certain pockets. But there are organizations that are trying. I can say today that it is a better place than it was twenty years ago. I see Jesus at work everywhere. I try to treat everyone I meet with compassion. You notice it here—that people will hold the door at the grocery store. There is an authenticity."

"We are not all hillbillies here," she added. "I've heard this part of Pennsylvania is called Pensatucky. There's more to it than that."

The Spirit's Power in Appalachia

I thought of Traci's words as I remembered the church service I'd attended in Hollidaysburg the night before. At first glance, I saw evidence of a decaying world. The service was quiet, and the crowd small. No one talked to others much. The interim pastor, filling in after the church had undergone deep conflict, was experienced but in poor health, barely able to complete the service. Everything felt stuck in the past, from the war and police memorials outside to the beginning of the sermon. "You do remember JFK, right?" the pastor asked, adding: "Jesus came not to do away with old-time religion. Jesus was a person who knew the law."

Midway through the sermon, the pastor looked as if he could fall asleep, as did much of the congregation. But he roused himself, and the service continued, even as the congregation sang the Alleluia liturgy and then the pastor, oblivious, read it aloud to himself a second time. Everything felt frustrating and out of touch. In front of me sat a girl who looked to be six years old, with a pink sequin dress and pink glitter shoes. I wondered what this service made her think about Jesus or about God. Did God even matter? We prayed—for people ill, hospitalized, or "struggling with some issues"; for Nate and Zack and Nick and Jeff serving the military overseas; for Kaylie, an eight-year-old with cancer; and for Michelle, with "life struggles."

Then, having completed the Communion liturgy a second time, the pastor hobbled around the altar for the Words of Institution. His unsteady gait contrasted with the glitzy stadiums I'd been accustomed to seeing across the South, following Red State Christians and Trump voters elsewhere. The pastor shuffled one foot in front of the other, his rumpled khakis and wrinkled shirt damp with perspiration. He leaned, hard, on the altar for support and then dramatically grabbed the bread as if his life depended on it (and maybe it did), and he lifted the bread into the sky. "THE BODY OF CHRIST, GIVEN FOR YOU!" With shaking hands, he set down the bread. He grasped the chalice, stronger now, in both hands and raised it above his head. "THE BLOOD OF CHRIST, SHED FOR YOU!"

As I stood there watching him, I felt ashamed. For all my saying that the other Christians got it wrong, I'd gotten it wrong, too. I'd failed to see the tiny signs of hope and possibility in this stifling church on a June Saturday night in economically depressed, socially backward central Pennsylvania. I saw it there, though, and it stayed with me the rest of my trip, with Amanda and Drew and Steve and Evie and Traci and the waitress whose son was away watching Kendrick Lamar in Pittsburgh.

Sure, the pastor almost keeled over during the service, and everyone was half asleep, but the Holy Spirit lived here, too. In that Spirit's power, Appalachia might finally speak for itself, with or without Trump's help.

CHAPTER 10

Conservative Catholics: Building a New American Kingdom and Defying the Pope

At one time in America, Catholics were the "other" Christians—mysterious, foreign intruders. In this view, they were not to be trusted; they were Irish drunkards or swarthy Italians, men who worked with their hands and women who presided over unruly large families, with children crawling out from underneath their skirts.

In much of American history, Catholics faced such persecution and lack of acceptance that they established their own educational system, developing a network of parochial schools known for their strict discipline and overflowing numbers. Catholic schools were unique in that they provided opportunities for poor families to send their children to private school at a reasonable cost. But that often meant—as my Catholic father once told me—classes of more than fifty students and nuns who used the stick to punish indiscriminately.

Anti-Catholic rhetoric was baked into early American tradition. The Pilgrims and Puritans first came to America to escape the tradition and stodginess of the Anglican Church and were loath to accept any form of clericalism, plus the early American Protestants often considered themselves superior to the "uneducated" adherents of the Roman Catholic Church, which had its roots in non-English-speaking countries. In 1780, John Adams wrote this after attending Mass at the cathedral in Brussels, Belgium, and seeing worshipers venerate a piece of religious artwork: "This insufferable piece of pious villainy shocked me beyond measure; but thousands were before it, on their knees, adoring. I could not help cursing the knavery of the priesthood and the brutal ignorance of the people; yet, perhaps, I was rash and unreasonable, and that it is as much virtue and wisdom in them to adore, as in me to detest and despise."[1] In Adams's writing you can see the dual reaction of many early Americans to the Catholic Church. They were both disgusted by what they saw as its blind ritual yet also attracted to its mystique and the faith it engendered among a diverse people.

As Catholic immigrants from Germany, Italy, and Ireland flooded American shores in the late nineteenth and early twentieth centuries, Catholics found a home in the Democratic Party. Lay Catholics in cities like Boston, Philadelphia, and Chicago often worked blue-collar jobs and were active in labor unions, which were allied with Democrats. This combination meant that most American Catholics were Democrats even into the late twentieth century. In the South, Catholics were considered a threat to the established white, Protestant order. The Ku Klux Klan included Catholics among its list of threats to "loyal Americans," believing that a Catholic could never be a true American, and Catholics were viewed with suspicion and mistrust.

I see this history of American Catholicism and mistrust of Catholics among American Protestants even in my own family. My father's ancestors were Catholics from southern Germany and moved to a predominately German Catholic small town in late-nineteenth-century Minnesota, where many people spoke German even into the mid-twentieth century. Then World War II forced German Americans, especially Catholics, to prove their allegiance to the United States. My dad's family didn't have a lot of money; with seven children, his parents struggled just to make ends meet. My dad remembers growing up on a diet of powdered milk and sharing his bedroom. Nonetheless, my dad and his siblings attended Catholic school.

My husband's dad also was part of a family of German immigrants—Lutherans who, once in America, joined what was then a mostly German-speaking Missouri Synod congregation. Ben was surprised the first time he came to church with me and we recited to the Apostles' Creed. We said, "I believe in the holy catholic church." Ben turned to me and asked, "Isn't it 'holy *Christian* church'?" He had grown up learning that to say "Catholic," even in the Apostles' Creed would be inappropriate, a betrayal of American Protestant tradition and the Reformation.

When John F. Kennedy became the first Catholic US president, he had to disavow his allegiance to the pope, famously saying, "I am not the Catholic candidate for president. I am the Democratic Party's candidate for president, who happens also to be a Catholic. I do not speak for my church on public matters, and the church does not speak for me."[2]

Kennedy said these words in 1960, in front of a group of ministers in Houston, which was then as it is today a hotbed of conservative Christian politics. But much has changed in America since Kennedy, an Irish American Democrat from Boston, distanced himself from the Catholic Church in order to be electable. By the second year of Trump's presidency, a majority of Supreme Court justices were Catholic; in fact, there hadn't been a Protestant on the court for years until he nominated Episcopalian Neil Gorsuch.

By the time of the 2016 election, Catholics had for decades been a reliable part of the Democratic Party, and the two most famous Catholic politicians were Nancy Pelosi and Joe Biden. Even so, things had changed. Like my late paternal grandmother, most Catholics were resolutely pro-life, placing them out of step with the Democratic Party. They also tended to differ on the morality of same-sex marriage. Perhaps this makes it unsurprising that, while Obama narrowly won the Catholic vote in 2008 and 2012, Trump in 2016 won Catholics over Hillary Clinton by a margin of 52 percent to 45 percent.[3] And among white Catholics, Trump won with a whopping lead of 60 percent to 37 percent.[4]

By the time of Trump's presidency, many conservative Catholics had won prominent positions in American politics. Paul Ryan, a devout Catholic, was the Republican speaker of the house. Vice President Mike Pence had been brought up Catholic, and while he attends an Evangelical megachurch, he calls himself an "Evangelical Catholic." The bonds between American conservative Evangelicals and American conservative Catholics could be easily seen at the March for Life each year in Washington, DC. There, thousands of Evangelicals and Catholics traveled from across the country to advocate for the overturning of *Roe v. Wade*, a prominent point of contention for Red State Christians who voted for Trump, despite their misgivings about his morality.

Many American Catholics, especially those living in red states, were finding out they had much in common with their conservative Evangelical brothers and sisters. Of course, they worship differently and view Communion much differently. For Catholics, Communion is Jesus's body and blood, unequivocally. For Evangelicals, Communion is more of a symbol, and their worship services center on preaching and music, rather than Eucharistic liturgy. Still, these theological differences were not top of mind for most Red State Christians before and during the Trump presidency. Many of them might not have even known the theological differences between their faiths. What they did know was that conservative Catholics and Evangelicals stood together on most major social issues, and they shared a common sense and fear that American culture was running away from them. For conservative Catholics, this included their more liberal brethren and even liberal Catholic clergy. Add in a potent sexual-abuse crisis and cover-up, and many conservative Catholics found themselves rudderless, looking for an anchor. Some of them found one in the Republican Party and in Donald Trump, even in unexpected areas of the country.

While New Hampshire narrowly gave its electoral votes to Clinton in the 2016 general election, New Hampshire Republicans had decisively paved the way for Trump's candidacy with his overwhelming primary win in New Hampshire that February. At the time of the primary, the Republican nomination was still very much up for grabs. Many expected standard bearer Jeb Bush to earn a win in the state among former Rockefeller Republicans. New Hampshire was known to be a renegade state, a place more socially liberal than the rest of the Republican electorate and neighboring some of the most liberal states in the nation. Nine Republican candidates were on the ballot in New Hampshire, including Sen. Ted Cruz, who had just won Iowa, and John Kasich, an Ohio governor and a favorite among moderate Republicans. Instead, Trump shocked the nation, getting more than double the votes of Kasich, the second-place primary finisher, and three times the votes won by Cruz. Upstart Sen. Marco

Rubio (R-Florida) finished fifth, behind a disappointing fourth place for Bush. After New Hampshire, the Trump train rolled on, and he won thirty-six more primary states en route to the Republican nomination and the presidency.

What was it about New Hampshire? So much about this state was different from the other places where Red State Christian voters handed Trump the presidency. Here, voters hadn't overtly turned on religion; New Hampshire has one of the country's highest rates of religiously unaffiliated people, known as the "nones"—36 percent, second only to neighboring Vermont.[5] New Hampshire voters also weren't influenced by megachurches, Southern Baptists, or a dying Appalachian economy. In New Hampshire, of the 56 percent of people who say they are Christians, 26 percent are Catholic, twice the percentage of those who call themselves Evangelical.[6]

So much about New Hampshire was unknown and unexpected. Of all the places I went to visit, I knew the least about New Hampshire and about its Catholics. I only knew that their story had to be told. I needed to return to the Mass of my father, to the roots of America, to the place where Trump first won and where two of American Catholicism's most conservative colleges were preparing to shape American politics for generations to come—here in these orange, red, and yellow forests of 2018 autumn in New England.

Liquor Store, One Mile

After landing at Boston Logan International Airport and as I walked out to the rental-car shuttle past an exhibit honoring JFK, I was reminded of the liberal, academic, polished air I'd always associated with New England, home to the Ivy League and America's stiffest upper lip. Quickly, however, I realized that Boston and New

England are much more than Harvard and Yale. Boston is home to some of America's most notorious gangsters, Southie, and, much longer ago, the revolutionary mobs who ignited the Boston Tea Party. That air of death-defying independence and blue-collar grit only increased as I crossed the state line from liberal Massachusetts into purplish New Hampshire, with its libertarian ethos and conservative political history. Later, during interviews with New Hampshire residents, I was told that part of the reason their state was becoming less conservative and less religious was that liberals were moving from Massachusetts into New Hampshire and bringing their politics with them.

New Hampshire is a unique state, circled by Dartmouth College on its western border, Boston to the southeast, fabled Portsmouth on the upscale Atlantic Coast, and French-Canadian Montreal to the north. Trump called New Hampshire a "drug-infested den" just days after being inaugurated; here, in educated and even elite New England, the opioid crisis is terrible. New Hampshire falls behind only West Virginia in drug overdose deaths per capita, and it leads the nation in overdose deaths per capita from fentanyl, a synthetic opioid many times more potent than heroin. The opioid crisis, fueled by drugs that mask both physical and emotional pain, is often associated with despair, and you can feel that despair here in New Hampshire. Despite having the highest median household income in America, as well as low unemployment and crime, the state is also plagued by what researchers at Dartmouth called "pockets of economic degradation"—rural areas where jobs are few and people rely on disability payments.[7]

On New Hampshire's meandering, forested roads, as I drove from Boston to Concord, I saw places that had been forgotten: addicts living in tents in Manchester, run-down buildings, and unique to New

Hampshire, highway signs that listed not only gas, food, and lodging, but also the distance to the nearest state-owned roadside liquor store. The opioid crisis may be new here, but New Hampshire has long had higher-than-average rates of addiction and alcoholism. A history of conservative state politics led to lower-than-average funding for resources like treatment programs and social workers. Later in the weekend, as I drove from Concord to Portsmouth, I would spend an entire drive listening to a New Hampshire Public Radio podcast about the crushing effect of the opioid epidemic on an overwhelmed state family welfare system, desperate for more foster parents and ways to help children of addicted parents.

That independent streak of New Hampshire and, really, America in general, evidenced by the state motto, "Live Free or Die," may also have contributed to the tight hold the opioid epidemic has on the Granite State. In a libertarian-leaning state, where people are reluctant to join together in churches or civic groups, they lack a safety net when families and individuals struggle. People are hesitant to ask for help or to meddle in someone else's business. Unlike many of my research trips to the South and the Bible Belt, here there would be no church Life Group where parents would pray together for an addicted daughter. Here, maybe the choice really was that stark. Live free—or die.

From my hotel in Concord across Franklin Pierce Highway, I could see New Hampshire's state buildings: the Departments of Corrections, Labor, and Health and the New Hampshire state hospital. Franklin Pierce, fourteenth president of the United States, had been a rare northern Democrat from New Hampshire; he opposed the abolitionist movement and enforced the Fugitive Slave Act.[8] His was a dubious legacy to the New Hampshire I'd visit in 2018—part of America's most liberal region yet also the state whose primary victory paved Trump's path to the presidency.

Sanctity of Life in New Hampshire

My first visit to Mass in New Hampshire was at 4:30 p.m. on the other side of Concord, at the Immaculate Heart of Mary. The presiding priest was a visiting priest from Rwanda; African priests are common here in New England Catholic churches, especially in rural areas. On one hand, the diversity was encouraging, and it represented an evolution in Catholic missions: once white Americans and Europeans traveled to Africa to share the gospel, and today priests travel from Africa to share the gospel with American Catholics, many of whom are white. On the other hand, the arrangement doesn't always work. African priests have been given little language training or opportunity to learn about American culture. American parishes were so desperate for priests that they would take someone immediately from seminary in Africa to a small town parish in America, where parishioners and priests alike would struggle with language and cultural barriers.

Catholics see the Mass itself as a sacrifice, making possible the gift of Holy Eucharist in the Communion meal of wafers and wine, Jesus's body and blood. The homily that evening emphasized sacrifice and service and the surprising truth about God's kingdom: "It is not about dominating, domineering authority; it is not about powerful authority. It is about sacrifice and service." The notion of sacrifice and service, outside of a military context, felt oddly anachronistic in twenty-first-century America, especially as governed by Trump, who at times has epitomized the idol of dominating, domineering authority. Still, many listening to the sermon that evening had likely voted for Trump, and I wanted to understand how they squared their Catholic beliefs with Trump's often opposite political tactics.

At the end of Mass, Kathleen Hedstrom walked forward to give an announcement. She wanted to invite people to join the parish's

Sanctity of Life group, a movement that focuses not only on anti-abortion advocacy but also protests capital punishment and euthanasia, both generally accepted in New Hampshire. Hedstrom said people who joined could have the chance to "adopt" an unborn child during an unplanned pregnancy, and after nine months, they could have a baby shower at the church, where the shower gifts would be donated to local families in need who were choosing to give birth.

The pamphlets for the Sanctity of Life group were on a table behind the sanctuary, next to brochures for families coping with the opioid crisis. I imagined that many of the state's unplanned pregnancies were related to addiction. These were such modern problems, facing families who looked much different than the 1950s nuclear and homogeneous family often evoked by traditional Catholics. I wondered how Hedstrom, herself a divorced mother of five, found the ancient Catholic faith helpful in facing New Hampshire's and America's problems of the early twenty-first century.

Hedstrom, age seventy-four, told me she was a midwesterner by birth, having grown up in Milwaukee as the middle of seven children in a large Catholic family. She attended Catholic schools throughout her life and graduated from Marquette University with a degree in nursing. Hedstrom had an adventurous spirit, and her early years as a nurse took her briefly to California, where she worked in Oakland during the height of the Vietnam War as well as the height of the hippie drug counterculture in San Francisco and Haight-Ashbury. "I saw men come back without limbs," she told me. "And then I saw all the war protesters and all the drugs. I couldn't stay. I remembered that I loved the fall foliage in New England, and so I decided to move to Boston."

There Hedstrom met and married her second husband, Dexter, later moving to New Hampshire. I wondered how Hedstrom, a devout

Catholic, could have attended Mass and taken Communion all those years, despite being divorced from her first husband and remarrying a second time without an annulment, an official church declaration that the first marriage had not been legitimate. "Well, he had died" before she got married again, Hedstrom said. "The church does not require an annulment if your first husband dies, even if you are divorced. My friends all told me when he died, 'You can get married again now.'"

For Hedstrom, her first husband's death brought a reawakening of her Catholic faith. Despite their divorce, Hedstrom's children had requested their mother's presence at their father's bedside before he died. "My daughter said, 'Say a rosary,'" Hedstrom remembered. "And even though she wasn't Catholic anymore, it meant something to her, and it meant a lot to me."

I found Hedstrom surprising and admirable—a woman who, despite divorce and personal hardship, had managed to cling to a faith that many would have let go long ago. I told her of Catholics I knew who felt their divorces had banished them from the church. "I never felt that way," Hedstrom said. "I was always still there."

More liberal about abortion in her earlier years, Hedstrom had a change of heart later in life, when she was pregnant with her fifth child at almost age forty. Early in the pregnancy, her obstetrician saw an abnormality in her son's skull and recommended an abortion. She traveled to another clinic to have an ultrasound and gather more information. There she was told the baby was fine. When he was born months later, Hedstrom's main doctor wasn't available, and she couldn't tell her obstetrician until later what had happened. In a follow-up appointment, Hedstrom broached the subject with her doctor: "Look at him; he's fine! You said I should have an abortion." She said her doctor didn't have much of a reaction at the time, other than apologizing and expressing his gratitude that the baby had been born healthy. "A few years later, though, he committed suicide," Hedstrom said. "He was divorced, but he had two daughters. I don't know why he did it. I don't know if I was the first one who made him start thinking about it all. I know he did abortions. I didn't know how he could deliver babies and do abortions."

Today, Hedstrom continues to live in New Hampshire, widowed after her second husband's death a few years ago. She still attends Mass regularly, and she's a proselyte for the Sanctity of Life group, shedding any shyness to speak boldly about the causes the group promotes. She said their parish group is small but joins with other local groups, and they're politically active with everything related to abortion, euthanasia, and capital punishment that comes before the state legislature. She told me about the group taking a bus together at five o'clock in the morning to travel to the March for Life. More recently, she said, she'd met with a hundred people in Manchester at Planned Parenthood, where the priest carried the Blessed Sacrament (the Communion host) through the streets of Manchester, praying for an end to abortion. "It was so peaceful and moving," Hedstrom said. "I thought people should see that as we were carrying Christ, this was what it meant to see Christ in us." She said some people there said they had regretted their abortions, and still others were "mad we were there, and they yelled at us."

The divided rancor and open wounds Hedstrom witnessed are emblematic of a divided populace in New Hampshire and a waning influence of the Catholic Church. Still, Hedstrom said, the gift of the Catholic Church to her is that she, a divorced woman, has always felt accepted. She wants others to experience that love and acceptance, even those who are on death row in New Hampshire, the only New England state that continues to practice capital punishment.

When asked about the 2016 primaries, Hedstrom said she had supported Ben Carson, a favorite of many Christian conservatives. When he lost and Trump became the Republican candidate, Hedstrom said she was influenced by a Catholic priest who addressed the Sanctity of Life Ministry, Father Frank Pavone, who is the national director of Priests for Life and president of the National Pro-Life Religious Council. He made headlines in 2012 for criticizing Cardinal Timothy Dolan for inviting then-President Obama to the annual Al Smith Dinner. (Two years later, after a financial-misconduct investigation of Priests for Life uncovered misdeeds, Dolan wrote to the Vatican and said that he wanted "nothing further to do with the organization.") The day after Trump's election, on November 7, 2016, Pavone presented what he claimed was an unclothed aborted fetus on the altar of the church where he was presiding, and he preached against abortion for forty-five minutes.[9] Subsequently, the Archdiocese of New York announced an investigation against Pavone, who is one of the thirty-three members of Trump's Catholic advisory council. The fact that Hedstrom, a relatively moderate woman in small-town New Hampshire, was influenced to vote for Trump by Pavone shows that the reach of conservative Catholic clerics is at the same level as that of more liberal Catholic clergy such as Pope Francis, who had sparred with Trump before and after his election. Hedstrom said Pavone had told the group to "look at the whole platform."

"My son says, 'Mom, you're a single issue voter,'" she told me. "But I'm not. I read the whole platform. The Republican side represented my values more. Trump is a loose cannon. But Father Pavone said we voted for him so that the voice of the people would be heard. Now you see, with the Supreme Court nominations, [Trump] is speaking up for the people."

Still, Hedstrom couldn't believe Trump almost won New Hampshire and later won the election. She watched almost in disbelief as he racked up more and more big states, flouting even the non-endorsement of New Hampshire's longtime conservative newspaper, the *Union-Leader*, which instead endorsed libertarian candidate Gary Johnson. "People didn't like that," Hedstrom said. "They said they were for Trump. It was the establishment against the people. The establishment was out of touch. They didn't see the despair of people due to the drug problem, and the despair of rural residents." Still, Hedstrom said New Hampshire remains a toss-up, and she laughed about Bernie Sanders's son Levi, who came over from Vermont to run in New Hampshire's first congressional district. Levi didn't do well in New Hampshire.

I asked Hedstrom if her Sanctity of Life group had done any work on immigration, in light of the border separation crisis and the Catholic Church's advocacy for refugees. Like other conservative Catholics I interviewed in New Hampshire, Hedstrom dodged the question. Immigration "is a complex issue," she said. "It was too hard, so I focused on abortion."

For Catholics who are also seniors and living outside America's major urban areas, all the change of modern life can feel overwhelming. The twenty-four-hour news cycle can also feel overwhelming, and it's easy to see why people would be drawn to the deceptively simpler issue of abortion, especially when they're unlikely to experience an unplanned pregnancy themselves. I noticed this, too, when I asked Hedstrom about the confirmation battle over Kavanaugh, a Catholic who was accused of sexual assault as a teenager while attending an elite Catholic prep school in Washington, DC. "I couldn't believe the way they treated him," Hedstrom said. "I thought the news media was just horrible. I had to rely on [Catholic channel] EWTN, because it's more peaceful. I didn't like that they joked about it on *Saturday Night Live*, and I didn't agree with the behavior of people on the [Senate Judiciary Committee]."

I noticed that efforts, like *Saturday Night Live* skits, that may appeal to younger, more liberal voters are often a turnoff to older Christian conservatives, who might otherwise be empathetic to victims of sexual assault. Hedstrom had trouble weighing the sexual assault accusations against Kavanaugh when the sexual abuse crisis within the Catholic Church itself was so much more horrific. Hedstrom said that for a while she had been bothered in her faith by the clergy abuse crisis, and she'd signed petitions to Pope Francis to "get a handle on it." She said to me, "I spoke to my confessor, too. I'm more at peace now. I don't come to the Mass for the priest. They aren't all wrong, but [the crisis] makes all priests look bad. The Catholic Church has gone through all kinds of horrible things, and it has survived. Still that doesn't make it right. We are in the present now, and we have to fix it."

While Hedstrom didn't explicitly note the conservative theory that homosexuality in the priesthood exacerbated and led to the clergy sex abuse crisis, she did move from talking about the crisis to talking about how "some people in the Catholic Church want the whole LGBTQ in the church now." She continued, "They say we have to be compassionate and accept it all. We do have to be compassionate, but I don't think we should accept acting that way. Sin is about the behavior, and that behavior is not acceptable. The pope is telling [priests and clerical leadership] that they have to resign. When we have to hold together, instead people are leaving and leaving the church altogether. Satan is destroying the church, and the shepherds are leaving instead of guarding the sheep."

I asked Hedstrom what she thinks of Pope Francis. "I think he is a holy man, but he comes from, you might say, a socialist country. Socialism has no place in the church."

I noted the ways in which our conversation moved quickly from Hedstrom's loving and peaceful advocacy for life in all its forms to repeating familiar conservative Christian tropes about socialism and the degrading effects of accepting people who are gay into the church. I wondered if, without the influence of conservative media, Hedstrom might think differently. After all, she had benefited from a more liberal understanding of divorce and the ability to remarry in the Catholic Church. Was it so easy to draw the lines of exclusion?

As our conversation ended, Hedstrom told me more about what she'd seen online—about protesters being paid as part of Antifa during the Kavanaugh confirmation trial and messages that the Women's March was all about Planned Parenthood. "My sister says that's not true, but it is. I can't convince my family."

I noticed the ways that conservative media and right-wing Catholic theology such as that espoused by Father Pavone were moving Hedstrom further from her family and putting her at odds with them. I could see the corrosive effect of conservative media. I was surprised to find that, for Hedstrom, a devout Catholic for decades, conservative media proved even more trustworthy than the Holy Father.

A Priest Testifies

Christ the King, where I attended Mass the following Sunday morning, and Immaculate Heart of Mary, where I met Hedstrom on Saturday night, are sister parishes in the town of Concord, New Hampshire. Christ the King was the result of the merger of three neighborhood parishes in 2011, and Father Richard Roberge, known locally as Father Rich, had been tasked with bringing this new community to life.

While the two parishes have much in common, I felt a significantly different energy at Christ the King Sunday morning than I felt at Immaculate Heart of Mary on Saturday night. This may have just been the result of a typical Saturday-versus-Sunday divide, but I noticed at Christ the King the increased presence of young children, families, and a spirit of openness to outsiders. Much of this was surely due to the irrepressible energy and optimism of Roberge.

I had entered this research trip with a fair amount of trepidation. Many of the well-known Evangelical pastors and leaders I'd spoken to in the past had been hard to track down, but I feared that speaking to a Catholic priest, operating in an institution known for secrecy and hesitancy to speak outside official parameters, could prove even more difficult. I'd already been turned down for a visit to a local conservative Catholic college.

Still, as I listened to Roberge preach and lead worship, I grew bolder in my desire to speak with him. Catholic priests, of course, have had great influence and power not only in American Catholic communities but also in American government, gaining the ear of politicians who were eager to earn Catholic votes and esteem. I knew a priest could help explain the phenomenon of, especially, white Catholic support for Trump and the burgeoning conservative Catholic movement in the Church that was challenging even the pope. A priest, situated in a seat of honor but also suspicion, would likely have a unique perspective to offer.

Like his priestly colleague the night before, Roberge spoke earnestly about the power of suffering in bringing us closer to Jesus and lifting one another up. Yet Roberge was also earthy in a way I haven't often experienced in a Catholic Mass. His homily was peppered with colloquial language, and he even quoted Pope Francis in saying that "shepherds should smell like sheep" and that Christians should not be afraid to dwell with "the least of these." Roberge seemed a priest who desired to be accessible and relevant even to his young or doubting parishioners. He showed also a desire to be painfully honest, surprising me when, in the Eucharistic prayer before Communion, he prayed for "victims of physical, emotional, and sexual abuse." His words were a recognition of the great trauma of the Catholic Church, a repentance of sorts, and an effort to uncover what had formerly been hidden.

After the Mass, I went up to Roberge on the way out of the sanctuary and asked if I could talk with him for a moment. "Sure," he said, after a moment's pause. "Let me take off my robes, and I'll meet you in the family room."

Unrobed, wearing a black clerical shirt, in a dated room behind the sanctuary where the altar boys had first gone to change after church, Roberge told me his own story of New England Catholicism and national politics. He had grown up not far from Concord, in rural Berlin, New Hampshire, an old mill town less than sixty miles from the Canadian border and closer to Montreal than to Boston. Most people in Berlin were descended from French Canadian roots, and over half of them speak a version of French called "Berlin French."

His earliest memories involve the death of his father, a poor Canadian laborer who died when Roberge was three, and the day after his father's death, when his youngest sister, Emilie, was born. Roberge's mother had five children in all, and she kept all the kids in Catholic school, even when they struggled to survive. The birth of his sister so quickly after the death of his father ingrained in Roberge at an early age the power of resurrection, and he was a child of deep faith. Even as he struggled to read, facing dyslexia and learning disabilities, he felt compelled beyond himself to be a priest. He threw himself into education, graduating from New Hampshire's Saint Anselm College, which famously hosts presidential debates prior to the New Hampshire primary.

After finishing seminary, in his first assignment as a priest, Roberge found out he had to preach at a rural parish in both English and French. He was terrified, and a local nun had to help him translate while he haltingly preached in French that Sunday morning. After the Mass, a woman came up to him. She said she recognized his last name, and she asked if he was from Berlin. "My husband was your father's best friend," she told Roberge. "He is dying. Will you come and visit him?" When Roberge came to their house, the dying man spoke to him with tear-filled eyes. "You are the answer to your father's promise," he told Roberge, who had never met the man or his wife before. The couple told Roberge that his father had wanted to be a priest, but his small Canadian town had no Catholic school and, his local priest said, no money to send him to one. So Roberge's father promised God that one of his children would be a priest.

This sense of divine calling has shaped Roberge's entire life, he told me. He was filled with a powerful sense of mission, both in his role as a parish priest and his role as a messenger of Jesus. As a result, Roberge, the priest of Christ the King in 2018, runs on pure adrenaline. If I squinted and listened to him talk about his plans for evangelism and renewal, I could conjure a similar small-town Southern Baptist church planter in Alabama, filled with missionary zeal.

Despite his energy and optimism, Roberge was not immune from the problems in the wider Catholic Church, especially the clergy sexual abuse crisis. He said that in his opinion, most of the problems with the Catholic Church abuse crisis are in the past, though they're only being uncovered now. He said the leadership of the church is working hard to clean up its act and end the crisis, and the conservative argument that homosexuality in the priesthood was the reason for clergy sexual abuse is "bunk" and "ludicrous." Catholic conservatives, he said, "are trying to dredge up more dirt because it fits their agenda. You'd have to be dumb not to realize there were lesbians in the convents and homosexual priests in the priesthood. If you are Catholic and gay, there aren't many other options. But the problem is not homosexuality; it is the schizophrenic culture. We've made sex and drugs recreational. That's the problem. You hear it all the time."

In a parish where brochures for families suffering the effects of the opioid crisis languish next to brochures for women facing unplanned pregnancies, you can see where drug abuse and more liberal sexual attitudes have led to difficulties in New Hampshire families. Roberge told me the opioid crisis in New Hampshire has not been overblown. "It's real. It's all that and more. I see it in my parishioners and their families," he said, describing a spiritually adopted son of his who was facing life in prison for selling drugs to feed his own habit. "He overdosed more than once, and unfortunately he has had a really difficult life. But I don't think there's a serious motivation to help the opioid crisis on the part of the government. Our state prisons are building up, but all the government talk about treatment clinics is a fake. They aren't hiring anyone. There's no counselors, no detox, no beds for people to stay. I see the addicts in jail, and they have nothing."

Roberge's compassion is great, and even as he tells me his offbeat worries about hormone-based birth control and male attraction to women, I generally find him to be refreshing and a welcome source of spirituality in a church that has historically been more focused on tradition than needed change. But even Roberge was at a loss when we talked about the problems facing Catholic clergy: a large clergy shortage, the inability to have families, the lack of acceptance for the

LGBTQ community. "Maybe we need to look at the celibacy of the priesthood," he said. "But my sister is married to a Baptist pastor, and he says sometimes the family suffers in ministry."

Even for Catholics, who have generally seen slower decline than mainline Protestants, there aren't easy answers. The past strength of the Catholic Church, even in America, has been its uncanny ability to prioritize unity over division. As American Protestants are quick to divide over relatively minor doctrinal issues, Catholics of a wide variety of theological and social viewpoints managed to stay together under the banner of the church. That unity today stands on shakier ground, and I noticed the divide and difference when I asked Roberge, a relatively progressive priest, about Pope Francis. In contrast to other, more conservative Catholics, Roberge didn't mention socialism or the clergy sexual abuse crisis. Instead, he praised Pope Francis for many of the places the pope has broken with Trump and with Republican Catholics.

"He cares for the poor and for the environment," Roberge said of Pope Francis. "The church is not capitalism. Capitalism is OK, but it's not the church . . . and some things in the church are socialism, like taking care of each other and feeding each other. When I hear Catholic politicians talk about health care and education, I don't think they are being honest. We need more outreach to people who are on the fringes and falling apart. And I don't think pro-life is going to be won in court. Some conservative Catholics and Evangelicals have gotten lost, and they don't think about pro-life issues beyond the womb. They're blind to all the pro-life issues. Addiction is a pro-life issue. Immigration is a pro-life issue. When people start to understand the sanctity of life, then the country will become pro-life. It won't happen because we are cramming in people with certain political viewpoints. It won't come by legislation."

When the conversation turned to Trump, Roberge was apoplectic. "Look at who we have running our country now. He is a billionaire with no moral compass. For the election, I just told people to look at all the issues. Trump said he had nothing for which he had to be forgiven. That guy has no conscience. I spoke out strongly against the family separations at the border. No government has the right to tear families apart."

Roberge said he was surprised by the amount of pushback he got from Trump supporters in the parish when he mentioned immigration. "They were angry I didn't support Trump," he said. At that, I wondered if I had overestimated the influence of local Catholic parish priests relative to conservative Catholic media and politics.

Educating the Conservative Catholic Elite

After spending Sunday night in coastal Portsmouth, New Hampshire, just south of Kennebunkport, Maine, I drove back into New Hampshire's rural and mountain heart, taking a wrong turn north toward Manchester before heading back east to quaint Merrimack. Less than sixty miles from Boston and home to picturesque New England winding roads and well-maintained colonial homes, Merrimack is an unlikely home for the conservative Catholic movement. I wondered if I was lost on a wild goose chase here, as I wound down a rural road past a strip mall, to a tiny sign and a gravel road, where Google Maps said to turn left.

When I arrived at what my map said was the destination, I looked for signs for the office of admissions, but all I saw was a small cluster of well-maintained older homes functioning as classrooms and dormitories, none of which had signs. I drove back out to the main road to ensure that the sign did indeed say Thomas More College.

I drove to the other end of the road and parked near a pickup truck with a Virginia license plate. I decided to leave; although I had spoken to someone at the college the previous week, she had never emailed me back to finalize a tour and interview. Just then, I heard a voice behind my car.

"Are you Angela?" A young man in a brown leather blazer and dress pants, with black-framed glasses and a haircut that reminded me of the "fashy" styles I'd seen on pastors at the River at Tampa Bay Church, was standing beside my door. His name was Dominic Cassella, and he had graduated from Thomas More the previous spring. When I asked him what he studied, he laughed. "We only have one major," he said. "Liberal arts."

It might be the only time the word *liberal* is used in a positive sense at Thomas More. When I had told Roberge that I planned to come here, he said the school is much more conservative than other local Catholic universities. "Most of the students are homeschooled," he said. "Their parents didn't think the parochial schools were conservative or Catholic enough."

Cassella, age twenty-three, said that wasn't the case for him. The oldest of six children, he was homeschooled until his freshman year but then graduated from a Washington, DC–area Catholic high school. It wasn't Georgetown Prep, the school made infamous for drinking and partying in Justice Kavanaugh's confirmation hearing, but Cassella did say he has friends who went there. Cassella originally had his sights set on the University of Virginia, until his best friend from high school attended Thomas More and convinced Cassella to join him. "It took some convincing for my dad," said Cassella, whose father is an engineer and a Princeton grad. "He didn't want me to go here at first. But now that he's seen the education, he wants all his kids to go here."

Cassella pointed out that the two nearby buildings were dormitories, one each for men and women. "Girls aren't allowed in boys' dorms, and boys aren't allowed in girls' dorms," Cassella said. "The atmosphere for dating here is good." He should know. Cassella met his wife, Carley, here, and he said seven people were married out of last year's graduating class of thirty, all of them to other Thomas More students.

The atmosphere here was strikingly different from the partying, hookup-friendly, alcohol-centered atmosphere at many of America's college campuses. It was easy to see how a place like this—far removed from the worries that plague many parents of college students—would attract conservative Christian families. "There is no drinking here," Cassella said. "We spend a lot of time having great conversation. Coming here has had a very large role in developing my Catholic faith. We focus on personal formation of the whole person. We learn virtues and practices. And it's really important to have a peer group that supports you."

He said not all students are Catholic: "There are some agnostic students. We did have a few Protestants, but I think they've converted."

Despite its tiny campus and small enrollment, Thomas More has a global footprint. All students spend three months of their sophomore year at the Rome program, where they share a campus full of olive groves with a group of Maronite monks. Students come to Thomas More from all over the world, Cassella said—from Brazil, the United Kingdom, Canada, and at least twenty-seven states.

The whole campus of Thomas More and its culture are oddly rooted in an ostensibly idyllic past while focused on shaping America's future. Cassella himself is personable, approachable, and polite. He introduced me to students, including a few young women, who were uniformly pretty, greeted me with a constant smile, and were all wearing skirts. Cassella had an almost European sophistication. He told me about the quality espresso served in the dining hall, introduced me to a chef, and offered me a sip of aromatic lemon-ginger tea. He told me about required courses on woodworking, sculpting, and art history. He said that in addition to reading classic literature like Aquinas, Aristotle, Cicero, and Augustine, Thomas More students read the whole Bible in their first year of college.

As we walked into the airy library, filled with well-dressed students reading quietly, the wide windows reflecting in the autumn light of maple groves outside the door, Cassella told me that the whole focus of Thomas More College is about free thinking and the value of thought. He said these are no longer liberal but conservative values—echoing the viewpoints of right-wing and conservative media outlets, which sometimes push the boundaries of what other media consider to be racist, sexist, or homophobic. "Today, if you want to be freethinking and value thought, you are a conservative," Cassella said. "You saw during the Kavanaugh trial that the left wing does not allow for free thought or freedom of the individual. . . . The Left no longer tolerates any idea except its own."

Cassella referred derisively to Biden and Pelosi, standard bearers for Catholics in American politics. "I mean, it's almost not worth mentioning [that they're Catholic]," Cassella said, shaking his head.

When I ventured to ask about Trump, whose boorishness is far removed from this prim and proper conservative Catholic environment, Cassella was initially hesitant. "The question was, Can you morally support someone who is not a moral person?" He noted the "mistrust" rampant in the 2016 election, but he said allegiances at Thomas More quickly shifted to Trump. "It wasn't fifty-fifty," Cassella said. "The majority were supporting Trump. You saw a lot of MAGA hats. We all went to a Trump rally together in Manchester."

Cassella and his fellow students' support of Trump did echo the same sentiments of their Evangelical brethren in the South and the blue-collar Red State Christians of America's heartland and Appalachia. They fear their culture is being threatened. For the conservative Catholic families who send their children to Thomas More, the truths that have sustained their power are changing, and they're losing their grip on Western society. Much of that fear is about changes in acceptable family structures and increased racial diversity, about the loss of absolute truth and what that means for a church that has been dependent on hierarchy and obedience.

Like many conservative Catholics, Cassella had more criticism for Pope Francis and Catholic hierarchy than he did for Trump. "The church is supposed to be the protector of families, and it's not doing that," he said. "We are fighting an internal battle right now. We have to have respect for families and defend families. It's painful to hear about the divide in the church, but Christ put Judas in the church for reason. He betrayed the church, and there will be more Judases in the church to come. The only solace is prayer."

Cassella said he believes homosexuality in the priesthood led to the clergy sexual-abuse crisis. "I have friends who joined the seminary and left because of what was going on. It made them sick," Cassella said, referencing seminary culture in the 1960s and '70s. "I have friends in seminary now, and they haven't said anything. I think it's getting better. But it's something people don't like to talk about."

I asked Cassella about Roberge's comments about gay priests and lesbian nuns—that because of their celibacy, they were welcomed into religious life. Cassella looked at me quizzically, at a loss for words for the first time in our walk around campus together. "Well, I don't know if [gay men] can be priests," he responded. "You want a naturally ordered man for the priesthood. [Gay men] need help. They should not be in the position of helping others."

For the first time, I clearly saw Cassella's handsome mask lifted and exposed for what lay beneath: a hatred of the other that is covered thinly by a well-practiced veneer of politeness and talk of "Western" culture. The idea that a gay man is not "naturally ordered" is not often expressed publicly in American culture, but Cassella said it without hesitation or shame.

Unsurprisingly, then, Cassella said Pope Francis has been a disappointment. When asked about the pope's advocacy for the poor, Cassella spoke at length about economic policy, saying it is "necessary and sufficient for a man to provide for his family." He said, "Greed is not good, but neither is abolishing property rights. Catholics who are socialists—it's just a confusion. Nobody has explained it to them well enough."

Listening to Cassella talk about theory and classical literature reminded me of myself after taking introductory ethics courses as an undergraduate or later when I was studying Greek philosophy and the New Testament in seminary. His sentences were peppered with academic phrases, but his Catholic heart had gotten lost in his Western brain. The idea of empathy or vicarious sacrifice did not find purchase. He was, as many young people are, taken in by rhetoric and the purity of the mind. It's easy to imagine Cassella's ideas softening as he ages. But if he continues to be surrounded only by conservative Catholic culture, and if he is afraid of anything that threatens his cultural identity, that softening is less likely.

Instead of describing partnerships between the school and more liberal Catholics, Cassella mentioned partnerships with conservative Evangelicals. He mentioned that five Thomas More students were selected as scholars for the Intercollegiate Studies Institute, which promotes conservative thought on college campuses. Cassella said he was no longer studying at Thomas More but was working with the Center for Restoration of Christian Culture, "promoting free education for people who can't afford it. We're offering free lectures around the country." This work is not purely altruistic; it's aimed at changing hearts and minds with conservative values.

As we walked back through the forest to the parking lot under the fall foliage, I said good-bye and thanked Cassella. He had been kind, patient, and open in his responses to my questions, and as I had been turned away from the other small conservative Catholic college in New Hampshire, I was especially grateful for the time Cassella had spent with me. Still, I felt uneasy. The campus was too pristine, too polished. The lemon tea and espresso couldn't cover up the disdain I heard for people who were gay; such amenities couldn't cover up the odd division of the sexes, the latent traditional gender roles that must stifle Thomas More's female students.

I was aware, too, that as a middle-class, married white woman and mother of two, I could be considered a friend of Thomas More's. Being accepted there was easy for me. For an afternoon, I could be considered one of them, though their acceptance would likely be short-lived.

Driving down the dirt road out of Merrimack, I kept thinking about the odd sterility of Thomas More's campus. It felt innocuous and strangely perfect—peaceful. I realized later what Thomas More and Cassella had reminded me of: the pristine, shimmering gardens of Hulu's breakout show about a conservative Christian takeover of America, The Handmaid's Tale. On the show, modeled after Margaret Atwood's book of the same name, unmarried women of childbearing age are forced to live as handmaids in the homes of the married, though sterile, conservative Christian elite. Once a month or so, when they're fertile, the handmaids are systematically raped in a religious ceremony pulled, in a twisted way, from the Old Testament. The male leaders of this nation, called Gilead, support their barbaric practices with sophisticated thought and analysis. They're temperate and well dressed, well organized and murderous, intolerant of any dissent.

I wondered what version of Gilead would be ideal for Thomas More's students and leadership, and I wondered what success they would have in sharing their vision more widely. As long as Trump is president, they'll have ample opportunity to promote their intolerance.

I wondered what the Catholic Savior would say about it all— the one who suffered and died meekly on the cross for a forgiveness rooted not in Western thought but in ancient love.

CHAPTER 11

Red State Arabs: Christians, Muslims, and Evangelicals in Houston

I sat in a SuperShuttle on my way to Los Angeles International Airport outside South LA in April 2017, whizzing past signs for Compton, Hawthorne, and Crenshaw Boulevard. The highway stretched fourteen lanes across at some points, filled with white, black, and brown Americans in a postracial Southern California melting pot. Sure, Donald Trump was president, but here in Los Angeles, where whites are the minority and Republicans are, too, Trump felt far away.

My SuperShuttle itself was a sign of America's future: the promise of immigrants and American dreams come true. The other passenger was Filipino. He had been in America working for ten years to gather up enough money to go home and bring his wife and two sons to America with him. His absence from his family had pained him so much that he had his wife install cameras inside their home in the Philippines, so he could log in and watch his family at any time.

Sometimes, his teenage son was absent when he was supposed to be at home, doing homework. Dad saw it and reprimanded his son later. But this morning, he was ebullient. Finally he was returning to the Philippines to bring his family back with him. He had done it. He was an immigrant success story. He was rescuing his family, I imagined, from the violent mobs of Philippine president Rodrigo Duterte. Elected six months before Trump, Duterte sanctioned the murder of drug dealers and users, killing more than seven thousand people by January 2017, when the government stopped recording data. I asked my shuttle-mate about Duterte. He hedged. "I think it's good," he said. "The drug dealers are destroying my community; they need to be punished."

Thus began my liberal education about immigrants, brown American Christians, and Trump, which was picked up by my Iraqi Christian driver. "Trump is the only choice," he said. "He is the only one who will beat ISIS. There is no other choice."

Understanding Arab American Christians

The idea that Arab Americans, or any brown-skinned Americans, would support Trump was unfathomable to paternalistic white liberals and inconsistent with their views on immigrants, many of whom are Christian and coming from Muslim-majority nations especially in the Middle East and the Arab world. Trump slandered Muslims and bowed before Israel and Saudi Arabia, ignoring the plight of the Palestinians and instituting a travel ban against people from Iran, Iraq, Libya, Somalia, Sudan, Syria, and Yemen just a week after taking office. Like Hillary Clinton, who lost Arab American–majority districts in Michigan to Bernie Sanders two-to-one, many white progressives fail to understand Arab Americans, particularly Arab American

Christians, who likely still outnumber Arab American Muslims in the United States. Census data from 2000 show Arab American Christians making up 63 percent of Arab Americans, compared with Muslims at 24 percent.[1]

In examining the Red State Christians who supported Trump, it would be neglectful and shortsighted to ignore Arab American Christians, particularly those living in red states. Arab Americans hold the keys to the birthplace of Christianity. Jesus was Middle Eastern. Maybe Middle Eastern and Arab Christians are best suited to bridge the divides between Christians in America today. Arab Christians, in America and the Middle East, have given up more to follow Jesus than most American Evangelicals. Risking it all, they cling to a faith that has led them to centuries of persecution and disenfranchisement, forcing many to flee their homelands. Although Arab Christians tend to be more affluent than their Muslim peers in the Middle East, Lebanon is the only Middle Eastern country where Christians have real power in the government, so Christians in the Middle East frequently face harassment, persecution, and even death because of their religion. Egypt is among the most perilous countries for Christians, with frequent bombings of Coptic Christian churches and forced conversions of Coptic Christian women, which have increased after the Arab Spring revolution and subsequent military rule in Egypt.

Arab American Christians may not have been Trump's target audience on November 12, 2015, in Fort Dodge, Iowa, when he told a campaign crowd, "I would bomb the shit out of [ISIS]. I would just bomb those suckers. And that's right. . . . I'd blow up the pipes. I'd blow up the refineries. I'd blow up every single inch. And you know what? You'll get Exxon to come in there. They'll build that sucker brand new, and I'd rig it, and I'd take the oil."[2] Most of Trump's Iowa audience wasn't Arab, but Arab Americans tuned in to Trump nonetheless.

They wanted to beat ISIS even more than he did. Their friends and countrymen and -women were terrorized by ISIS, bludgeoned to death for having beards too short or not memorizing the Qur'an or not wearing the proper headscarf. Their children were murdered on mountains and left to starve in abandoned towns, with black flags waving from the tops of poles in homes where Christians used to live.

Issa Kabar, a Jordanian Evangelical Christian, immigrated to the United States in 2017. His grandfather was a Palestinian from Bethlehem, but Issa has never been allowed to travel there because of the Israeli annexation of the West Bank. He said he went once as a baby and then never again. Still, for Kabar, extremist Muslims have posed a greater threat to Arab Christians than Israel has. "In the Middle East, you have three choices," he said. "You can be a Muslim, you can pay very high taxes, or you can be killed. That's it."

In light of such stark choices, Democratic rhetoric about Islam as a peaceful religion fell on deaf ears among Arab American Christians, and many of them, particularly those I spoke to in red states, voted for Trump, despite his anti-Palestinian and anti-immigration rhetoric. "We thought Trump would take this country to the next level," Kabar told me, a year into Trump's presidency. "I thought what made America great, greater than any other country, was that two hundred years ago, it was based on the Christian faith. But [politicians] keep pushing God away."

Speaking at the Arabic Church of Houston, where he is associate pastor, Kabar was resigned—clear in his faith but uncertain of his politics. He says he is not fully Americanized yet: "You cannot live like the Middle East here." And Kabar said that disappointment in Trump is widespread in Houston. "There is disappointment all over. The disappointment is not just for Middle Eastern Christians. Nobody can keep promises. But it will all come out as God's will."

The Arab Americans of Houston, Texas

In the 2000 US Census, just ten states had Arab American populations of more than forty thousand. Only one of those states was consistently red: Texas. And just one city in Texas boasts a significant Arab American population: Houston, the fourth-largest American city and one of the largest minority-majority cities in the country. As of 2010, just 25 percent of Houstonians were non-Hispanic whites, with 44 percent Hispanic or Latino of any race, 26 percent African American, and 6 percent Asian. Those nonwhite percentages have gone up in the decade since the last census, when Houston was already the most racially and ethnically diverse major metropolis in the country, surpassing New York. Houston's Muslim population also is growing: as of 2012, Houston had the largest Muslim population in the southern United States.[3]

Houston's population is predominately Evangelical Christian, with 73 percent of Houstonians claiming to actively practice their Christian faith—50 percent telling the Pew Research Center they attend Protestant churches, and 19 percent Catholic churches.[4] Five of the country's largest megachurches call Houston home. If you want to understand nonwhite Evangelical Christians who likely consider themselves conservative but may not adhere to strict partisan beliefs, Houston is the place to go. It's also a great place to get a glimpse into Trumpism, Evangelicals, and Arab Americans, as well as the surprising ways people break out of the boxes we put them into.

If Houston is the future of Red State America, Jeannette Lahoud is a face of that future. I met Jeannette in Missouri City, Texas, just outside Houston, on a sunny Sunday morning in April 2018. It turned out I'd already met her uncle, Issam, and her mother, Jacqueline, a couple of nights earlier at an Arabic-language Bible study, where a

Presbyterian Egyptian immigrant parishioner named Hend stood in the back of the church and painstakingly translated the entire study for me through headphones. I found the whole experience remarkable. Here I was, a white-bread midwestern Lutheran woman, in one of the reddest states in America, surrounded by Arab Americans studying the Bible in Arabic. For the many Americans who associate Arabic with the Islamic State and terrorists screaming "Allahu Akbar" before blowing themselves up, this Bible study was a humbling reminder that Jesus was not a white European but rather a Palestinian Jewish man who spoke Aramaic, a precursor to Arabic and a derivation of Hebrew.

I came to Houston specifically to visit this church, unique among American churches both for its language and its style. Most Arab American churches reflect the Orthodox traditions of Middle Eastern countries, steeped in tradition and ritual. But the Arabic Church of Houston is different. While the Friday-night Bible study and Sunday-noon services were both in Arabic and attended primarily by middle-aged Arab American immigrants from Middle Eastern countries, the congregation is also decidedly Evangelical, both in style and practice. For all Arabic services, live translation is readily available. The church also boasts an equal number of English-language services and studies, with English-only retreats and music. Most members of the church consider themselves not just Christian but Evangelical, as well as politically conservative, though as Hend pointed out to me, "Arabs are diverse. We don't all agree on anything!"

The Arabic Church of Houston is a member of the Baptist General Conference of Texas, the oldest surviving Baptist convention in Texas, which partners with the Southern Baptists and the Cooperative Baptist Fellowship, among others, on mission support. The BGCT is considered politically moderate, differing with the SBC on issues such as biblical inerrancy and women in ministry. However, the

BGCT does not make official statements on doctrine, so diversity exists among individual congregations. I spoke with Pastor Issa a few weeks before coming to Houston, and his openness to me as a female pastor was a sign to me that this church was slightly more moderate than many of its Evangelical counterparts in Texas.

Of his church, Pastor Issa said to me, "We are definitely not liberal. We are not exactly conservative. We are in the middle. We are multidenominational. We believe that salvation is only by Jesus Christ obtained only through faith. Our faith is clear, but we don't talk much about doctrine, and we are not controversial." In Jordan, Pastor Issa had been baptized as a baby into the Greek Orthodox Church. Many Arab Christians are officially Greek Orthodox, despite the fact that their churches originate in the Middle East. Issa began attending an Evangelical church at age fourteen. "When I got saved is when I came to know Jesus," he said. "At fourteen years old, I knew Jesus Christ as my Savior." The phrases Issa used are trademark American Evangelical, yet they originate in a place just miles from Jesus's birthplace.

Issa said Texas reminds him of the Middle East in one way beyond the hot climate: "I love the Evangelical churches here," he told me. "In Texas, they have a big heart for giving and for helping. They have open and loving hearts." The world at large does not always view Evangelicals this way, but Issa's words ring true in Houston, where faith communities of all backgrounds came together in August 2017 to clean up after floods of biblical proportions devastated homes and families all over Houston.

These groups included Houston-area Muslims, whom I met just over four miles away in Stafford, Texas, in the corner of southwestern Houston that is home to many of the city's Arab Americans. The parking lot was packed for Friday prayers, and as I drove up, I saw that the mosque was next door to Everest Academy, a private Islamic school established in 2007 for students from pre-kindergarten to eighth grade. Together the school and mosque make up more than fifty thousand square feet of property.

The campus looks modern, but the prayer service is a mix of ancient and contemporary. As is customary at Islamic prayer services, men and women worship in separate rooms, with the imam's sermon simulcast on a screen in the women's room. Those attending the women's gathering range from young girls under age five to elderly women, all of whom are wearing head scarves, as prescribed on the doors. However, few of them wear the long, flowing abaya robe prescribed in Saudi Arabia, though all are dressed conservatively, many in long skirts and dresses. I listen as Imam Sheikh Syed talks repeatedly and at length about global politics and personal faith. He repeatedly uses the word *mujahid*, which means warrior. Non-Arab-speaking Americans might be familiar with the term *mujahideen*, which was first widely used in English during the Soviet-Afghan War of 1979–89, when Americans cheered the brave Islamic warriors for defeating the evil Communist empire. Today, the word *mujahid* connotes a more negative image, especially in light of global jihadist terrorist acts. Nonetheless, Imam Syed uses it in the sense of being a warrior for faith, a warrior for God in peace and not in violence. The imam speaks about Syria, the Gaza Strip, and Palestine. The problems of the Middle East loom larger here than in white Christian America. Then, abruptly, he changes tack: "We want to be people who give more than we receive from anyone else. We want to be the *mujahid*. We want to have our own plan."

The plan involves something strikingly different from the terrorism and isolation often associated with American Muslim communities: "We are having an open house coming up on April 28. Some people think that if there are non-Muslims, we need to have toughness against them. But that's not what the book [the Qur'an] says. There is a time for toughness, but now is not that time. God started the book by saying that God is the God of all people. We have to come together. Don't become like the people who would gas children [in reference to chemical weapons used in Syria in 2018]. We should invite all to come and share stories with them. It's not just about us, but about all of us."

I was curious about the relationship between Muslim and Christian Arab Americans in Houston. I found out later that the Arabic Church of Houston would be attending the mosque's open house. Pastor Issa said that the Arabic Church often works with refugees, particularly from Middle Eastern countries, because they share the same language. He pointed out that the couch we sat on that day in the church was new because the previous one had been given to a refugee family from Iraq.

"Most of them are Muslims," Issa said. "We have about five families who have converted, and some of them who haven't still attend church here. In the Middle East, you can be killed for leaving Islam. But here they can ask questions, and they do." I sense an internal religious tension between the Arab American Christians and American Muslims, and Issa said it goes back to the Middle East. "We love Muslims, but we are against Islam as an ideology," Issa said. "The refugees we take in, they say, 'Why are you doing this? We are killing you in the Middle East.'"

In America we have hope for reconciliation, though Issa told me later that American liberals are naive about the persecution wrought by Islamic leadership in the Middle East. Still, what both Arab American Muslims and Arab American Christians share is an American patriotism that blurs religious lines. In a survey by the Pew Research Center, 92 percent of American Muslims said they're proud to be

American, and 70 percent professed faith in the American dream, saying most people who want to get ahead can make it in America if they are willing to work hard.[5]

In his sermon on the day I visited the Masjid Sabireen Mosque, Imam Syed ended on a progressive note, explaining what he wants the rest of America to know about his faith community: "American Muslims are the most ethnically diverse community in America. We can be together. We need to be proud of that. Seventy-three percent of our women have post-high-school degrees. Women are more likely than men to have post-high-school degrees. We need to celebrate that and share that!"

As proof of these statements, Imam Syed introduced Farha Ahmed, a local lawyer who was running for city council in nearby Sugarland, Texas. Standing in the men's prayer room and speaking to the assembled crowd, she said, "I want my kids to be proud that they're Americans. I want them to know that this country belongs to them as much as everyone else. I don't want them ever to be ashamed of their faith or their culture." I found it curious that, here in this sexually segregated mosque in Texas, I heard an imam champion women's education and gender equality and lift up a female lawyer and candidate for public office. These sentiments were not ones I'd often heard expressed or practiced in my worship experiences at Evangelical Christian churches.

The imam's desire for dialogue and reconciliation with his non-Muslim surrounding community was not an abstract desire but a safety concern. Javed Malik, the mosque's director, told me that just two weeks before this prayer service, the local police had notified the mosque of a security threat. An outside group wanted to come and protest in front of the mosque, and this being Texas, they wanted to protest while carrying guns.

"Nothing came of it," said Malik, a native of Pakistan who has been an American citizen since 1988 and works as a structural engineering manager. "But we have an excellent relationship with the churches and faith communities near us. The synagogue was the first to call us and offer support after the threat was made." Malik recounted 2017's Hurricane Harvey as a time when all faith groups of Houston came together.

In a different way than other large American cities such as New York or Los Angeles, Houston is self-consciously faith based, anchored not only by white Evangelical Christians and Latino Catholics and Evangelicals, but also by ethnic faith groups, including the Muslims at Masjid Sabireen plus Jews and Sikhs and Hindus, all of whom banded together to save flood victims. Harvey's shadow was still long when I visited. As Pastor John Gray had said earlier that Sunday morning at Joel Osteen's Lakewood Church, "When it all goes down, you have to fight for people who aren't like you. Remember Hurricane Harvey? Nobody who had a boat was, like, 'Are you saved?'" Or, I would add, "Are you Muslim?"

In light of the recent security threat, Houston's Muslim community doubled down on openness. The open house was a direct response to the protest threat. Malik, for his part, said he is more Texan than Pakistani, and he has three native-born Texan daughters and a native-born Texan grandchild. While Malik said he has noticed an increase in anti-Muslim sentiment since Trump's election, he also doesn't shy away from sharing his own conservatism. "Nobody was expecting Trump to win, even here," he said to me. "But I think the Evangelical Christians just really hated Hillary."

Malik said the challenge for Arab Christians and Muslims is to begin anew in America. He has worked with Arab Christians and says they've always had a good relationship. But Malik disagreed with

Kabar's assessment of the persecution faced by Christians in the Middle East, or at least with the viewpoint of Islam as dangerous. "Most of the negative opinions about us are based on wrong information. [Evangelical Christians] think we want to bring Sharia law. We don't. I hope for more dialogue and talking to each other. We are citizens, and this country was based on religious freedom. I think it will be a lot easier when we talk to each other more."

As for Trump, Malik was dismissive, saying the travel ban has not affected his community. "Trump is our president now. So we think of him—well, he is our leader."

Shedding Stereotypes

While data show that Arab American Christians still outnumber Arab American Muslims, the Christians I met at the Arabic Church of Houston all shared a similar, painful story of being mistaken for Muslims. They lamented that because of their brown skin, dark features, and native language, Americans assume they follow Islam, forgetting that Jesus shared that same brown skin, dark features, and a similar native language. Issa and Jeanette both told similar stories.

Issa recalled, "I met a guy the other day at a restaurant who said, 'You are speaking Arabic, and you're a Christian?'" The man was shocked, Issa remembered.

"I am from the Middle East," Issa replied.

"Were you a Muslim before?" the man asked.

"No. You forget that Christianity started in the Middle East," Issa told him. "Jesus was born in our backyard."

Jeannette Lahoud, a nineteen-year-old Evangelical Christian and drummer for the Arabic Church's worship band, told me she was mocked by a high-school teacher for saying she went to the Arabic Church. "All the time," Issa said. "People assume I am Muslim because I am Arab."

Their pain is an indictment of the shortsightedness and simplistic thinking of too many ethnic European, white, American-born Christians. While liberals often assume brown-skinned refugees are poverty-stricken invalids in need of saving and education, conservatives too often see them as radical Muslims in need of conversion. What we all need is to listen more. That's what I did that Sunday morning in Houston, following the advice of the Arabic Church's senior pastor, Dr. Issam Raad, a native of Lebanon and a noted doctor and researcher at the University of Texas M. D. Anderson Cancer Center. At Friday night's Bible study, translated from Arabic for me by Hend, Raam taught this lesson:

Avoid being prejudiced. Sometimes we are prejudiced in following people who consider everyone else the enemy. We are so zealous of our own beliefs that everyone else becomes the enemy. The Lord changed me so that I could see that I don't have any enemies. My heart is grieved even if someone is killed from an enemy nation. My father told me prejudice is like putting a blindfold over your eyes. We need to lose our prejudice, and don't be blind to the truth. People rally around the flag, and people follow some leaders blindly without criticizing what we are following. It is important to follow and examine. If we are too worried about our own position, we can fall into that same trap. When you think bad people are in control, God uses them. Think of Joseph. Don't lose heart. Things are not beyond hope.

The Biggest Church in Texas

With these words in mind, I started Sunday morning at Joel Osteen's Lakewood Church, the predominant Evangelical megachurch in Houston, with nearly sixty thousand parishioners worshiping every weekend in the former Compaq Center, former home to the NBA's Houston Rockets. Osteen is beloved around the world, responsible for thousands of baptisms and Christian conversions, one of which I was about to experience firsthand at the Arabic Church later that morning. Osteen is also often criticized for preaching the prosperity gospel, which suggests that giving money to the church and following Jesus will result in financial rewards for believers. It certainly worked out that way for Osteen, whose net worth was estimated to be between $40 million and $60 million.[6]

I didn't hear Osteen the morning I visited. Instead, I heard the final sermon from Pastor John Gray, Lakewood associate pastor and star of *The Book of John Gray*, a reality series on the Oprah Winfrey Network. Gray, an African American man, was one of Lakewood's most popular pastors and drew huge crowds for his Wednesday-night Bible studies before departing to lead Redemption Church in Greenville, South Carolina.

The crowd was predominately African American. I did hear some prosperity-style preaching from Joel Osteen's sister, Lisa Osteen Colmes, who introduced the collection of the offering by praying for well-paying jobs with full benefits, a worthy petition indeed. However, she also promised the crowd, "I believe this is going to be your best year financially. You're the best givers ever. I believe 2018 will be your best financial year yet, and God will bless you as you give."

Gray's sermon was devoid of political or doctrinal controversy, focused on discipleship and living as Jesus wanted people to live. He concluded by responding to Lakewood's critics who claimed the church was light on preaching sacrifice. Gray ended his tenure with a call to discipleship, sacrifice, and love of neighbor. On leaving Lakewood for a smaller church and community, Gray claimed a higher calling: "I don't care what it looks like to you or to anyone else. I'm not trying to build a career; I'm trying to be faithful to my God. If I'm gonna be like Jesus, I'm gonna have to die to personal ambition, to external validation. You think, 'Who wouldn't like Jesus?' Well, people didn't like him. He healed too many people. But he was not looking for the applause of some; he was looking for the applause of one."

"When it all goes down, you have to fight for people who aren't like you," Gray concluded. He had preached a curious sermon—a rejection of popularity and fame for a megachurch built on numbers, fame, and popularity.

The Converted Arab Muslim Charlatan

Lakewood Church and the Osteens' arms reach far into Houston and beyond, and I was about to meet one of the first Muslim converts of Joel's father, John Osteen. Or at least that was the story, although he had actually converted a few years before meeting the Osteens. Prior to Sunday morning's English-only service at the Arabic Church, I had been awed by the Christianity of the Arab Americans I'd met in Houston. Their faith was like a deep well, with reservoirs of resilience and fortitude to endure even the greatest suffering and persecution. When their voices rose up to sing a hymn, they sang as though their lives depended on it. They were singing because how could they not sing? They were singing because for centuries, they'd been the guardians of the Holy Land, caught between a murderous battle for land and blood, pushed into corners in Lebanon and Bethlehem and Nazareth, protected by American Christians with words rather than deeds, and forced away from their homes by the thousands, yet still they were faithful, resolute, even hopeful.

After visiting Lakewood on Sunday morning, I headed to the Arabic Church for the English-language service first. We began with worship music from Elevation and Bethel, megachurches in North Carolina and California. Surrounded by Arab American millennials, as well as African American men and women and a young white family, I was impressed by the service's diversity and quality music. Then I met my first Arab American prosperity gospel preacher. The day's guest preacher was Saleim Kahleh, the assistant minister for the Department of Student Life at Houston Baptist University, where he had earned a bachelor's in Christian studies and recreational sports.

Kahleh was born to Palestinian and Lebanese Muslim parents. He converted to Christianity as a teenager, having heard the gospel at a Christian coffeehouse. He then attended Houston Baptist, where he connected with John Osteen, who served as his spiritual mentor for nearly ten years. Kahleh was ordained by Lakewood Church, where he served as a volunteer minister and helped with baptisms. He told me that he had played softball with Joel Osteen, who performed the wedding of Kahleh and his wife, Melanie. Kahleh's life and ministry melded his Middle Eastern background with Evangelical, Osteen-esque glitz. Melanie is ten years younger than her husband, blond, and not of Middle Eastern background, though she did graduate from Houston Baptist. On Saleim's website, Melanie posts blogs about mission trips, but on her own website, she focuses on natural medicine, noting that she has given birth to six children without pain medication.

Not even pain medication could have prepared me for Kahleh's sermon that morning. He began by opening his Bible filled with Post-It notes, and he spent most of the sermon rummaging from Post-It to Post-It, trying to find the right verse. He employed a technique I'd seen used by Osteen, White, and other televangelists: "Turn to your neighbor and say . . ."

Kahleh's sermon began jarringly, as the song "The Lion and Lamb" finished with "Who can stop the Lord almighty?" Kahleh quipped, "Well, we can, I think." He moved on to his trademark illustration, involving three sheets—one black, one white, and one red. He asked for a volunteer to assist, and then he demonstrated, draping the white sheet around himself to represent God, the black sheet around the volunteer to represent sin, and the red over the black to represent blood. His demonstration was overly simplistic, but in retrospect, I could see how it would be helpful to introduce the basics of the gospel to a non-Christian audience. However, I could find no redemption for Kahleh's odd behavior or sayings, as he pantomimed, "Daddy God kissing on you," to his volunteer and said, "Obviously, there's levels in heaven." At one point, he searched his wallet for money, wondering aloud, "Did my bride take it all?" Later on, he pulled out a rope he said he'd bought that morning at Walmart. "This rope represents eternity, and the handle represents your life," Kahleh said. "What you do in this handle represents how you'll live for eternity. Some will be street cleaners because they barely got in, but hey, at least the streets are gold."

I wondered later if Kahleh really believed all he was saying. His bizarre message seemed at odds with his ministerial credentials in Houston. He had been in ministry for decades, at one time serving as the principal chaplain for the Houston Rockets, when members of the team asked him to witness to Hakeem Olajuwon. He must have had better material at some point.

As he wrapped up his sermon, he couldn't find the Post-It he wanted to end with, so he went with his own summary: "God is coming with rewards," he said. "Faith is salvation, but works

261

determines placement. We're gonna get more specific about the rewards next week."

When I talked to Kahleh after the service, he was overwhelmed, a little tired, but basically earnest and kind. He denied that the rewards he had mentioned would be financial, though it sure sounded like the prosperity gospel was alive and well in Houston. Luckily, the service ended on an upbeat note, with an invitation to a church retreat—and this being Texas, there would be skeet shooting.

The Christian Lebanese Drummer Girl

After the disappointment of Kahleh and his rewards-based preaching, I was glad to talk with Jeannette Lahoud following the Arabic-language service that Sunday morning. I'd spotted her during the English service, drumming in the corner, wearing a graphic T-shirt and skinny jeans, with wild brown curls that tumbled past her frank, though delicate face. Jeannette was nineteen, daughter of a former Lebanese rock star and drummer turned ExxonMobil executive who'd moved the family to Houston before Jeannette was born. She'd spent almost her entire life in Texas, with two short stints in Saudi Arabia and Dubai for her dad's work.

More than anyone I met in Houston that weekend, Jeannette represented for me the future of American Christianity. Her life as a second-generation American was marked by promise and loss. Her family had been wealthy due to her father's career, yet she had also known terror, agony, and debilitating grief. When she was three, the family was living in Saudi Arabia during a compound bombing that killed 39 people and wounded more than 160 outside Riyadh. Jeannette's family lived near the center of the devastation, and she said she watched buildings crumble while huddling behind a concrete wall. "It was like that wall right there," she said, pointing to the wall of the room we were in, about eight feet away. "We were on the other side, and the wall protected us. Everything was destroyed. We left immediately."

Jeannette's family had become Evangelical after her father's sister became an Evangelical Christian. Jeannette's parents had both come from Orthodox and conservative Christian families but had not been brought up with a personal faith. Initially, Jeannette said her father's family made fun of her aunt for her Evangelical views. But eventually, the whole family converted. Her father had been a pillar of the Arabic Church of Houston; her uncle is Senior Pastor Raad. Jeannette's world was shaken again in high school, when her dad contracted leukemia and died. During his battle with cancer, he kept a blog to keep friends and family updated on his health and his faith. He signed each note, "In His Grip," and after his death, the family received a note from a reader in Australia, also a leukemia patient, who said her faith had been renewed through reading Jeannette's dad's blog.

Jeannette told me she got her rhythm from her dad, but she got so much more, too: her confidence, her faith, her groundedness. "I was consistently looking to my dad for everything," she said. "And I didn't feel I had to be as close to God. To lose my father and the father figure in my life, I had to seek the Lord and have him fill the emptiness in my heart. I was forced to be dependent on God."

Hers is an Arab American Christian story—a story of loss, of faith forged in fortitude. Jeannette's story is also the story of a young Gen Z woman struggling to find her place in Red State Christian America. When we spoke in April 2018, Jeannette was a sophomore at the University of Houston, studying organic chemistry. She said she wanted to become a pharmacist, to help on medical missions led by her uncle to the Middle East. Like many second-generation Americans, and like many American Christian millennials today, Jeannette is caught in the middle. She says she is conservative but gets tongue-tied when asked about Evangelical Christian support of Trump. "I have some people in my life who support him, but that was earlier [when we thought he'd support Christians in the Middle East], and things have changed," she said. "I think they mostly support the Republican side of things. Politics stress me out. I have more of an American mind-set, because I was raised here. I am more moderate, but there is still the conservative side of me. [In the election,] we had Trump, who was very conservative, and Hillary, who was very liberal. I guess I go back to the conservative side."

Jeannette wrestles with the conservative social mandates of her faith and the friendships she has with people who exist outside the rules of her church. She gives an outlook and an explanation that is often absent from dialogue about the thought process of Red State Christians. "The country is changing," Jeannette said, bringing up progressive social issues. "It's becoming more liberal anyway. I thought with the conservative side, it would just change a little more slowly."

CHAPTER 12

On the Border:
Donald Trump and
Latinx Christians

"Build that wall!" The chant started quietly, in the background, as then-presidential candidate Donald Trump extolled the story of his supposed Border Patrol endorsement.

They've never endorsed a candidate for president ever in their history, and 16,500 Border Patrol agents endorsed me," Trump said.

Hushed chants. "Build that wall. Build that wall."

"We're told to just stand back and let them flow across like Swiss cheese," Trump continued. The crowd booed. "We're gonna build the wall. We have no choice. We have no choice." Cheers rose up.[1]

The chant was getting louder, carried now by a chorus of youngish-sounding male voices. "Build. That. Wall. Build. That. Wall." Trump half smiled, half grimaced. Straightened up his shoulders a little bit, then leaned forward as the chants got steadily louder. "Build that wall. Build that wall. Build that wall. Build that wall. *Build that wall.*" Trump looked pleased with himself as he stared into the crowd. He raised his arms out. Two thumbs, straight up—that old politician's gesture, repurposed for effect—and the California heat rose inside the Anaheim Convention Center, where 46 percent of the city's population is of Mexican descent and three people had been stabbed three months earlier during a February 2016 Ku Klux Klan rally.

Trump leaned forward, closer to the microphone, his shoulders slightly hunched, his lips pursed, his coiffure impressively unmoved. "BUILD THAT WALL! BUILD THAT WALL!" He gestured once more, then turned away, satisfied, as the crowd continued to chant. The chant was almost hypnotizing in its simplicity; the message boiled down to these three words, and only then would America be great again. You could imagine that if you were there, you'd want to join in. You'd leap in the air, shake your fist. Yes! BUILD THAT WALL!

Trump's other favorite rally chant involved a call and response. After "Build that wall," the crowd sufficiently whipped into a frenzy, Trump would smile that carny smile, his eyes would twinkle, and then he'd ask them: "Who's gonna pay for the wall?"

He pointed to the crowd, and they responded gleefully, "Mexico!"

"Who's gonna pay for the wall?"

"Mexico!"

"Who's gonna pay for the wall?"

"Mexico!"

They were having so much fun, more fun than at a Hillary Clinton rally or any church service anyone had been to recently. Even if you found it alarming, the sinister nature of the chant and the crowd was undermined somewhat by the ridiculousness of it all. Mexico's former president, Vicente Fox, was constantly trolling Trump on Twitter: "@ realDonaldTrump: I won't pay for that f*cking wall!" It felt like a joke. Build that wall! Ha! It's all fun and games. Take him seriously but not literally. Mexico won't pay for the wall.

Meanwhile, as the campaign continued, Trump's rhetoric on immigration continued to grow more and more bitter. He wasn't just talking about drugs and criminals; he wanted to limit legal immigration, too. Mexico was a particular scourge. Later, Trump would battle a judge of Mexican descent. He'd call immigrants "animals" and say refugees hailed from "shithole" countries. He'd separate thousands of immigrant children from their parents at the border and then deny responsibility or culpability. He'd blame illegal immigrants for all sorts of American woes, and he'd latch onto any illegal immigrant who committed a violent crime. Meanwhile, Trump's own properties were staffed by immigrants, many of them in the country illegally. Still, for the Red State Christians who backed Trump, many of whom lived hundreds or thousands of miles from the Mexican border, everything felt somewhat theoretical. Build that wall? Yeah, right, OK.

The Border in Your Backyard

For Dee Reardon, a longtime Evangelical Christian minister and intern at Del Sol Church in El Paso, Texas, things look different, for the debate isn't theoretical. Like many El Pasoans, Reardon is Mexican American and a conservative Christian. Her dad came "over the river," as they say here, from Durango, Mexico, and Reardon has been in El Paso almost forty years. She grew up Catholic and became the first of her family to convert to Evangelicalism.

"I wanted to know more," she said. "What is this relationship thing they're talking about? I found out that's what Christianity is. It is a relationship with Jesus." Reardon, with her husband, later became involved with a ministry that equips laypeople, non-clergy, to lead congregations in spiritual growth. She brought the ministry to Del Sol Church, a multisite Evangelical congregation in El Paso that is part of the Southern Baptist Convention. Reardon, who says she is politically conservative, was supported by her church years ago as she left an abusive relationship. She says her faith has set her free, and now she is the only woman from Del Sol who attends the El Centro jail ministry.

"One woman and ninety-nine men," she says proudly. Reardon, who plays keyboard and sings in the worship band at Del Sol Church's East Montana location, is vivacious and dynamic, confident in her Christian faith and passionate about evangelism. She says her longtime goal has been to be a missionary to Mexico, to share with other cradle Catholics like herself the more personal relationship-centered gospel that is central to American Evangelical Christianity. In any other part of America, Reardon would be a Trump voter. She's pro-life. She's a conservative Evangelical Christian. She lives in a red state.

Reardon's bright eyes darkened when I mentioned the 2016 presidential election. Her voice got lower; her personality lost that spark. I asked her about hearing the chants from Trump rallies. She isn't angry or fired up. She's not that type of person anyway. Instead, she is resigned. A dream has died. "I was sad," she told me quietly. "I was really sad." Reardon remembers growing up in a different America. "I could see Mexico from my house," she said. "And I saw families who crossed the border. Sometimes kids would come. I wasn't afraid. I wasn't upset. If anything, I was like, 'You made it! Way to go!'"

In that moment, watching them come, Reardon no longer saw a wall but a finish line, the end of a long race, and there at the finish line stood this Mexican American conservative Evangelical woman, and she was beaming because they would be Americans, and she was so proud to be an American. "I would flash my porch lights when I saw them," she said. "Just to let them know they were welcome."

Thousands of miles away, the Statue of Liberty raises her fist in solidarity, carrying her own light across the New York Harbor:

> Mother of Exiles. . . .
> "Give me your tired, your poor,
> Your huddled masses yearning to breathe free,
> The wretched refuse of your teeming shore.
> Send these, the homeless, tempest-tost to me,
> I lift my lamp beside the golden door!"[2]

The masses who had once poured through Ellis Island, millions of them like the Drumpfs of Bavaria, Germany, are now brown skinned, speak Spanish, and are huddled across the Rio Grande. They yearn for new hope, like all immigrants; they yearn for escape from persecution and sure death, like the Salvadorans and like Joseph and Mary and Jesus, who escaped to Egypt shortly after the first Christmas. Joseph and Mary had to leave, to immigrate illegally, to bring their baby to safety after King Herod had threatened the lives of all newborn Hebrew baby boys in Israel.

The Borderlands in El Paso and Juarez

After driving a short distance from the small El Paso airport down Airway Boulevard, past an immigration detention center, to El Taquito Mexican restaurant, I lifted the door handle on my rental car. As soon as I opened the door, the heat rushed in, hitting my face like the air from a hair dryer.

Not knowing more than a few words *en español*, I was a minority in El Paso, its culture a wondrous mix of Lone Star State pride (big highways, big trucks, military pride), Native American and Southwest Pueblo tranquility, and Mexico itself, just around the corner, its haciendas and flautas and mangos and watermelons nestled in plastic cups, waiting patiently for the gringos to come. You cannot be frantic in the Southwest. I mean you can try, but it doesn't work out well, because you sweat too much. Even amid the chaos of the border, the dubious history of Ciudad Juarez (El Paso's Mexican sister, the most murderous city in the world, according to some sources, from around 2008 to 2012),[3] the drug war, the undocumented, and the Border Patrol, in El Paso nonetheless I felt a southwestern spirituality, a oneness, and a calm that hid the swirling storm near and far away in Washington, DC.

That mix of Native American and Texan and Mexican is evident in studying El Paso's religious-adherence rates. According to the Association of Religion Data Archives, just 57 percent of El Paso County residents claim a religious affiliation.[4] The county is officially 43 percent Catholic and just over 10 percent Evangelical Protestant.[5] Of the 485 congregations listed in the 2010 ARDA data, 129 are Southern Baptist.[6]

Abundant Living Faith Center, El Paso's best-known megachurch, is nondenominational, loosely affiliated with Hillsong Family, a Pentecostal church movement that began in Sydney, Australia, and a prominent producer of contemporary worship music. Native El Pasoan Charles Nieman, who looks like an aging Texas cowboy, started Abundant Living Faith Center with his wife, Rochelle, in 1977 in a small railroad union hall with fewer than twenty people. Today, the church boasts more than thirty thousand members. Rochelle died in 2012, and Nieman's children, Shannon and Jared, continue to lead the church; Nieman himself remarried in 2016.

Like many Pentecostal-based megachurches, Abundant Living Faith Center is more diverse and less doctrinal than its Southern Baptist counterparts. For his part, Nieman still carries a chip on his shoulder about being criticized for his wealth and for the church's size. When I visited in May 2018, he was still complaining during his sermon about negative press, saying, "Can you imagine that we've been criticized? We need a building. I'll be honest, I wouldn't be there standing on the parking lot with you. I'm just being honest with you." (Just a reminder: Jesus's best-known sermon was preached on the side of a mountain on what was likely a balmy day in the Middle East.)

I visited Abundant Living because I wanted to experience the city's most well-attended congregation, which is popular with many El Pasoans of color, even if its pastoral family was white. I attended Saturday-night worship the day after a school shooter killed ten people at Santa Fe High School on the opposite side of the state, just outside Houston. While other congregations were praying about gun violence, Jared Nieman took a more Trumpian tack in his opening prayer: "We're gonna pray for our country, because we believe that it's strong and prosperous. We're gonna pray to protect those who protect us and serve in the streets."

While El Paso tends to be a blue town in a red state, this prayer felt right at home with the popular right-wing talking points of the day. With his nod to the school shooting complete, Jared Nieman turned it over to the video news: "Church news! Church news!" went the jingle. "What's the best news of the week? Church news! It's guaranteed to be the most positive news of the week." After church news, Jared handed the microphone over to his father, and with a characteristic

Texas drawl, Charles Nieman gave the sermon, during which he noted that those who purchased a teaching series set for fourteen dollars also got a bag of Communion cups and wafers to begin taking Communion at home. Even though his style was different from even most megachurch pastors I'd heard before, you could see Nieman had a certain camaraderie with his congregation that pastors anywhere would envy. As he swung through the book of Ephesians, he turned to his main point for the night. He gazed out into the crowd and said, "C'mon! Is you is or is you ain't? I don't care what Brother Ding Dong said on TV."

Nieman would not be criticized for being politically correct. The point of his sermon was that taking Communion could cure physical ailments, and true to his Pentecostal background, Nieman was a wild card. He lifted up eating organic, natural, and said he wanted to ban soda. He said the Bible warns against extremism and partisanship, and he decried the anti-abortion activists who used to blow up clinics. "Look," Nieman said. "If you disagree with me, that's fine. But can we not fight?" He had his congregation oohing and aahing as the sermon came to a close, with Nieman promising to explain more next week. "Have you enjoyed this tonight?" he asked. "Isn't that incredible?"

I left the service feeling a little confused. Nieman had that slick, slightly unsavory, megachurch pastor glisten, delivered with that rich-white-man Texas drawl that convinced you he would stand staunchly behind everything that Trump had said and ever would say. Still, Nieman's heart was pastoral. I had little doubt of his love for his church. So would he turn in a Mexican migrant standing before him? I didn't know. That was the mystery of El Paso and its many shifting borders. I staggered back to my hotel in the night desert air, strangely quiet though the city quaked all around me. As I walked up the concrete stairs to my room, I passed gaggles of teenagers in formal dresses. Prom? I wondered. Then, I saw the sign: "This way for Anna Maria's Quinceañera."

A Female Bolivian Texas Pastor Straddles Borders

Contradictions and inconsistencies were many in El Paso. While Trump's election brought fear and apprehension to undocumented Hispanic immigrants across America, his election also meant opportunity. Early in his presidency, Trump called for hiring five thousand more Border Patrol agents. Many of the people to answer Trump's call were Hispanic, and by 2016, more than 50 percent of the Border Patrol was Hispanic.[7] According to a *Los Angeles Times* report, ten of the eleven people taking part in a Border Patrol citizens' academy in early 2018 were Hispanic as well.[8]

A Southern Baptist pastor I talked to in El Paso, Ariel Martinez, said this wasn't surprising. Border Patrol is a steady job that pays well, sometimes hard to come by in a border town. It is easy to take stands and choose mercy when posting on Facebook thousands of miles from the border, but life choices are harder for those closest to the center of the action. For Hispanic Americans, the choices looming during Trump's presidency have often been loaded. This reminded me of the sadness I'd felt when talking with Reardon, the Evangelical minister and worship leader who used to blink the lights for families crossing the border. I noticed heaviness among the Hispanic Christian leaders I spoke to in El Paso. Their choices were hard ones. They felt somewhat disempowered and tired.

Rose Mary Guzman has been ministering to people on the border in El Paso for more than twenty years. When I met her later that Saturday evening for Mexican food, sitting next to a loud band singing in Spanish, I had to lean in close to hear her. She spoke softly. Pastor

Rose Mary had spent most of the day at her church, a short walk from the Mexican border in downtown El Paso, in a neighborhood where many refugees and migrants pass through. Guzman herself is not Mexican. She was born to a prominent Bolivian family; her parents were both conservative Evangelical pastors and teachers, and her mother was raised by American missionaries. She told me she had wanted to come to America since age thirteen, when she yearned to be a missionary to the same Americans who taught but also sometimes mistreated the Bolivians with whom they worked.

Rose Mary's American chance first came on a student visa to a Lutheran Bible college in Los Angeles, then to Chicago, and finally in 1997 to Iglesia Luterana Cristo Rey, where she leads border immersions and teaches groups of white midwestern Lutherans who come to visit. Here she ministers and cares for migrants and refugees who come across the border in need of assistance. She has filled out more than a hundred applications for Deferred Action for Childhood Arrivals (DACA), and she finds herself straddling the many borders in her life: Bolivian, American, Texan, Mexican, Lutheran, Catholic, Evangelical, conservative, liberal. Guzman's mother recounted stories of growing up and living with the American missionaries, doing housework for them, and seeing the price of her Evangelical faith. She said the Bolivian Catholic priests would throw stones at the new Evangelical churches, and Christians were bitterly opposed to one another.

Nonetheless, Rose Mary's parents ascended in the ranks of their Evangelical church, and her father became president of the church's university, as well as a lawyer and a pastor. Her parents instilled in Rose Mary a free spirit and a sense that more could always be done for love and for the gospel. After Trump's election, Rose Mary dug in deeper to her work. She says the calls for border immersions—experiences for

Americans living far from the border, who come to the area to meet migrants, see the fence, and talk with Border Patrol guards about immigration—doubled after Trump's election. "But it's too bad," Guzman said, ruefully. "We needed them before the election."

It's quickly obvious that she is not a Trump voter, which is not uncommon in this county that voted solidly for Hillary Clinton. But Guzman is still a Red State Christian, and she says in many ways, she is conservative. Guzman has Hispanic friends who voted for Trump. "I do understand it," she says slowly, "because of how I grew up. He was having Bible studies in the White House, and [Latino Evangelicals] want to be seen. It's really important to show that you're a real Christian, and he seemed to be doing that." Since the election, one of Guzman's friend's sons has become a vocal Trump supporter and an outspoken opponent of immigration, particularly border crossers from Mexico and Central America. "I feel awkward whenever I go to her house now," Guzman said sadly. "I don't know, what does he think about me?"

One of Guzman's biggest financial backers, a large midwestern Lutheran megachurch, removed its support of Iglesia Luterana Cristo Rey after Guzman sent a letter critical of Trump's immigration policies. One of the church's pastors had been a friend of Guzman's, and Guzman responded to the email noting the end of support by saying, "I have been really hurting with all that is happening here. Why didn't you reach out?"

The pastor responded, from her perch in midwestern Lutheran utopia, surrounded by cornfields and homogeneity, "Well, why didn't you reach out to me?"

Their conversation concluded with the midwestern pastor repeatedly telling Guzman, "This guy [Trump] is going to do great things. Just wait."

Meanwhile, Guzman had lost major support for her ministry—money that had paid for food and clothing for refugees, money that had paid for summer camp for children. Already an anomaly in a denomination that is more than 90 percent white and English speaking,[9] Guzman felt even more alone. She ultimately found family where she wouldn't have expected it, among the other pastors of downtown El Paso, many of them conservative Evangelicals. In the face of needy migrants, border deportations, and a lack of federal direction, the churches banded together to create a coalition for border issues. They meet once a month, often discussing help for asylum seekers from Central America. Guzman has recently befriended a young Baptist church planter. She smiles while talking about it. Texans are not just conservative, they are also warm and hospitable, partially attributable to the warmth and family values of Hispanic culture.

The El Paso church coalition has been working to make space in America for asylum seekers from Guatemala, El Salvador, and Honduras. El Salvador is home to the notoriously violent MS-13 gang, and Guatemala and Honduras have been crippled by poverty and political corruption for generations. Migrants from these countries have often been unaccompanied minors who risked their lives to ride on top of trains through Mexico to reach America. They are not usually the hardened criminals, rapists, drug lords, or murderers Trump regaled his crowds with at his rallies. They are more often skinny children and teenagers, mothers carrying toddlers, and pregnant women.

Face-to-face with tragedy and dire need, Guzman said her efforts haven't even been about politics. She has no other choice but to help. "It takes [decades] for family reunification," Guzman said. "If you're from Mexico trying to immigrate legally, they're just now [in 2018] processing papers filed in 1992. People have died waiting to immigrate. If you have the money, it's easy. If you don't, it's nearly impossible."

Guzman told me about one of her first members at Cristo Rey. "She lived in the US for twenty-six years. I met her when her kids were babies. She married an American citizen; she spent tens of thousands of dollars applying for legal immigration." But Guzman's friend, running away from an abusive relationship, scared and alone, had fibbed to Border Patrol agents on her initial border crossing, claiming she was an American citizen. Even though she quickly recanted, she can now never receive citizenship. "Her son joined the military. They were adopted by her American husband and got citizenship. Her son was pleading and crying with the immigration officer," Guzman told me. "She'd been going in for check-ins and getting extensions, and after Trump got elected, they deported her right away. She was in Juarez, but now she has moved further into Mexico with family. She has lost her entire life."

For Guzman, Trump's stance on immigration boils down to racism. She recognizes it as the same ailment that caused the American missionaries to force their Bolivian converts to clean their homes and take tiny salaries. "He's a racist," she said. "When he welcomed those [neo-Nazis] in Charlottesville, I knew it. He is one of them. He is lying. He calls [the migrants] animals."

She said El Paso is filled with military families, most of whom support Trump, even the Hispanic families. Her friend who has the pro-Trump sons who make Guzman uncomfortable also has a daughter-in-law who is Mexican and who is also pro-Trump. Dividing lines here are unclear. Borders are crossed all the time. "I hate to say it, but Mexican immigrants who have succeeded and become middle class because of owning businesses are often the ones who abuse their brothers and sisters the worst, as wait staff or by not paying them fairly," Guzman admitted. "Many Mexican people abuse other Mexicans."

The issues are complicated. Christians and Hispanics and Texans find themselves on multiple sides of the same issues. Guzman, rooted in her Evangelical faith, turns again to Jesus. "Sometimes it seems we are reading a different Bible," she said of her Hispanic conservative Christian friends who support Trump. "I wasn't afraid before. Now I am. There are no more open doors in this country where I wanted to come for so long. I am afraid of him getting reelected, and I never used to think that."

Still, do not accuse Guzman of a lack of patriotism. "I am still proud of being an American. My hope [for Hispanic Christians] would be to have a middle ground and create coalitions. What we've done here in El Paso is not focus on the issues that divide us, like abortion or gay marriage, but concentrate on serving and helping the other. It's not about making the other person believe what you believe. It's about helping the other. If we form groups that help the neighbor, the Holy Spirit will create belief in the midst of it." For Guzman, it is still about creating disciples, but she sees that happening in a different way than she used to see it.

"I was all black-and-white as a Christian in the past," she said. "I always wanted to be a pastor, but I discovered I was a racist. My skin is lighter because I have more Spanish heritage than Indian heritage. Bolivia is divided, and whiter people discriminate against darker-skinned people. And I discriminated against people who didn't have education. I thought Mexicans were people wearing sombreros, breaking the law and being lazy. That's what I saw on TV in Bolivia. I've changed. Now I'm all gray, not black-and-white. And God is OK with that."

Before we paid our bill and left the table, Guzman asked me to return to an earlier question she hadn't been able to answer. What would Jesus do about immigration in America? What would Jesus do on the US-Mexican border? "Jesus would say that when it comes to immigration, nobody is illegal in the world. We all have rights," she said. "Jesus broke all kinds of rules. He touched the lepers. One came back, and the law said not to come back, but he did, and Jesus blessed him. The law said the Samaritan woman should have been stoned. The law said Jesus shouldn't heal on the Sabbath. For Jesus, compassion and love were more important than the law. We are not there to judge [at the border]. God will be the judge. Jesus said to feed the hungry and clothe the stranger. That is it. Who are we to pick who to feed and clothe?"

The Southern Baptists of El Paso

I headed east of downtown El Paso the next morning, attempting to find Del Sol Church's East Montana location, but I saw it might be possible to drive right into Mexico without realizing it from El Paso, or at least it felt that way. Note to readers: Do not follow Google Maps' directions to Del Sol Church–East Montana. I found myself on a dead-end dirt road in a forsaken, dust-covered, newish area of East El Paso. Tumbleweeds and abandoned, broken-down cars lined the street, and I realized I had to turn around and backtrack.

Then, rising like a mirage in the distance, I saw it—the boxy, newish building with a flashy logo that signified a new Evangelical church plant. I'd arrived. I chose Del Sol Church to visit in El Paso because it was sort of the other end of the megachurch spectrum from Abundant Living Faith Center. Where Abundant Living looked flashy, Pentecostal, and huge, Del Sol was doctrinally Southern Baptist, more traditional in function if not in form, and committed to the multisite church multiplication model, refusing to let any one campus grow too large. I came to this East Montana outpost of Del

Sol because I wanted to speak with its founding site pastor, Ariel Martinez, who was also the pastor of administration and a recent (distance-learning) graduate of Liberty University.

At first, Martinez was hesitant to talk, noting that Del Sol's congregation tended to be evenly split politically. He also noted the increasing divide among Southern Baptists: "There are two groups of Southern Baptists. One is more accepting and willing to try new things; the other is not accepting or willing to change." Martinez did not say which group Del Sol or Liberty University fit into or if it was the same group.

Born into a second-generation American family (Martinez's paternal grandfather came from Chihuahua, Mexico), Martinez said his dad, maternal grandfather, and brother all served in the US military—his grandfather in World War II, his father in Vietnam, and his brother in Afghanistan. His family has known more sacrifice for America than many white American families, yet Martinez sometimes feels torn between his patriotism and his role as a pastor, especially in a congregation with a large military and Border Patrol population. "We decided at Del Sol Church a long time ago that our work and calling is the kingdom of God, not America," Martinez said. "It's tough, because we support our country and our military. But America is not my allegiance. I've seen so many people and churches be torn apart because they think their allegiance and focus is to their country and not to God."

Again, in El Paso, the borders run close together. Border control is not a theoretical argument, especially when most families have conservative Christians, American military members, and Mexican immigrants all together in one family and, likely, one congregation. Martinez says he is personally interested in politics and active in local races, including one coming up for a new judge. He doesn't want to squander his pastoral influence on politics, but he also sees social and ethical issues brush up against politics and against Christianity, and he finds areas where he feels the church must speak.

Interestingly, for a congregation located just across the border from thousands of refugees and asylum seekers from Central America, Del Sol Church has chosen to support refugees from thousands of miles away in northern Europe, giving money to an Austrian church plant for Middle Eastern refugees. "It's actually a Mexican pastor, married to a German woman," Martinez said. "The church ministers to refugees from the Middle East, from Iraq and Syria, and we are vocal about supporting it."

Given the issues at the US-Mexican border, it is surprising and even delightful that Del Sol Church has chosen to support a church full of Muslim refugees halfway across the world. Still, Martinez did not mention public ministry support at Del Sol for refugees closer to home, and he hesitated when asked about the asylum seekers across the border from El Paso, traveling primarily from Central America. Martinez took a deep breath. "I think the most important thing to remember is that they're people. The asylum seekers coming across are people. It's easy to call names or put people in categories, but they're people first, and we do need to have compassion. We have Dreamers in our church in leadership positions. I see things people write on social media, and I think, 'If you knew that [Joe] was here illegally, would you still think that way?' People need to have a name and face. I think you should know who they are before you talk about them. As Christians, we don't have the right to dehumanize people. We don't have a right to write people off. As Americans, you can do whatever you want. But as Christians, we have to show the compassion of Christ."

As part of a family that had risen from poverty, Martinez said that sometimes socioeconomic status influences Mexican Americans' viewpoint on immigration more than anything else. When you have money and live in middle-class El Paso, you are isolated from the concerns of asylum seekers and economic migrants. You have a different perspective than people living in the *colonias*, or impoverished dwellings clustered on both sides of the border, where people often live without electric power, indoor plumbing, sewage, or trash pickup. Martinez pointed to Jesus's story. Jesus was a political refugee, fleeing people who were trying to kill him. But his family also went to register with the government.

The Liberty University graduate, Southern Baptist megachurch pastor, second-generation Mexican American, native Texan, and El Pasoan smiled that wry smile again. "So you can see both sides," he said. "But our country has lost the sense of compromise. It's very easy to say Hispanics or Christians vote one way, but it's more complicated. We have a pastor here from Mexico on a visitor's visa who is doing great ministry. We are trying to get him through immigration legally, so that he can stay and do ministry, and it is almost impossible. It's easy to say people should do it the right way, but I saw how difficult it was for us to bring Pablo here legally and keep him here. It was extremely expensive. The system is broken. If people knew this, they would think differently. The legal way to immigrate is much harder than people realize."

I walked out of Del Sol Church and into the dusty parking lot, the Franklin Mountains rising brown in the distance. I realized I am left with more questions than answers, certain only that the divisions drawn by pundits and pollsters don't fit neatly here in this border town, where Mexican American Southern Baptists and military members and Border Patrol members and Dreamers worship a former political refugee Savior together. I had only one place left to go before my flight would leave the next morning. I had to cross my own border.

I had to learn to straddle it and stand in both places the way everyone in El Paso learned to do out of necessity, out of love, and out of a pragmatic yet hopeful stubbornness that belies conservative or liberal talking points and is linked inextricably to the Savior who crossed even the border of life and death.

¡Bienvenido a Mexico!

That Sunday afternoon, after worship at Del Sol, I met Rose Mary, her husband Fernando, a former Bolivian pro soccer player, and two of their three daughters, and we piled into the Guzman van, cranked up the air conditioning, and drove toward the border. I settled into my seat, expecting a long drive, staring into my purse. When I looked up, no more than two minutes later, we were driving around a curb with orange cones. Two men in military fatigues looked at us and yawned. Fernando slowed down the car on the bridge. I noticed a plaque to my right side: *Limite de Los Estados Unidos Mexicanos. ¡Bienvenido a Mexico!*

I felt a little misled. All this hype about the border, and that was it? We were here. Where were the drug gangs? The rapists lined up? The bedraggled masses and caravans? All I saw were more brown mountains rising in the distance. Fernando and Rose Mary chuckled, explaining that the wait to get back into the United States would take considerably longer, but no more than an hour at most today. Their family often spent afternoons, especially on Sundays, in Juarez. They'd walk the downtown, have a dessert at the cafe, consider buying trinkets, take in a show of dancing and horses at Vive Mexico restaurant. To them, Ciudad Juarez was just another town.

Ciudad Juarez has indeed become significantly safer in recent years, no longer the most murderous city in the world. It boasts a middle class and wealthy citizens of its own, as well as industry and education. Its downtown had some attempted revitalization, an Instagram-worthy photo op at the center of the square with a red sculpture reading, "I <3 JRZ." The road through downtown is pedestrian-only, and on this Sunday afternoon, Juarez was bustling, with people everywhere—people selling melon and mango in plastic cups, people drinking Cokes and eating Papa John's pizza, even people dancing in the middle of the street, wearing old-fashioned early-1950s Mexican clothing.

The city, a vestige of its murderous past and the acrimony between warring drug cartels that terrorized Mexico, did have a distinctly lawless feel to it, especially noticeable as we wandered through the downtown. Nothing happened to me that was untoward, but I had a sense that if it had, if I had been robbed or assaulted, I might have been out of luck. Everyone, including the police, would just keep walking and ignore what was happening. I also had a sense I could quite easily acquire any number of illicit items upon asking. Still, Trump painted Mexico in general, and Juarez in particular, as a particular horror, but I didn't experience anything like that. After walking the downtown a while and eating a delectable piece of cheesecake in a heavenly air-conditioned open-air restaurant, we drove to Vive Mexico for the show. For nearly two hours, we heard mariachi live music and watched dancing, equestrians, glorious costume changes, and hilarious skits. Gleeful, joyful, delightful— it was all there together: live entertainment the like of which I had never experienced in America. Welcome to middle-class Juarez: big families gathered for big dinners, dressed up, bringing gifts and birthday presents and blowing out candles.

As the emcee of the performance—a big, boisterous Mexican man with a Vicente Fox mustache and a giant cowboy hat—rode past gallantly on a black stallion, whipping and waving the Mexican flag in the air to shouts and cheers and applause from the crowd, I realized something disquieting. I had been quite a xenophobe, imagining in my quasi-charitable progressive-ish mind-set that only two sorts of people inhabited Mexico and Central America: the impoverished masses, who needed to immigrate and needed our help, and the warring drug lords, who were tearing their country apart. Oh, and there was a third sort—a fabulously wealthy set of isolated Mexicans who occasionally appeared in Southern California and on reality TV. But here in this restaurant were Mexicans and some Americans, families and children and mothers and fathers and grandfathers and grandmothers, all generally patriotic and caring about their families and this place in the world they had come to call home. I had clouded my mind with my American narrative and thought it applied to everyone, and here I was reminded that Mexico has its own story to tell, its own history, and its own pride, and we all know only pieces of the one big story that God is trying to tell us, which we can grasp only if we first love and listen to one other.

My conversation from earlier that morning with Dee Reardon, the conservative Christian minister and worship leader at Del Sol Church, floated back into my head as I luxuriated in the lavish show and delectable dessert tray that was Juarez now for me, in all its three-dimensional wonder and mystery.

Dee was remembering how it felt in El Paso when she was a kid—a Mexican American kid who could see the border from her window. "It's different now," she said. "We are the ones who are jailed in. I think the wall is not to keep Mexicans out but to keep us in jail. It's a pity. We used to go to Mexico and see El Paso on the other side, and we felt connected. Now there is a wall to keep us apart. Why? I have no idea."

Truthfully, I felt relieved to return to the United States that night, crossing the bridge into familiar territory and safety. But I know, too, that I am glad a wall did not keep me from Juarez and that the wall I had built around my heart, without even knowing it, to keep out people who were different from me was beginning to fall down.

Conclusion

When I started researching Red State Christians, I had a plan for the last story I wanted to tell. I wanted to end with the story of my college roommate, Lindsey, the one who saved me from partying too much in Greektown and being bullied by sorority sister roommates, the one who brought me to Bible study and, incidentally, reminded me to clean the toilet more often. Lindsey was two years older than me and came from a suburb of Saint Louis. She related to everyone in a grounded and impeccably kind way; she had a gift for positivity and hope even in the most difficult situations. Lindsey was there for me in so many ways, and I know she changed my life at a vulnerable time, offering me a place to live and a safe place to rediscover my deep Christian faith with a group called Christian Campus House.

Lindsey was, and is, a Red State Christian. We've stayed in touch over the years, sometimes better than others, and we were on opposite sides of the 2016 presidential election. I remember when she shared an article online that made a Christian case for voting for Trump, and at the time, I just couldn't fathom it. She posted it shortly after Trump's vulgar comments about women, recorded on a bus with Billy Bush, were made public.

I wanted to tell Lindsey's story in this book, because it's often stories like Lindsey's that go untold. She works as a preschool teacher and fitness instructor; she's a mom of three and a university graduate.

Her husband, who graduated with us and discovered his own Christian faith thanks to his relationship with Lindsey, works as an engineer. They're both bright and open-minded in many ways, and they live in a major metropolitan area. They live in Missouri, which is a red state that is also home to a diverse mix of political and social viewpoints at the crossroads of America.

When we met up in Missouri over the summer of 2018, I was reminded of everything I loved about Lindsey and the richness of her faith. She told me about how her parents had once been hippies but had been converted to Evangelical Christianity, and how her grandma had been an attendee of one of Joyce Meyer's first Bible studies. Meyer today is famous among Evangelicals, including my mom, for her devotional books and speaking engagements, especially to women's groups. I was also reminded about how much Lindsey and I still have in common, including the ways both of us struggled with the extremes of our chosen political and religious tribes. We desperately want the best for our kids; we desperately want to pass on the love of Jesus and the joy we've found in Christian community. As we talked, neither of us was ever quite certain that we knew the best way to do that.

That summer, we made rough plans that I'd join Lindsey and her family for Thanksgiving in Saint Louis that year. Thanksgiving represents our country's inextricable political divides and the way those divides play out in individual families, as well as representing the time-honored American tradition of togetherness and generosity despite difference. I was eager to see how other families were dealing with the different conclusions their faith led them to regarding American politics, and I was hopeful to see examples of love winning out over even entrenched political positions and different social backgrounds.

But when I called Lindsey a week or so before Thanksgiving, we realized it just wasn't going to work out. She had four Thanksgiving dinners to attend, spread across Missouri, and it was going to be too hectic to mix in book interviews among newborn babies, grandmas and grandpas, aunts and uncles and cousins.

Something else was bothering me, too. I realized that I was being pushed a certain direction—a direction I'd resisted since I'd begun writing and researching. I had spent most of 2018 traveling around the country, interviewing and researching Christians living in red counties, many of whom had supported Trump, yet I had shied away from talking about the very thing that made this book so important to me in the first place. When it came to writing about Thanksgiving and about family, I was being driven back to the one place I had yet to go. I was being pushed to tell the story not of Lindsey's family but of my own, a story that cuts straight to the heart of America and its Christians and their politics.

I kept remembering something an editor of a Christian magazine had written to me, after reading a story I'd published elsewhere: "You do write about 'red state Christians' as if they are an 'other' that you are trying to sympathize with and explain to people like you, who are implicitly different." That bothered me, because I didn't quite think it was true. To tell the stories of Red State Christians in this book is like telling pieces of my own story and the stories of my family. I am the granddaughter of a German American Lutheran pastor who ministered on the Kansas-Missouri state line in the midst of the civil rights movement. On the other side of my family, I am the granddaughter of a German American Catholic deeply faithful woman who voted and advocated against abortion. I am the daughter-in-law of a Vietnam veteran and Lutheran school graduate from rural Missouri who put a Trump sign in his lawn and a MAGA hat in his garage. I am the niece of an aunt who sparred with her father, my grandfather, over the possibility of a Christian supporting Trump, an aunt who felt ostracized by her father because of her political and religious beliefs. I am the wife of a man who is the only one among his high school friends who voted for Hillary and who was mocked for doing so. I am the sister-in-law of an African American woman who protested with Black Lives Matter in Chicago. I am the sister-in-law of a half-Hispanic woman who lives in deep-red rural America and is conservative herself.

My family makes a patchwork of red and blue, Evangelical and mainline, urban, suburban, and rural. I resist the idea that we must continually make one another the other. In our own families, to do so means devastating separation and estrangement. It's not worth it. It never is. Red State Christians are not the "other" any more than my own family members are not the "other." I have been a Red State Christian when I've lived and worked in conservative communities and churches, as well as when I wrote a paper in seminary wrestling with my then-undecided viewpoint about gay marriage, shortly before serving at a church with a music minister who is a gay man and who changed my life and my perspective. Red State Christians are my family. They're your family. They're you. For me, this book is not about some other America that I had to excavate and uncover, like an archaeologist. Rather, for me, this book is about America itself and ultimately about uncovering myself, my family, and my faith.

When I look back at my travels across America, from Dallas megachurches to Appalachian small towns, I realize that I was overwhelmingly welcomed and accepted. Not by everyone. A conservative Catholic college in New Hampshire forbade me from visiting, and Rick Warren's Orange County megachurch, Saddleback, told me explicitly not to conduct interviews. But the everyday people I spoke to across America in red counties welcomed me. I wanted to talk to some big names, like Paula White, Jack Graham, and Russell Moore—people who were often quoted when it came to talking about politics and conservative Christianity and Trump. But my overriding purpose was to tell the stories of people who had been ignored in national media, people like the young Hispanic Evangelical pastor in El Paso who talked to me about immigration, people like the Jordanian Arabic-speaking pastor in Houston who had supported Trump but had some misgivings, people like the small-town New England Catholic priest, like the African American assistant principal and football coach in Florida who responded to an altar call at a funeral in a white Baptist church, and like the young Lutheran farmers and high-school students in rural Missouri. In these moments, with these strangers and friends, I found that all across America, people were willing to engage in conversation. I heard stories of tragedy, stories of relentless faith in the face of terrifying adversity, and stories of individual people making resurrection and new life possible even in places where new life seemed awfully unlikely.

Sometimes I heard people say things that sounded intolerant or racist or mean. It usually happened when they were telling me about something they'd heard on TV or on the internet. And at the same time, I learned too that people's general beliefs often didn't apply in the particular. People who voted against gay marriage or gay rights often welcomed people who were gay into their own church communities or families. Even racism was hard to quantify. Liberals knew all the right words to say and theories to quote, but I noticed patterns of structural racism that white liberals benefited from all the time yet no one acknowledged. Meanwhile, the white conservatives I spoke with often had more diverse family and neighborhood experiences than the white liberals I spoke to. Which was worse, racism in general or racism in particular? I learned that the dividing lines we draw don't mean so much in practical, everyday American life. Of course we find that out only when we cross the dividing lines.

In saying this, I refuse to whitewash the troubling incidents I witnessed and heard during the course of my research. Primarily among pastors and media figures, among wealthy and powerful people, I heard people use Christianity to justify American Christian Nationalism that would seek to harm the weak among us: refugees, the poor, women, people of color, the LGBTQ community. I saw Bible passages twisted; I heard the story of Israel used as justification for the historical significance of America and heartless foreign policy. These manipulative pastors and Christian leaders wanted money, power, and control, and they saw Trump as a means to these ends. Their victims were women, their own churches, minority communities, and America itself. As a follower of Jesus, I found it unconscionable that a story of humility, grace, kindness, and God's sovereignty would be told in such a way as to lift up human strength, wealth, power, and manipulation.

Still, as I come to the end of this journey, what sticks with me are the stories of surprise. All across America, people are doing surprising things that don't fit into our prescribed boxes that we use to categorize people. Evangelicals are not a monolith, not universally any one thing, and Red State Christians defy categorization. Eighty-one percent of white Evangelicals voted for Trump—some because they wanted to overturn *Roe v. Wade*, some because they hated Hillary, and many because they felt like Trump was talking directly to them and speaking for them, whereas Democrats and others didn't even seem interested in engaging with them in a conversation that wasn't laced with pejorative or patronizing insults. In neglecting to have that conversation, many Americans miss out on the stories of the people I've introduced you to in this book. America is a big country, and the

Holy Spirit is alive—not primarily in Washington or on TV screens, but in El Paso and Naples and Cole Camp and Altoona.

The voices that I believe will heal America's wounded heart are the voices that can speak truth to power in places far from seats of power. I am encouraged by Wes, the half-Hispanic, half-Tongan youth pastor at one of Orange County's largest churches, who bristles at those who assume he's on the grounds crew but who relentlessly proclaims the difficulty of the gospel anyway, and thousands listen. Evangelicalism depends on an experience of the Holy Spirit and a dynamic display of God's power. For many years, that power has been caged inside churches and power-hungry pastors, but what I found across America while talking to Christians in red counties is that American Evangelicalism is beginning to break out of its cage. Jesus always sought out those in society who were unpopular, who were neglected, who were considered deplorable. Among them, Jesus preached his revolutionary message of God's power, of human weakness, and of unimaginable sacrifice for one another, for the weakest among us.

At the heart of it all is my own Red State Christian family and the ways it divides and comes together and surprises even me with its love and forgiveness. When I felt most nervous, most vulnerable throughout my writing and research, then God revealed truth and surprise to me through the people I was with. This happened far away and close to home. It happened through everyday moments of grace, like the Delta customer service agent who got me a last-minute flight home from New Hampshire to care for my flu-ridden six-year-old son or like the Bolivian family who took me across the border to Mexico and reminded me that grace squeezes through walls.

A moment of grace that sticks with me happened during something I said I wouldn't write about, my own family reunion for my father-in-law's side in rural Missouri. His family is staunchly Missouri

Synod Lutheran, a cousin of sorts to the Evangelical Lutheran Church in America where I grew up. The Missouri Synod does not ordain women pastors, and its theology is a great deal more conservative than the ELCA's. The two groups often fight like the siblings they are, and the ELCA pastor in the small Missouri town where we held our reunion told me that the two Lutheran churches had dueling stands at the town fair, serving different versions of the exact same food.

If you believe the stories you're told about the impermeability of American political and religious division, you might believe that spending time with my husband's family would be hard for me. Their church says people from my denomination aren't even supposed to take Communion at their churches, that my ordination itself is invalid. But people are much more capable of nuance than theological documents or news stories about faith groups are.

The first time I met my husband's dad's family, I was captivated by the rolling hills of rural Missouri—by the farm and the fiddles and the music and the hugs I received. When we got together again for the big reunion this past summer, in a red county in a red state surrounded by Red State Christians and Trump supporters, I figured I should just be a mom and take off my author and pastor hats. I was greeted with the usual family hugs and warmth. When it was almost time to eat, my two-year-old son had a potty accident, and I found myself in the bathroom in the basement of the Missouri Synod church. Everyone would want someone to lead us in prayer, and one of our relatives had been an accomplished Missouri Synod pastor. I figured we were good to go. When I came out of the bathroom with my son, everyone had started eating. My husband came up to me with a puzzled look on his face. "Where were you?" he said. "Everyone was looking for you. They were waiting for you to pray for us."

When I think back on my whole year researching Red State Christians, that story stands out. It reminds me that all Americans, Christian or not, conservative or not, have a remarkable gift for acceptance. If given the chance, we can accept one another, learn from each other, and build an entirely new country built on justice and freedom for all.

My Red State Christian story began with Trump, with his bombast and his uncanny ability to mollify moral concerns and unite an Evangelical Christian coalition of voters. Still, the place my story ends is far from Trump. It ends in places in America where people are forming unlikely alliances, surprising each other and surprising political pundits, to build a future that looks nothing like the Republicans or Democrats of the past.

Grace, for American Christians and for all of us, is a difficult thing. It means starting from a place where all of us have been wrong, and knowing that we all have something to learn from each other. If you are a liberal reading this book, I hope you've learned about the humanity and diversity of Red State Christians, and you can see parts of yourself in them. If you are a conservative reading this book, I hope you've learned about the dangerous edges and manipulation apparent in parts of American Red State conservative Christianity, and I hope you see that in some places, Jesus's message of love and sacrifice has been perverted to lift up power and hatred. I hope, whoever you are, that your beliefs prior to reading this book have been challenged and that you're open to further conversation.

ACKNOWLEDGMENTS

For me, *Red State Christians* begins and ends with family—with my own family and with our American family and the ways that politics and faith tear us apart while we fight through love to grow closer together without hiding our wounds.

So I have to begin by thanking my family: my husband, Ben, and my sons Jacob and Joshua, who ate fruit snacks and crackers in my office while I wrote and edited chapters, who played baseball outside the backyard window while I interviewed sources, who dropped me off and picked me up at the airport with smiles, hugs, and unconditional love. Ben read every chapter of the book as I wrote it, and I sent him a spare copy of all my interview notes—just in case. He is my guardian and my soul-keeper, my resting place, and often my health-insurance carrier as I pursue more creative vocations.

I also have to thank my parents, Rick and Claudia Busch. We moved back to Minneapolis to be just thirty minutes from them, and while I wrote *Red State Christians*, they were the loving and supportive parents they've always been, taking care of Jake and Josh while I traveled during weekdays while Ben was at work. My mom told all her friends and everyone she met—including in the sauna—about my book, convincing even people who seemed uninterested that they just had to read it. Her love and boundless optimism encouraged me even on frustrating or anxiety-filled days. My dad bemoaned my leaving sports writing nearly ten years ago, and he initially had trouble envisioning his daughter as a pastor, as he grew up among Catholic priests and nuns. Still, he too followed each step of my *Red State Christians* journey with joy, celebrating with me and taking my boys sledding and providing childcare on Tuesdays, chatting with preschool moms at pick-up.

I want to thank my mother-in-law and father-in-law, Linda and Dennis Denker, who have accepted me and loved me as part of their family since Ben and I started dating in 2004. While we often view politics differently, we never let our political differences color the love and mutual respect we share as a family, and I cherish the relaxation and comfort of our family trips to their home in Kansas City. Our commitment to family despite political differences was a major inspiration for my work in *Red State Christians*, and thus I must also thank the entire extended Denker and Reagan families. Thanks for loving this Minnesota "liberal," as you call me.

Red State Christians would not exist without the vision and drive of my editor, Tony Jones, at Fortress Press. He took a risk on a first-time author with a whacky idea about Orange County Christians and the 2016 presidential election, and he gave me legs to carry out his dream of writing about Red State Christians across America. Thanks, Tony, for texting me during unconventional and disturbing church services, for believing in me and in the project, and for helping me to believe in my voice.

Thanks, too, to everyone at Fortress Press. To Lisa, who picked up the end of the project where Tony left off, to Emily and Mallory and Layne and the entire marketing team for making me feel valued and for investing in the travel this book required.

Thanks to my sources and fixers around the United States. To Jenny Yang, who connected me with *Evangelicals for Life* and some of my most important interviews around Christian Nationalism and the Southern Baptist Convention. To Daniel Darling, who let me in to the conference and helped me set up elusive interviews with conservative Christian leaders.

To Jason Micheli, Steve Larkin, and Brad Todd, who made me feel like a DC insider and treated me with dignity and respect.

To Adam Fisher, who connected me with sports sources and old friends in Naples, Florida.

To the Arabic Church of Houston and your boundless generosity and wisdom.

To Rose Mary Guzman and family, who took me over the border and broke down my walls in more ways than one.

To Dean Inserra, who trusted me and reshaped the focus of my book to begin with Christian nationalism on Fourth of July weekend in Dallas.

To Amanda and Drew McCaffrey, who made me feel like family in outsider-wary Appalachia and Central Pennsylvania.

To Willie Rosin, Beth Pottratz, and Greg Yeager, who talked to me about guns in their own lives and guns in their rural congregations.

To Kimberly Knowle-Zeller and Stephen Zeller, who welcomed me into their small-town Missouri church and helped me to see the beauty of rural Christian America.

To the *Red Letter Christians* family, who gave me my start as a faith blogger and writer, who connected me with some of the Evangelical world's most important voices.

To the people of Messiah Lutheran Church in Yorba Linda, California, and Pastor Bob Mooney, who walked with me through the sometimes contentious carnage of the 2016 election and who taught me to love freely above all and who will always be family.

To the countless people across America, from rural New Hampshire to opulent Orange County, who opened their hearts to me, who answered my questions, who shared with me their fears, their hopes, and their faith—that together we might build a better America and listen to one another.

To the people of Easter Lutheran Church and former lead pastor Kris Capel, who called me as an interim teaching pastor during the writing and promotion of this book, who accepted me as one of their own and also gave me the freedom to do the writing God had called me into.

To all those who read early and late editions; to former sports editors Mark Wollemann, Joe Walljasper, and Greg Hardwig; to journalism professors Steve Weinberg and Mary Kay Blakely; to all those who believed in me as a journalist, a writer, and as a pastor, who gave me courage and ability to write these stories and speak the truth. To mentor pastors Peter Geisendorfer-Lindgren, who baptized, married, and ordained me, and Mark Wickstrom, who molded me into an Evangelical preacher who could never go back to the pulpit. To Karoline Lewis, who gave me courage to leave full-time ministry and jump without a net. To Lisa Sharon Harper, who encouraged me to take up my own space and leave the comfortable for the unpredictable. To Beth Lewis, who opened doors for me at 1517 Media.

To my online writing groups, made up mostly of women, who inspired me, encouraged me, and picked me up when I got knocked down.

To the Holy Spirit and a forgiving God, who carried me and healed me and provided unexpected and surprising solutions to all the problems I encountered along the way.

And finally, to my grandpa Jerry, who died five months before *Red State Christians* was launched. He was a Lutheran pastor desperate to share the word of God in the red states where he pastored, to speak out in the political realm, even on topics that were unpopular in his congregation and his community. He was never afraid to speak his truth, even when it cost him jobs and popularity. In my grandpa's shadow, I write this book on a contentious and divisive topic, assured that out of the shadow of evil and division, God's light will shine.

NOTES

Chapter 1

1. "Full Text: 2017 Donald Trump Inauguration Speech Transcript," *Politico*, January 20, 2017, https://tinyurl.com/yatpzd4k.
2. Jessica Martínez and Gregory A. Smith, "How the Faithful Voted: A Preliminary 2016 Analysis," Pew Research Center, November 9, 2016, https://tinyurl.com/h5zd2fl.
3. "The Religious Typology," Pew Research Center, August 29, 2018, https://tinyurl.com/ycgr8eka.
4. Pew Research Center, "The Religious Typology."
5. Martínez and Smith, "How the Faithful Voted."
6. Will Hall, "Texas Congregation Escrows CP over Concerns about Direction of SBC," *Baptist Message*, February 16, 2017, https://tinyurl.com/ycgkc7p5.
7. Hall, "Texas Congregation Escrows CP."
8. Hall, "Texas Congregation Escrows CP."

Chapter 2

1. David Brody, "Brody File Exclusive: Donald Trump Explains Pro-Life Conversion," interview with Donald Trump, Christian Broadcasting Network, April 8, 2011, https://tinyurl.com/y766rnk8.

Chapter 3

1. Maya Rhodan, "Gun-Related Deaths in America Keep Going Up" *Time*, November 6, 2017, https://tinyurl.com/y6en97as.

2. A. J. Willingham and Saeed Ahmed, "Mass Shootings in America Are a Serious Problem—and These 9 Charts Show Just Why," CNN, November 6, 2017, https://tinyurl.com/yxshnda6.
3. William Cummings and Bart Jansen, "Why the AR-15 Keeps Appearing at America's Deadliest Mass Shootings," *USA Today*, February 14, 2018, https://tinyurl.com/yyjxn2c8.

Chapter 4

1. David Whiting, "O.C. Divorce Rate One of Highest in Nation," *Orange County Register*, June 25, 2012, https://tinyurl.com/yyfr8zvt.
2. Richard Flory, "How California's Megachurches Changed Christian Culture," Center for Religion and Civic Culture, University of Southern California, January 10, 2018, https://tinyurl.com/y6b7t9pa>.
3. Flory, "How California's Megachurches Changed Christian Culture."
4. Flory, "How California's Megachurches Changed Christian Culture."

Chapter 5

1. Eugene Kiely, "'You Didn't Build That,' Uncut and Unedited," FactCheck.org, *Annenberg Public Policy Center*, July 24, 2012, https://tinyurl.com/yd4r6v5h.
2. Kiely, "You Didn't Build That."

Chapter 6

1. Aric Jenkins, "Read President Trump's NFL Speech on National Anthem Protests," *Time*, September 23, 2017, https://tinyurl.com/yb85sapo.
2. Shaun R. Harper, "There Would Be No NFL without Black Players: They Can Resist the Anthem Policy," *Washington Post*, May 24, 2018, https://tinyurl.com/yy9olbwv.
3. We are talking, however, about Trump, a man who has always been fascinated by football and has a sordid football past of his own. Trump, after all, once schemed to join the owner's club by purchasing a United States Football League team, the New Jersey Generals, in 1983. He spent millions trying to lure players and coaches to the USFL from

the NFL, three years later joining forces with his fellow USFL owners to compete directly with the NFL and sue for antitrust violations. Trump was hoping for a multimillion-dollar judgment that would force the NFL to merge with the USFL. But the court sided against Trump and the USFL, awarding a judgment of only $3, a decision that led to the folding of the USFL. Trump would lose more than $20 million, and he would never own a football team again, despite participating in bidding wars for the New England Patriots and Buffalo Bills.

4. Michael Bamberger, Ben Baskin, and Pete Madden, "First Golfer: Donald Trump's Relationship with Golf Has Never Been More Complicated," *Sports Illustrated*, August 7, 2017, https://tinyurl.com/y5j55fc4.

Chapter 7

1. Gregory Korte, "Trump Is the 'Most Pro-Life President in American History,' Pence Says," *USA Today*, January 18, 2018, https://tinyurl.com/y7nqoz5q.

2. Martínez and Smith.

3. Kate Shellnutt, "ERLC Defends Russell Moore, Who Apologizes for His Role in Trump Divide," *Christianity Today*, March 20, 2017, https://tinyurl.com/y5h9b7yv.

4. Will Hall, "Texas Congregation Escrows CP over Concerns about Direction of SBC," *Baptist Message*, February 16, 2017, https://tinyurl.com/ycgkc7p5.

5. David Roberts, "The Real Problem with the New York Times Op-Ed Page: It's Not Honest about US Conservatism," *Vox*, March 15, 2018, https://tinyurl.com/y24oafdt.

6. Jenny Jarvie, "Here's How the Poor People's Campaign Aims to Finish What MLK Started," interview with Rev. William J. Barber II, *Los Angeles Times*, May 11, 2018, https://tinyurl.com/yy9gcm6v.

7. Jarvie, "Here's How the Poor People's Campaign Aims to Finish."

8. Sarah McCammon, "White Evangelicals Discuss Intersection of Faith and Political Leadership," *All Things Considered* (National Public Radio), April 1, 2018, https://tinyurl.com/y6xo2jpl.

Chapter 8

1. Jane C. Timm, "Trump on Hot Mic: 'When You're a Star . . . You Can Do Anything' to Women," *NBC News*, October 7, 2016, https://tinyurl .com/y77pjlby.

2. Morgan Lee, "My Larry Nassar Testimony Went Viral; But There's More to the Gospel than Forgiveness," interview with Rachael Denhollander, *Christianity Today*, January 31, 2018, https://tinyurl.com/y6dowv5z.

3. Lee, "My Larry Nassar Testimony."

4. Lee, "My Larry Nassar Testimony."

5. Lee, "My Larry Nassar Testimony."

6. Sarah Bessey, "I Am Damaged Goods," *A Deeper Story*, January 29, 2013, https://tinyurl.com/y3nfemz2.

7. Bessey, "I Am Damaged Goods."

8. Bessey, "I Am Damaged Goods."

9. Rachel Martin, "Former Evangelical Pastor Rethinks His Approach to Courtship," interview with Josh Harris, *Weekend Edition Sunday* (National Public Radio), July 10, 2016, https://tinyurl.com/yynqfeuk.

10. Lyz Lenz, "'I Kissed Dating Goodbye' Told Me to Stay Pure until Marriage; I Still Have a Stain on my Heart," Acts of Faith, *Washington Post*, July 27, 2016, https://tinyurl.com/y4359xko.

11. Lenz, "'I Kissed Dating Goodbye' Told Me to Stay Pure."

12. Lynne Hybels, "The Truly Global Sisterhood of #SilenceIsNotSpiritual," LynneHybels.com (blog), December 23, 2017, https://tinyurl .com/yyk9a8bm.

13. For more on this, see Angela Denker, "How You Know Jesus Has Left Your Church," *Sojourners*, January 11, 2018, https://tinyurl.com /y4l3mdyy.

14. Beth Moore, "A Letter to My Brothers," Living Proof Ministries blog, May 3, 2018, https://tinyurl.com/yagahl3m.

15. Moore, "A Letter to My Brothers."

16. Moore, "A Letter to My Brothers."

17. Moore, "A Letter to My Brothers."

18. Julia Duin, "She Led Trump to Christ: The Rise of the Televangelist Who Advises the White House," *Washington Post Magazine*, November 14, 2017, https://tinyurl.com/yybgoagj.

Chapter 9

1. "President Obama's 2008 Altoona Gutter Ball," WTAJ, October 15, 2012, https://tinyurl.com/y4orbjtf.
2. "Pennsylvania: Presidential County Election Results," Election Results 2008, *New York Times*, December 9, 2008, https://tinyurl.com /y2l3mwtk.
3. Aaron Thomas, "Trump Makes Stop in Altoona," WTAJ, August 13, 2016, https://tinyurl.com/yy9de73z.
4. Chip Minemyer, "Trump Promises to Save, Restore Jobs during Campaign Stop in Altoona," *Tribune Democrat*, August 13, 2016, https:// tinyurl.com/y3fbqz6z.
5. Katie Reilly, "Read Hillary Clinton's 'Basket of Deplorables' Remarks about Donald Trump Supporters," *Time*, September 10, 2016, https:// tinyurl.com/yxq6rbvs.
6. Betsy Rader, "I Was Born in Poverty in Appalachia; 'Hillbilly Elegy' Doesn't Speak for Me," *Washington Post*, September 1, 2017, https:// tinyurl.com/y3jxuvnn.

Chapter 10

1. Donald R. McClarey, "John Adams and the Mass," *Catholic Stand* (Little Vatican Media), May 24, 2016, https://tinyurl.com/y4lt4zrq.
2. "Transcript: JFK's Speech on His Religion," *National Public Radio*, December 5, 2007, https://tinyurl.com/y4vnncpr.
3. Gregory A. Smith and Jessica Martínez, "How the Faithful Voted: A Preliminary 2016 Analysis," Pew Research Center, November 9, 2016, https://tinyurl.com/h5zd2fl.
4. Smith and Martínez, "How the Faithful Voted."
5. "Adults in New Hampshire: Religious Composition of Adults in New Hampshire," Religious Landscape Study, Pew Research Center, 2014, https://tinyurl.com/y45z7flr.
6. Pew Research Center, "Adults in New Hampshire."
7. Katharine Q. Seelye, "How a 'Perfect Storm' in New Hampshire Has Fueled an Opioid Crisis," *New York Times*, January 21, 2018, https:// tinyurl.com/y4n9zext.
8. *Wikipedia*, s.v. "Franklin Pierce," https://tinyurl.com/yy26qant.

9. Brian Roewe, "Fr. Frank Pavone Uses Aborted Fetus in Message for Election Day," *National Catholic Reporter*, November 8, 2016, https://tinyurl.com/y33x2gre.

Chapter 11

1. "Arab Americans," Arab American Institute, 2005, https://tinyurl.com/yye7n98j.
2. "Donald Trump on ISIS—'I would bomb the SHIT out of 'em!'" YouTube, 0:44, uploaded by "#MAGA," November 12, 2015, https://youtu.be/aWejiXvd-P8.
3. Kate Shellnutt, "U.S. Sees Rise of Islamic Centers," *Houston Chronicle*, March 8, 2012, https://tinyurl.com/y2s6mkcn.
4. "Adults in the Houston Metro Area: Religious Composition of Adults in the Houston Metro Area," Religious Landscape Study, Pew Research Center, 2014, https://tinyurl.com/yyh3epen.
5. "U.S. Muslims Concerned about Their Place in Society, but Continue to Believe in the American Dream," Pew Research Center, July 26, 2017, https://tinyurl.com/y5of3eqa.
6. Dwight Adams, "Joel Osteen in Indianapolis: Why the Televangelist Is So Beloved and Controversial," *IndyStar*, August 19, 2018, https://tinyurl.com/yxpxov3u.

Chapter 12

1. "Trump Leads 'Build That Wall' Chant in California," NBC News, May 25, 2016, https://tinyurl.com/yybx6mct.
2. Emma Lazarus, "The New Colossus," November 2, 1883, National Park Service, https://tinyurl.com/zmdrzp8.
3. Sam Quinones, "Once the World's Most Dangerous City, Juarez Returns to Life," *National Geographic*, June 2016, https://tinyurl.com/y4afw35s.
4. "County Membership Report: El Paso County, Texas," Association of Religion Data Archives, 2010, https://tinyurl.com/y4zq5255.
5. Association of Religion Data Archives, "County Membership Report."
6. Association of Religion Data Archives, "County Membership Report."

7. Brittny Mejia, "Many Latinos Answer Call of the Border Patrol in the Age of Trump," *Los Angeles Times*, April 23, 2018, https://tinyurl.com/y28gsqkt.

8. Mejia, "Many Latinos Answer Call."

9. Michael Lipka, "The Most and Least Racially Diverse U.S. Religious Groups," Pew Research Center, July 27, 2015, https://tinyurl.com/y6ys39tl.